Frequency Domain Filtering Strategies for Hybrid Optical Information Processing

ELECTRONIC & ELECTRICAL ENGINEERING RESEARCH STUDIES

PATTERN RECOGNITION & IMAGE PROCESSING SERIES

Series Editor: **Professor Josef Kittler,** *University of Surrey, UK*

4. An Introduction to Infrared Image Acquisition and Classification Systems
   L. F. Pau *and* **M. Y. El Nahas**

8. Image Processing System Architectures
   Edited by **Josef Kittler** *and* **Michael J. B. Duff**

9. Image Segmentation and Uncertainty
   Roland Wilson *and* **Michael Spann**

10. Frequency Domain Filtering Strategies
    for Hybrid Optical Information Processing
    C. R. Chatwin *and* **R. K. Wang**

ML

Frequency Domain Filtering Strategies for Hybrid Optical Information Processing

C. R. Chatwin
University of Sussex, UK

and

R. K. Wang
University of Glasgow, UK

RESEARCH STUDIES PRESS LTD.
Taunton, Somerset, England

JOHN WILEY & SONS INC.
New York · Chichester · Toronto · Brisbane · Singapore

RESEARCH STUDIES PRESS LTD.
24 Belvedere Road, Taunton, Somerset, England TA1 1HD

Marketing and Distribution:

Australia and New Zealand:
Jacaranda Wiley Ltd.
GPO Box 859, Brisbane, Queensland 4001, Australia

Canada:
JOHN WILEY & SONS CANADA LIMITED
22 Worcester Road, Rexdale, Ontario, Canada

Europe, Africa, Middle East and Japan:
JOHN WILEY & SONS LIMITED
Baffins Lane, Chichester, West Sussex, England

North and South America:
JOHN WILEY & SONS INC.
605 Third Avenue, New York, NY 10158, USA

South East Asia:
JOHN WILEY & SONS (SEA) PTE LTD.
37 Jalan Pemimpin 05-04
Block B Union Industrial Building, Singapore 2057

Library of Congress Cataloging-in-Publication Data

Chatwin, C. R. (Chris R.)
    Frequency domain filtering strategies for hybrid optical
information processing / C.R. Chatwin and R.K. Wang.
        p.   cm. — (Electronic & electrical engineering research
studies. Pattern recognition & image processing series ; 10)
    Includes bibliographical references and index.
    ISBN 0-86380-177-3 (alk. paper) (Research Studies Press). – ISBN
0-471-95743-7 (alk. paper) (John Wiley & Sons)
    1. Optical pattern recognition.   2. Optical data processing-
-Mathematics.   3. Computer algorithms.   4. Digital filters
(Mathematics)   I. Wang, R. K. (RuiKang)   II. Title.
III. Series.
TA1650.C53   1996
006.4'2—dc20

British Library Cataloguing in Publication Data

A catalogue record for this book is available from the British Library.

ISBN 0 86380 177 3 (Research Studies Press Ltd.) *[Identifies the book for orders except in America.]*
ISBN 0 471 95743 7 (John Wiley & Sons Inc.) *[Identifies the book for orders in USA.]*

Printed in Great Britain by SRP Ltd., Exeter

To: Catherine Agnes MacGregor
        & Qing Shang

Preface

Hybrid optical/digital computers offer enormous potential for the future of numerically intensive computational problems as they are able to perform totally parallel computations at the speed of light. The greatest investment in this highly active research area has taken place in the USA, Japan, Europe and China. Under the auspices of the Advanced Research Projects Agency (ARPA), a major research effort is currently underway in the USA, this is called: Transitioning of Optical Processing into Systems (TOPS), it is pursuing programmes for both military and industrial pattern recognition. In Europe, research into: rapid fingerprint recognition, passive spacecraft docking control, automatic recognition of roadsigns and industrial inspection is being funded under the CEC-ESPRIT research programme. CEC-BRITE-EURAM are funding research into hybrid optical-digital systems for high speed industrial quality control.

Customised solutions exploiting optical information processing systems have delivered a number of notable success stories, for example: reconstruction of synthetic aperture radar (SAR) images; particle sizing; particle velocimetry; robot end effector guidance; rapid searching of databases stored on compact discs, general pattern recognition problems. Jenoptik, GmbH-Germany, produce an incoherent optical image processing system (OIPS), which has been exploited for: surface inspection of white bread; inspection of textiles for weaving defects; incompleteness of filling of plastic boxes; detection of waste paper types for auto re-cycling; the orientation of wood shavings during the strewing process in the production of oriented-strand boards; in-process control of the "degree of grinding" of roast coffee beans. In the short term we believe that hybrid optical processing will produce greatest success when systems are designed to solve specific problems; in the longer term more general solutions will emerge.

There is an ongoing requirement for substantial investment in optical to electronic interface technology; for particular problems, existing interface technology is frequently adequate, but general solutions require high-quality, high resolution, fast spatial light modulators capable of multiple level quantisation of phase and amplitude. Existing binary SLMs (spatial light modulators) satisfy many of these requirements but compromise finesse in solutions. There is a lack of investment in SLM research for the actual application of optical computing; devices currently in use have been designed and optimised for other purposes such as: image display devices and optical interconnects. Performance of optical computing systems would benefit greatly from investment in SLM research which delivers devices optimised for optical computing.

As the title of the book suggests we focus our attention on the development of optically implementable frequency domain algorithms that may be exploited to enhance the performance of optical information processing systems; these are developed for implementation in systems using either the VanderLugt type architecture or the joint transform arrangement; however, this is not a restriction and a number of new architectures are suggested. The objective of filtering is to overcome limitations in performance that are generated by problems relating to: input image distortion i.e. scale mismatch, in-plane rotation and out-of-plane rotation; input image noise and clutter; discrimination between in-class and out-of-class images, especially similar objects; object localisation accuracy; multi-class recognition requirements; optical efficiency; frequency plane dynamic range. This litany of difficulties, which are equally applicable to fully digital approaches, occurs to a greater or lesser extent depending on the application. For example, an industrial inspection problem is far less likely to suffer from problems of noise, clutter and scale mis-match than a military targeting application. Thus, the solution must be adapted to the requirements of the application; it is this system customisation approach that has achieved the greatest success in applications. Thus the frequency plane filtering algorithms, presented herein, should be applied within this context. More general systems need to be re-configurable and benefit greatly from the use of knowledge based systems for adaptation. This text is aimed at: the research community, industrial and military systems builders and post-graduate courses in opto-electronics.

The authors would like to thank the University of Glasgow, Laser and Optical Systems Engineering Group, which operates out the Mechanical Engineering Department, for access to the resources that made this work possible, and also the Commission of the European Communities; BRITE-EURAM research programme, which funded parallel activities that facilitated this research. We would like to thank Dr. Ming-Yaw Huang for his contribution and last, but not least, we would like to thank one of the least well known world experts in optical computing, Dr. Rupert Young, who made a considerable contribution to the work herein.

C.R. Chatwin and R.K. Wang
22 August 1995

Nomenclature

(x, y)	—	coordinates in the space domain
(x_0, y_0)	—	origin coordinates in the space domain
(u, v)	—	coordinates in the frequency domain
(x_f, y_f)	—	coordinates in the frequency domain
(Δ_x, Δ_y)	—	sampling intervals in the space domain
(Δ_u, Δ_v)	—	sampling intervals in the frequency domain
$*$	—	complex conjugate operator
Δ	—	discrimination capability
σ	—	standard deviation
λ	—	wavelength of light
θ	—	phase angle
ηH	—	Horner efficiency
f	—	focal length of Fourier transform lens
$\star$	—	convolution operator
$\odot$	—	correlation operator
$\mathcal{A}$	—	SLM amplitude coding domain
$\mathcal{F}$	—	forward Fourier transform operator
$\mathcal{F}^{-1}$	—	inverse Fourier transform operator
$\mathcal{M}$	—	modulation operator
$\mathcal{N}$	—	modulation operator
$\mathcal{P}$	—	SLM phase coding domain
ACMF	—	amplitude-compensated matched filter
ACR	—	auto-correlation result
ADF	—	adaptive discriminant filter

AMF	—	amplitude modulated filter
APC	—	armoured personnel carrier
API	—	auto-correlation peak intensity
BFP	—	back focal plane
BJTC	—	binary joint transform correlation
BPOF	—	binary phase-only filter
BR	—	beam ratio
BSO	—	Bismuth Silicon Oxide
CGH	—	computer generated hologram
CJTC	—	conventional joint transform correlation
CMF	—	classical (complex) matched filter
CPI	—	correlation peak intensity
DC	—	discrimination capability
DC_w	—	worst case discrimination capability
DOG	—	difference of Gaussian
DFWM	—	degenerate four wave mixing
DFT	—	discrete Fourier transform
ECP	—	equal correlation peak
FAF	—	fringe-adjusted filter
FAFJTC	—	fringe-adjusted filter joint transform correlator
fSDF	—	filter synthetic discriminant function
FTP	—	Fourier transform property
FT	—	Fourier transform
FWHM	—	full width half maximum
IF	—	inverse filter
IIC	—	intra-in-class
$Imag[\ ]$	—	imaginary part of a complex function
IOC	—	intra-out-of-class
JPS	—	joint power spectrum
JTC	—	joint transform correlation

LCTV	—	liquid crystal television
LCLV	—	liquid crystal light valve
MACE	—	minimum average correlation energy
MFAF	—	modified fringe-adjusted filter
MFAJTC	—	modified fringe-adjusted joint transform correlator
MfSDF	—	modified filter synthetic discriminant function
MVSDF	—	minimum-variance synthetic discriminant function
MLAP	—	multi-level phase and amplitude
POF	—	phase-only filter
PNI	—	pixel number inside correlation peak at full width half maximum
PNO	—	pixel number outside correlation peak at full width half maximum
PRMS	—	peak to the root mean square ratio
PSR	—	peak to secondary peak ratio
PSR_w	—	worst case peak to secondary peak ratio
$Real[\ ]$	—	real part of a complex function
SBWP	—	space bandwidth product
SDF	—	synthetic discriminant function
SLM	—	spatial light modulator
SNR	—	signal to noise ratio
TMF	—	tenary matched filter
TPR	—	tuneable photo-refractive
VLSI	—	very large scale integration
WF	—	Wiener filter

Contents

Preface   vii

Nomenclature   xi

List of Tables   6

List of Figures   7

1 Introduction   15
   Bibliography 23

2 Optical Pattern Recognition: Fundamentals   25
   2.1 Introduction 25
   2.2 Fourier Transform   25
        2.2.1 Continuous Fourier transform   25
        2.2.2 Discrete Fourier transform   27
        2.2.3 Properties of the Fourier transform   30
   2.3 Fourier Transform Property of a Lens   33
   2.4 Complex Spatial Filtering   37
        2.4.1 Coherent Optical Processor   37
        2.4.2 Complex spatial filtering   39
        2.4.3 Holographic recording   40
        2.4.4 Coherent optical correlation   42
   2.5 Matched Spatial Filters   43

1

    2.5.1   Classical matched filter 44

    2.5.2   Phase-only matched filter 45

    2.5.3   Binary phase-only filter 46

   Bibliography 49

3 Spatial Frequency Tuning for Pattern Recognition by Correlation 50

   3.1   Introduction 50

   3.2   Tuneable Photo-refractive (TPR) Filters 51

    3.2.1   TPR filter based correlator 52

    3.2.2   Performance of the TPR filter 58

   3.3   Difference of Gaussian (DOG) Filters 61

    3.3.1   Theoretical aspects 64

    3.3.2   Performance of the DOG filter 66

   3.4   Comparison of the TPR Filter with the DOG Filter 68

   3.5   Noise Robustness of TPR filters 74

   Bibliography 83

4 Adaptive Filtering Technique 85

   4.1   Introduction 85

   4.2   Filter Synthesis 86

   4.3   Performance Simulations and Results 89

   4.4   Implementation 99

   4.5   Conclusion 101

   Bibliography 103

5 Synthetic Discriminant Functions (SDFs) 104

   5.1   Introduction 104

   5.2   Historical Background 105

   5.3   Synthetic Discriminant Functions 106

    5.3.1   Frequency plane correlator 107

    5.3.2   Equal correlation peak SDF 108

	5.3.3	Two class problem	109
	5.3.4	Training image set size	111
	5.3.5	Selection of training images	112
	5.3.6	Computational issues	113

5.4 Generalised Synthetic Discriminant Functions 115

5.5 Minimum Average Correlation Energy Filters 117

Bibliography 120

6 Modified Filter-SDF Filter and its Real Time Implementation 123

6.1 Introduction 123

6.2 Background — Filter SDF 125

6.3 Modified Filter SDF (MfSDF) 126

6.4 Data Base 129

6.5 Implementation Study of MfSDF Filters Using a Binary Spatial Light Modulator 130

	6.5.1	Simulation considerations	132
	6.5.2	Filter construction	133
	6.5.3	Distortion range of filters	136
	6.5.4	Target discrimination	144
	6.5.5	Conclusions	146

6.6 Implementation Study of MfSDF Filters Using a Liquid Crystal Television as a Modulator 150

	6.6.1	Consideration of multilevel LCTV constraint	151
	6.6.2	Simulation considerations	153
	6.6.3	Distortion range of filters	154
	6.6.4	Discrimination capability of filters	159
	6.6.5	Training image spacing	165
	6.6.6	Noise resistance of filter	167
	6.6.7	Conclusions	173

Bibliography 179

3

7   The Wiener Filter and Its Application to Optical Correlation   182

7.1   Introduction 182

7.2   Wiener Filter Based Correlation 184

    7.2.1   Wiener filter formulation 184

    7.2.2   Application to the optical correlation 186

7.3   Wiener Filter–Synthetic Discriminant Functions 191

    7.3.1   Wiener filter SDFs 192

7.4   Simulations and Results 193

7.5   Wiener Filter Applied to Laser Cutting Process Control 200

    7.5.1   Experimental result 212

7.6   Conclusions 213

Bibliography 216

8   Joint Transform Correlation   219

8.1   Introduction 219

8.2   Joint Transform Correlation 222

    8.2.1   Basic concept 222

    8.2.2   Input noise characterisation 225

8.3   Modified Fringe-adjusted JTC 226

    8.3.1   Multi-object modified fringe-adjusted JTC 230

8.4   Results from Modified FAFJTC 232

    8.4.1   Input scene with noise free single object 232

    8.4.2   Input scene with a single noise corrupted object 235

    8.4.3   Multi-object input scene with background noise 239

8.5   Synthetic Discriminant Function MFAJTC 242

    8.5.1   SDF-based JTC 243

    8.5.2   SDF-based modified fringe-adjusted JTC 245

    8.5.3   SDF-based MFAJTC with multi-object input 247

    8.5.4   Results from SDF-based MFAJTC 248

Bibliography 259

Subject Index   262

Author Index   266

List of Tables

2.1   *Properties of two-dimensional Fourier transform* 33

3.1   *Filter performance measures* 72
3.2   *Comparison of discriminatory abilities for the four filters* 72
3.3   *Quantitative comparison of filter performance* 78
3.4   *Quantitative comparison of filter discrimination ability* 82

4.1   *Quantitative comparision of filter performance* 95
4.2   *Quantitative comparision of filter's discrimination ability* 99

6.1   *Final coefficient parameters for BPOF/MfSDF* 133
6.2   *Final coefficient parameters for BPOF/fSDF* 136
6.3   *Comparision of different training image spacings* 167

7.1   *Quantitative comparison of the filter performance* 190
7.2   *Relative cross-correlation peaks heights* 208
7.3   *WF based SDF filter weighting coefficients* 211

8.1   *Quantified results from an input scene with a noise free single object* . 235
8.2   *Quantified results from an input scene with a noise corrupted single object* 236
8.3   *Quantified results from an input scene with multiple noise corrupted objects* 240
8.4   *Quantified results using individual training set images as the input scene* 250
8.5   *Quantified results from an input scene with multiple objects* 255

List of Figures

1.1   *General optical correlator* 16

2.1   *Sampling a continuous function* 28

2.2   *Eigenfunctions of a linear shift invariant system.* $\Phi = exp[j2\pi(ux + vy)]$, $H_\Phi = H(u,v) = $ *Fourier transform of* $h(x,y)$. 31

2.3   *Configuration for analysing the Fourier transform property of a lens. The fields adjacent to the various surfaces are indicated by dashed lines.* 34

2.4   *Coherent optical processor.* 38

2.5   *Interferometric arrangement for recording a holographic filter.* 41

2.6   *Output of an optical processor with a holographic filter.* 43

3.1   *Schematic of up-dateable photorefractive correlator* 53

3.2   *Cross-sections through reconstruction field values of the TPR filter with the BR indicated. These figures were obtained from a square block image that was band pass filtered using the TPR filter with various BR values and then reconstructed.* 58

3.3   *Test image defined on a 128×128 array* 59

3.4   *(a) and (c) are the cross-sections through the TPR filter in the frequency domain with BR set to 5 and 10 respectively. (b) and (d) are corresponding cross-sections through the field values directly behind the TPR filter.* 60

3.5   *(a) and (c) are the cross-sections through the TPR filter in the frequency domain with BR set to 20 and 32 respectively. (b) and (d) are corresponding cross-sections through the field values directly behind the TPR filter.* 61

3.6   *Autocorrelation results obtained using the input image Fig.3.3 with the BR set to 5, 10, 20 and 32 respectively.* 62

3.7   *Cross-section through a DOG function in the space domain with* (σ_1, σ_2) *set to (0.1, 0.16)* 65

3.8 Cross-section through the Fourier transform of the DOG function shown in Fig.3.7 65

3.9 (a), (c) and (e) are cross-sections through the frequency domain DOG function with standard deviations (σ_1, σ_2) set to (0.1, 0.16), (0.075, 0.1) and (0.05, 0.07) respectively. (b), (d) and (f) are cross-sections through the reconstructed square after it has been convolved with the adjacent DOG. 67

3.10 (a), (c) and (e) are the cross-sections through the DOG filter in the frequency domain with (σ_1, σ_2) set to (0.1, 0.16), (0.075, 0.1), and (0.05, 0.07), respectively. (b), (d) and (f) are the corresponding cross-sections through the field values directly behind the DOG filter. 69

3.11 Autocorrelation results obtained using the input image of Fig.3.3 with (σ_1, σ_2) set to (0.1, 0.16), (0.075, 0.1), and (0.05, 0.07), respectively. 70

3.12 Image used for the test of filter discrimination. 73

3.13 Real images encoded at 128×128 pixels: (a) Bradley APC vehicle, (b) Abrams MI tank. 74

3.14 Correlation functions: (a) and (b) are from correlating the target and non-target images with the TPR filter (BR set to 32), respectively; (c) and (d) are from correlating the target and non-target images with a DOG filtered version (with (σ_1, σ_2) set to (0.05, 0.07)), respectively. . 75

3.15 (a) The noise free image of the Bradley APC vehicle. (b) The noise corrupted image of the Bradley APC vehicle with $20 \log SNR_I = -17.4dB$. 78

3.16 Correlation intensity outputs for (a) TPR with BR=32, (b) POF and (c) CMF; correlated with noisy images of the Bradley APC vehicle with $20 log SNR_I = -17.4dB$. 80

3.17 Abrams MI tank images used as the non-target object input, (a) noise free, (b) corrupted by noise with $20 log SNR_I = -17.4dB$. 82

4.1 Schematic diagram of iterative procedure for optimum filter construction 88

4.2 Input images with different noise levels (a) noise free, (b) 0.4dB, (c) -13.6dB and (d) -17.4dB 90

4.3 Correlation filter with different threshold values $\varepsilon =$ (a) 0.01, (b) 10^{-4}, (c) 10^{-5} and (d) 10^{-6} 91

4.4 Impulse response of correlation filter with threshold values corresponding to the values in Fig.4.3 92

4.5 Correlation results from ADF correlation filter using input image of Fig.4.2(d) with different threshold values $\varepsilon =$ (a) 0.01, (b) 10^{-4}, (c) 10^{-5} and (d) 10^{-6} 93

4.6 *Filters: (a) optimum ADF correlation filter ($\varepsilon = 10^{-4}$), (b) POF and (c) CMF* 95

4.7 *Correlation results from (a) optimum ADF correlation filter, (b) POF and (c) CMF using the input image of Fig.4.2d* 96

4.8 *Abrams MI tank used as the nontarget image, (a) noise free image, (b) noise corrupted image with $20logSNR_I = -17.4dB$.* 99

4.9 *Optimum threshold values vs. input image noise levels. x denotes noise level values in the input scene, and y denotes the logarithm of optimum threshold values. R^2 = residual error square* 100

4.10 *Hybrid correlation system diagram. AM-SLM denotes the amplitude modulating spatial light modulator, and PM-SLM denotes the phase modulating spatial light modulator.* 102

5.1 *Schematic of the frequency plane correlator* 107

5.2 *Representation of the SDF equations using hyperplanes. Here the number of training images $N = 2$* 114

6.1 *Flow chart of the MfSDF design procedure* 127

6.2 *Flow chart of the iterative procedure to produce MfSDF function* . . . 130

6.3 *Examples of the in-plane rotated images of the Bradley APC vehicle. (a), (b), (c) and (d) are the vehicle views at $0°$, $30°$, $60°$ and $90°$, respectively* 131

6.4 *Examples of the in-plane rotated images of the Abrams MI tank. (a), (b), (c) and (d) are the tank views at $0°$, $30°$, $60°$ and $90°$, respectively* 132

6.5 *Stages in the filter design procedure for the MfSDF-BPOF made from the phase-only training set images in the frequency domain. (a), (b) and (c) are the composite image $S(u,v)$, real part of the composite image $S(u,v)$ and final binary version of MfSDF, respectively* 134

6.6 *Mapping procedure from complex values of $S(u, v)$ to the binary values of $(+1,-1)$* 135

6.7 *Stages in the filter design procedure for the fSDF-BPOF made directly from training set images in the frequency domain. (a), (b) and (c) are the composite image $S(u,v)$, real part of the composite image $S(u,v)$ and final binary version of fSDF, respectively* 137

6.8 *Impulse responses of the (a) BPOF/MfSDF and (b) BPOF/fSDF functions* 137

6.9 *Peak correlation and peak clutter responses with a distortion range from $0°$ to $45°$: (a) binary phase-only MfSDF and (b) binary phase-only fSDF* 139

9

6.10 *The 3-D representations of the correlation functions which present the highest possibility of erroneous correlation peak detection over the range from 0^0 to 45^0; (a) and (b) are the cases of lowest correlation peak and highest second peak for the BPOF/MfSDF respectively; (c) and (d) are the same cases for the BPOF/fSDF respectively* 140

6.11 *The worst correlation peak to secondary peak ratio (PSR_w) over distortion ranges from $0°$ to $90°$ for the MfSDF method* 143

6.12 *The worst correlation peak to secondary peak ratio (PSR_w) over distortion ranges from $0°$ to $90°$ for the fSDF method* 143

6.13 *Average modulus of the correlation peaks over distortion ranges up to $90°$* 144

6.14 *Average values of the signal to noise ratio (SNR) over distortion ranges up to $90°$.* 145

6.15 *Discrimination capability of filters over distortion ranges up to $90°$; the target and non-target inputs are at the same rotation angle. (a) average value of inputs at $5°$ increments, (b) average value of inputs at $1°$ intervals* 147

6.16 *The 3-D representations of the correlation functions obtained from correlating the target image and non-target image at the rotation angle of $40°$ with both MfSDF and fSDF designed for $40°$ in-plane vehicle rotation invariance. (a) and (b) are the results from the MfSDF filter for the target and non-target input images respectively; (c) and (d) are the results from the fSDF filter* 148

6.17 *Flow chart of the filter coding procedure* 152

6.18 *Peak correlation and secondary correlation peak responses over a distortion range of $90°$: (a) MLAP/MfSDF and (b) BPOF/MfSDF* . . . 156

6.19 *Best-case and worst-case correlation functions of the filter constructed for a distortion range from $0°$ to $90°$ with the input images at $1°$ intervals, (a) and (b) are the best-case and worst-case for MLAP/MfSDF respectively, (c) and (d) are the best-case and worst-case for BPOF/- MfSDF respectively* 157

6.20 *The worst correlation peak response to secondary peak response ratio (PSR_w) over the distortion ranges from $0°$ to $130°$* 159

6.21 *Average modulus of the correlation peak responses over the distortion ranges up to $130°$* 160

6.22 *In-class correlation peak and out-of-class correlation peak responses over a distortion range of $90°$: (a) MLAP/MfSDF and (b) BPOF/- MfSDF* 161

6.23 *Worst-case discrimination correlation functions of the filter over the range from 0^0 to 90^0, (a) and (b) are from correlating the MLAP/-MfSDF with the in-class input at 2^0 orientation and the out-of-class input at 60^0 orientation respectively, (c) and (d) are from correlating the BPOF/MfSDF with the in-class input at 88^0 orientation and the out-of-class input at 72^0 orientation respectively* 163

6.24 *The worst discrimination capability (DC_w) of filters between in-class and out-of-class images over the distortion ranges up to 130°* 165

6.25 *(a) The intensity distribution of the MLAP/MfSDF filter constructed for a distortion range from 0° to 60° with training images spaced at 5°; (b) and (c) are its real and imaginary parts respectively, where the grey levels vary from 0 to 255. (d) is the BPOF/MfSDF constructed from the same training images but in which the white pixels denote the values of 1 and black pixels denote the values of -1* 168

6.26 *Impulse responses of the (a) MLAP/MfSDF and (b) BPOF/MfSDF functions* 169

6.27 *Views of (a) Bradley APC vehicle and (b) Abram MI tank at the orientation angle of 0°, corrupted by noise with an image energy to noise energy ratio of 0.5* 170

6.28 *Correlation functions from correlating the input images of Fig.6.27(a) and Fig.6.3(a) with the filters of Fig.6.25(a) and Fig.6.25(d) respectively. (a) and (b) are the results from correlating the filter Fig.6.25(a) with the inputs of Fig.6.27(a) and Fig.6.3(a) respectively; (c) and (d) are the results from correlating the filter Fig.6.25(d) with the inputs of Fig.6.27(a) and Fig.6.3(a) respectively* 171

6.29 *Correlation peak, secondary peak and out-of-class correlation peak responses with a distortion range from 0° to 40°, where ICCP means the in-class correlation peak, ICSCP is in-class secondary correlation peak and OCCP is out-of-class correlation peak. (a) MLAP/MfSDF and (b) BPOF/MfSDF* 174

6.30 *Correlation functions from correlating the in-class and out-of-class input images of the APC vehicle and MI tank, at a 35^0 orientation, with the filters of MLAP/MfSDF and BPOF/MfSDF respectively* . . . 175

6.31 *The worst correlation peak response to secondary peak response ratio (PSR_w) and the worst discrimination capability (DC_w) of filter between in-class and out-of-class images over the distortion ranges from 0° to 60°: (a) MLAP/MfSDF and (b) BPOF/MfSDF* 177

7.1 *Characters used to produce the Wiener filter, (a) in-class image, (b) out-of-class image* 187

7.2 *Input image used in correlation* 187

11

7.3   *The computed intensities at the correlation output plane when the scene shown in Fig.7.2 is input into the correlator; (a), (b) and (c) are the correlation results using the Wiener filter, CMF and POF, respectively* 188

7.4   *(a) The form of the Wiener filter in the Fourier domain $W(f_x, f_y)$; (b) The impulse response of the Wiener filter $w(x, y)$* 190

7.5   *Examples of the out-of-plane rotated in-class training images of the Bradley APC vehicle. (a), (b), (c) and (d) are at $0°$, $60°$, $120°$ and $180°$ aspect angles respectively* 194

7.6   *Examples of the out-of-plane rotated in-class training images of the Abrams MI tank. (a), (b), (c) and (d) are at $0°$, $60°$, $120°$ and $180°$ aspect angles respectively* 195

7.7   *Results of the WF SDF designed with training image spacing of $30°$ for the distortion range $0°$ to $180°$. IMP and OMP are the in-class and out-of-class maximum correlation peaks, respectively* 197

7.8   *Results of the WF SDF designed with training image spacing of $15°$ for the distortion range $0°$ to $180°$. IMP and OMP are the in-class and out-of-class maximum correlation peaks, respectively.* 198

7.9   *Results of the conventional SDF designed with training image spacing of $15°$ for the distortion range $0°$ to $180°$. IMP and OMP are the in-class and out-of-class maximum correlation peaks, respectively* . . . 199

7.10 *Results of the POF/SDF designed with training image spacing of $15°$ for the distortion range $0°$ to $180°$. IMP and OMP are the in-class and out-of-class maximum correlation peaks, respectively* 199

7.11 *The 3-D representations of correlation functions obtained with the $15°$ training image spacing of WF SDF ((a) and (b)), conventional SDF ((c) and (d)), and POF/SDF ((e) and (f)) for the same in-class and out-of-class tank images respectively. The figures (a), (c) and (e) are the in-class correlations; and (b), (d) and (f) are the out-of-class correlations.* 201

7.12 *A typical spark cone image from mild steel cutting process* 204

7.13 *Spark cone image of 2 mm mild steel cutting process — good cut* . . . 204

7.14 *Spark cone image of 3 mm mild steel cutting process — good cut* . . . 205

7.15 *Spark cone image of 4 mm mild steel cutting process — good cut* . . . 205

7.16 *Spark cone image of 5 mm mild steel cutting process — good cut* . . . 205

7.17 *Spark cone image of 6 mm mild steel cutting process — good cut* . . . 206

7.18 *Spark cone image of clean cut process — mild steel* 206

7.19 *Spark cone image of low dross cutting process* 207

7.20 *Spark cone image of medium dross cutting process* 207

7.21 *Spark cone image of heavy dross cutting process* 208

7.22 *Cross-correlation result using a WF filter — 4 mm mild steel: (a) from good cutting process, (b) from poor cutting process* 209

7.23 *Relative cross-correlation peak heights* 210

7.24 *Maximum out-of-class to in-class image cross-correlation peak ratio* . 211

7.25 *Schematic diagram of updateable correlator* 212

7.26 *Cross-correlation result using a WF based SDF filter — 4 mm mild steel: (a) from good cutting process, (b) from poor cutting process* . . 214

7.27 *Kerf surfaces of different thickness, mild steel 6mm, 5mm, 4mm, 3mm, 2mm, 1mm (without SDF filter imaging control system)* 215

7.28 *Kerf surfaces of different thickness, mild steel 6mm, 5mm, 4mm, 3mm (with SDF filter imaging control system)* 215

8.1 *Schematic of the joint transform correlator* 222

8.2 *Schematic of the fringe-adjusted joint transform correlator* 225

8.3 *Schematic of an alternative real time fringe-adjusted JTC* 231

8.4 *Bradley APC images used in the simulation, (a) noise free APC image, (b) noise corrupted APC image with the signal energy to the noise energy ratio of 0.21* 233

8.5 *3-D plot of correlation output functions when the input scene is free of noise, (a) the MFAF based JTC, (b) the FAF based JTC* 234

8.6 *3-D plot of correlation output functions with no power spectra subtraction when the input scene is noise corrupted, (a) from the MFAF based JTC, (b) from the FAF based JTC* 237

8.7 *3-D plot of correlation output functions with power spectra subtraction from a noise corrupted input scene, (a) from the MFAF based JTC, (b) from the FAF based JTC* 238

8.8 *Noise free multiple object input scene used in the simulation* 239

8.9 *Noise corrupted multiple object input scene with signal energy to noise energy ratio of 0.4 used in the simulation* 240

8.10 *3-D plot of correlation output functions with power spectra subtraction from a noise corrupted multi-object input scene, (a) from the MFAF based JTC, (b) from the FAF based JTC* 241

8.11 *Views of the Bradley APC vehicle (from left to right and top to bottom) at 0°, 15°, 30°, 50°, 70° and 90°* 249

13

8.12 *Spatial SDF reference function $r(x,y)$ from (a) the fringe-adjusted JTC, (b) the classical JTC and (c) the binary JTC* 250

8.13 *The worst-case correlation results for the SDF-based MFAJTC: (a) from first class set, (b) from second class set; the SDF-based CJTC: (c) from first class set, (d) from second class set; and the SDF-based BJTC: (e) from first class set, (f) from second class set; respectively* . 252

8.14 *Multiple-object input scene used in simulation* 255

8.15 *3-D plot of correlation output functions with a multi-object input scene, (a) from the SDF-based MFAJTC, (b) from the SDF-based CJTC, (c) from the SDF-based BJTC, respectively* 257

14

Chapter 1

Introduction

The ability of optical elements and filters to implement a broad range of computationally intensive complex mathematical operations in parallel, and at the speed of light, has great significance for the future development of hybrid optical/digital computer architectures. For example a lens, Fig.1.1, is able to compute the Fourier transform of a 512×512 data array in fractions of a nano-second, this is equivalent to a throughput of about 2×10^{16} mathematical operations per second; this estimate is based on the number of digital multiplications and additions required to perform the same transform using the FFT algorithm. Significantly, when exploiting optical computational schemes the computational time does not increase if the data array size increases; it is this potential that has stimulated and sustained international research in the area. Until recently, the ability to use optical systems as a general computational tool was severely constrained by the ability to get data into and out of the system. Fortunately, recent developments in hardware (spatial light modulators) have provided a potential solution to this problem, and spurred a flurry of research activity in the field.

In 1964 VanderLugt proposed using a Fourier plane mask for pattern recognition [1]. This architecture is usually referred to as a frequency plane correlator, as shown in Fig.1.1. His system performed a cross correlation between two functions and is based on the autocorrelation theorem and the Fourier transform property of a lens using monochromatic coherent light. VanderLugt's insight was realising a way to write a

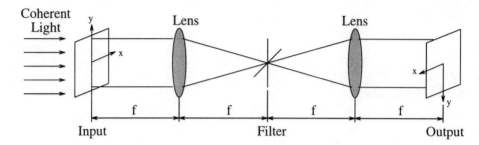

Figure 1.1: *General optical correlator*

complex function (i.e. the Fourier transform of an input image or signal) onto an energy sensitive medium, photographic film. The method proposed was holography, which results in encoding a complex transform function of a reference object onto a spatial carrier frequency. With the introduction of computer-generated holography (CGH) [2, 3], it became possible to fabricate matched filters of mathematically synthesised objects, but the CGH filter was still written onto photographic film, and therefore could not be implemented in real time.

Real time implementations are critical for practical applications of optical correlation. Due to the rapid development of spatial light modulators, optical materials and filter design techniques, real time pattern recognition exploiting hybrid optical correlation is increasingly attractive. The spatial light modulator (SLM) enables signal or image patterns to be encoded as amplitude and/or phase modulation patterns across a directed coherent optical beam. It is the vast computational potential of optical information processing that provides the motivation for the design of spatial filters suitable for implementation on currently available SLMs.

Probably the most challenging SLM requirement is that of real time matched filter modulation at the Fourier plane of a VanderLugt correlator. The matched filter generally is a complex function, requiring independently controlled phase and amplitude spatial modulation. Most SLMs, such as the LCTV in its normal mode of operation, only provide amplitude modulation which is usually accompanied by incidental phase modulation that is not independently controllable.

As stated above, practical application of the matched filter was limited because the filter is complex, and no effective means existed to implement such a filter in real time. Caufield [4] and Horner [5] originally conceived the idea of using only the phase of the Fourier signal to make a matched-type of filter. Horner and Gianino first demonstrated the feasibility of this idea through computer simulations [6], and named it the phase-only filter (POF); it gives a correlation peak that is anywhere from 50 to 500 times higher than that from a classical matched spatial filter. An optical filter which operates with pure phase modulation is very attractive as it does not attenuate the light passing through it. In contrast, the amplitude portion of a matched spatial filter attenuates the light since it is written on a positive device such as film or an SLM, and the peak transmission cannot exceed 100 percent, which usually occurs at the origin of the frequency plane. Also the light budget of a holographically recorded matched filter is further eroded by its poor diffraction efficiency, particularly if one tries to implement it on a spatial light modulator. Thus, the 100% light efficiency of the POF is a distinct advantage in a low-powered optical correlator. However, the high frequency bias of the POF adversely affects its signal-to-noise ratio (SNR) performance, making it very sensitive to noise in the input scene. A good correlation filter should not only produce a sharp localised correlation peak in the output plane, but also be robust to noise in the input scene. This optimisation is of great importance in an optical correlator system and is a major focus of the research herein.

The concentration of most of the energy at low frequencies, for common objects, is responsible for the broad correlation peaks generated by a classical matched spatial filter; that is, it behaves as a low pass filter. The influence of the input image noise in the frequency plane of the correlator is greater for high spatial frequencies. Thus the POF, which is an all pass filter, is very susceptible to noise in the correlator. This suggests that a filter with a band-pass characteristic is likely to be tolerant to noise and also give good localisation of the correlation peak.

Since convolution based edge enhancement is equivalent to a band pass filtering operation in the frequency domain, optical processing exploiting a photo-refractive material as a tuneable holographic filter provides a simple and effective method for implementing low noise (low noise in the sense that it does not introduce artefacts in the reciprocal domain) edge enhancement concurrently with correlation. This approach was recently implemented as part of a matched spatial filter by Young and Chatwin [7]; this method exploits selective erasure of spatial frequencies at the Fourier transform plane in the photo-refractive material Bismuth Silicon Oxide (BSO). The use of the widely available BSO has several important consequences for the overall system design.

In order to emphasise the importance of the BSO tuneable photo-refractive (TPR) filter, Chapter 3 investigates this tuneable bandpass type filter recorded in BSO and evaluates its noise robustness. In addition, an approximately equivalent bandpass filter, based on the difference of Gaussian (DOG) function is also reported and compared with the TPR filter.

An alternative approach to the BSO TPR filter is to use commercially available programmable SLMs which are limited to binary quantization of amplitude and/or phase; this has been a popular approach in the past ten years which has introduced binary phase-only filters for practical pattern recognition. However, this approach only partially exploits the finesse of filters designed for processing images with continuous phase and amplitude information. An optimal filter, that is tolerant to noise in the input scene and able to produce high quality localised correlation peaks, requires continuous phase and amplitude information. Implementing correlation filters on a binary phase-only SLM compromises the correlation performance. Recently, it was found that the liquid crystal television (LCTV), —for example the Epson LCTV panels, which are part of a commercial video projector, — can encode approximately continuous (i.e. multilevel) amplitude or phase information from Fourier transformed images. The Seiko Epson LCTV works quite well in the amplitude mode if the attached film polarizers are removed and replaced with high quality external polarizers. When the usual polarizers are removed the phase mode of operation can be operated over the range of $0°$ to $540°$. Thus, slightly modified LCTVs can implement almost continuous functional representation of the designed optimal filters, which usually require continuous amplitude and/or phase information to be encoded. This technology led to the design of the adaptive discriminant filter (ADF), which is reported in Chapter 4. The ADF is designed so as to optimise the sharpness of the correlation peak and the filter's tolerance to noise in the input scene.

Matched spatial filters are sensitive to distortion of the input images relative to the reference image. For example, in-plane rotations of several degrees, or scale changes of several percent, typically result in a 50% reduction in the correlation peak intensity. Filter sensitivity depends strongly on specific parameters such as object shape and the spatial frequency bandpass of the correlation filter. In any practical application not only must the expected distortions of targeted, or in-class, patterns (objects) be accommodated (usually by virtue of a high correlation peak response), but the filter should be robust to noise, and able to reject out-of-class objects (usually by virtue of a relatively low correlation peak response). The classical matched spatial filter is the optimal solution for the case of a single in-class pattern with significant background stochastic noise; a case having limited practical application.

A realistic and typical application is to recognise specified types of vehicle, regardless of orientation, in scenes which include other vehicles (nontargeted) and natural or man-made clutter such as trees, bushes, buildings, roads, etc. Random noise may also be present in the input patterns as a result of the imaging system or viewing conditions. Thus, the need to reject out-of-class patterns places serious constraints on the design of widened in-class responses (distortion invariance).

Many applications would benefit from the use of the space-invariant feature of Fourier-based correlation to furnish a location estimate of each recognised target, based on correlation peak location in the output plane. This involves additional trade-offs in filter design since, in general, optimisation of peak localisation (i.e. achieving narrow peaks) is inconsistent with maximising classification accuracy (e.g. achieving highest signal-to-noise ratio).

The synthetic discriminant function (SDF) [8] was a significant milestone in filters designed to cope with target distortion problems. The SDF filter is a composite filter in which the weights are set, using linear discrimination techniques, to yield specified on-axis correlation responses over the in-class and out-of-class training image sets. In its original form, called the equal correlation peak (ECP) SDF, the on-axis covariance matrix for the training set is formed and linear algebra techniques are applied to solve for composite filter weights which ensure equal-correlation-peak responses for all the in-class training set images. Problems with sidelobe correlation responses being larger than the desired on-axis response were addressed by the correlation-SDF filter which incorporates control of sidelobe responses not included in the ECP formulation [9].

Variants of the SDF have been developed, several of which are called optimal linear discriminant function filters [10]. Notable recent developments include the minimum average correlation energy (MACE) SDF [11] and the minimum-variance SDF (MVSDF) [12]. A generalised SDF formulation, which encompasses most of the previous types as special cases, was recently reported [13].

Generally, these SDF filters are continuous complex-valued filter functions. However, at present, spatial light modulator technology does not readily support the real time implementation of continuous complex-valued functions. Thus, the device limitations must be incorporated into the SDF filter design. In this regard, the POF and BPOF play an important role in real time implementations.

The phase-only concept is a very general principle that can be applied to any complex filter function by merely retaining the phase (or binarizing it) and setting the modulus to unity, as first proposed by Horner et al for the POF-SDF filter [14], which is implemented by converting the continuous complex-valued ECP-SDF to a phase-only type (or binary phase-only type). However, the POF-SDF does not give equal correlation peaks over the entire in-class training image set; this limits its practical application. To solve this problem, Jared and Ennis [15] developed an *ad hoc* iterative technique, called the filter-SDF (fSDF) which adjusts the heights of a composite transform, based on the training image set, so as to control the on-axis correlation response of the POF-SDF or BPOF-SDF over the training image set, i.e. it ensures that the SDF satisfies the equal correlation peaks goal. The formulation process is numerically relatively simple; however, convergence is not guaranteed. Fortunately, it was successful in nearly all the cases studied. Thus this iterative relaxation algorithm is a powerful tool when designing SDF filters with nonlinear characteristics that satisfy the ECP rule.

Jared and Ennis's idea was to ensure that the filter-encoding constraints imposed by the actual device with which they are implemented are taken into account at the design stage of the SDF filter. Unlike the fully complex SDF filter, the fSDF filter can be implemented on commercially available spatial light modulators and used in an optical correlator; they are therefore of particular interest for real-time optical pattern recognition systems employing rapidly updateable SLMs.

It is well known that, for common objects, the concentration of most of the energy in the central zone of the spectrum, i.e. low frequency components, is responsible for poor correlation performance. There is no doubt that the conventional SDF, which is a linear combination of the training set images, is dominated by the lower frequency components of individual training set images. The fSDF implements the filter modulation constraints (i.e. POF or BPOF) on the conventional SDF and partially ameliorates the problem; however, correlation performance is still inadequate. To overcome this problem, Wang and Chatwin [16, 17] very recently gave further consideration to the filter-encoding constraint applied to the equal correlation peak SDF design. Their idea was to synthesise the SDF from the linear combination of a set of training images which are already filter modulated, i.e. pre-processed, so that the constructed SDF is dominated by the higher, not the lower, frequency components of the individual training set images. This idea and its implementation on commercially available devices (spatial light modulators) is fully elucidated in Chapter 6.

An extremely important performance criterion for a correlation system is its ability to discriminate between in-class and out-of-class objects. Normally the discrimination capability of a filter depends on the sharpness of the correlation peak produced. Thus, the CMF, which is optimal for the recognition of objects in additive noise, gives a low discrimination ability between an object of the class to be detected and an out-of-class object which is to be rejected, especially when the objects are similar. In order to overcome this problem, several methods [18, 19, 20] have been proposed. An optimal filter, which maximises the discrimination capability, was reported by Yaroslavsky [21] and gives better performance than the POF. For this reason, Chapter 7 introduces the Wiener filter, which has been successfully implemented to enhance the filter discrimination ability. In this implementation, the

Wiener filter is formulated so as to incorporate the out-of-class image, to be rejected, as the Wiener filter noise term. Furthermore, an SDF filter constructed from the proposed Wiener filter is also investigated by applying it to vehicle recognition and laser cutting process control.

The joint transform correlator (JTC) provides a popular alternative to the Vander-Lugt architecture; Chapter 8 introduces some techniques to improve its performance. A modified fringe-adjusted filter (MFAF) based JTC is introduced and (with multi-object input) shown to ameliorate the noise sensitivity of the fringe-adjusted filter (FAF) based JTC; this provides a solution that overcomes the difficulties encountered with binary JTC techniques. In order to allow the JTC to accommodate a high degree of image distortion, Chapter 8 introduces a SDF based MFAF-JTC and demonstrates its ability to deal with noisy multi-class, multi-object inputs.

Bibliography

[1] A. VanderLugt, "Signal detection by complex spatial filtering", IEEE Trans. Inf Theory **IT-10**, 139-145(1964).

[2] G.R. Brown and A.W. Lohmann, "Complex spatial filtering with binary masks", Appl. Opt. **6**, 967-969(1966).

[3] A.W. Lohmann and D.P Paris, "Binary Fraunhofer holograms generated by computer", Appl. Opt. **6**, 1739-1748(1966).

[4] H.J. Caufield, "Role of Horner efficiency in the optimization of spatial filters for pattern recognition", Appl. Opt. **21**, 4391-4392(1982).

[5] J.L. Horner, "Light utilization in optical correlators", Appl. Opt. **21**, 4511-4514(1982).

[6] J.L. Horner and P.D. Gianino, "Phase-only matched filtering", Appl. Opt. **23**, 812-816(1984).

[7] R. Young and C.R. Chatwin, "Design and simulation of a synthetic discriminant function filter in an updateable photorefractive correlator", in Optical Pattern Recognition III, D. Casasent and T. Chao Eds, Proc. SPIE **1701**, 239-263(1992).

[8] C.F. Hester and D. Casasent, "Multivariant technique for multi-class pattern recognition", Appl. Opt. **19**, 1758-1761(1980).

[9] D. Casasent and W.T. Chang, "Correlation synthetic discriminant functions", Appl. Opt. **24**, 2343-2350(1986).

[10] V. Sharma and D. Casasent, "Optimal linear discriminant functions", Proc. SPIE **519**, 50-55(1984).

[11] A. Mahalanobis, B. Kumar and D. Casasent, "Minimum average correlation energy filters", Appl. Opt. **25**, 3633-3640(1987).

[12] B. Kumar, "Minimum-variance synthetic discriminant functions", J. Opt. Soc. Amer. **A3**, 1579-1584(1986).

[13] Z. Bahri and B. Kumar, "Generalized synthetic discriminant functions", J. Opt. Soc. Amer. **A5**, 562-571(1988).

[14] J.L. Horner and P.D. Gianino, "Applying the phase-only concept to the synthetic discriminant function correlator filter", Appl. Opt. **24**, 851-855(1989).

[15] D. Jared and D. Ennis, "Inclusion of filter modulation in synthetic discriminant function filters", Appl. Opt. **28**, 232-239(1989).

[16] R.K. Wang, C.R. Chatwin and M.Y. Huang, "Modified filter synthetic discriminant functions for improved optical correlation performance", Appl. Opt. **33**, 7646-7654(1994).

[17] R.K. Wang, and C.R. Chatwin, "Multilevel amplitude and phase encoded modified filter synthetic discriminant function filters", Appl. Opt. **34**, 4094-4104(1995).

[18] G.G. Mu, X.M. Wang & Z.Q. Wang, "Amplitude-compensated Matched Filtering", *Appl. Opt.* **27**, 3461-3463(1988).

[19] A.A.S. Awwal, M.A. Karim and S,R.Jahan, "Improved Correlation Discrimination Using an Amplitude-modulated Phase-only Filter", *Appl. Opt.* **29**, 233-236(1990).

[20] F.M. Dickey, B.V.K. Vijaya Kumar, L.A. Romero and J.M. Connelly, "Complex Ternary Matched Filters Yielding High Signal to Noise Ratio", *Opt. Eng.* **29**, 994-1001(1990).

[21] L.P. Yaroslavsky, "Is the Phase-only Filter and Its Modifications Optimal in Terms of the Discrimination Capability in Pattern Recognition", *Appl. Opt.* **31**, 1677-1679(1992).

Chapter 2

Optical Pattern Recognition: Fundamentals

2.1 Introduction

Due to its central importance in optical and digital image processing, this chapter reviews the Fourier transform and some of its properties. This is followed by an explanation of the Fourier transforming property of a lens, as this is frequently a key element in optical processing systems. Complex spatial filtering and some basic, but important, spatial filters are then reviewed.

2.2 Fourier Transform

2.2.1 Continuous Fourier transform

One- and/or two-dimensional Fourier transforms are of fundamental importance in optical and digital image processing as will become evident in the subsequent chapters. Let $f(x)$ be a continuous function of a real variable x. The Fourier transform of $f(x)$, denoted by $\mathcal{F}\{f(x)\}$, is defined by the equation

$$\mathcal{F}\{f(x)\} = F(u) = \int\limits_{-\infty}^{+\infty} f(x)exp[-j2\pi ux]dx \qquad (2.1)$$

where $j = \sqrt{-1}$.

Given $F(u)$, $f(x)$ can be obtained by using the inverse Fourier transform

$$\mathcal{F}^{-1}\{F(u)\} = f(x) = \int\limits_{-\infty}^{+\infty} F(u)exp[j2\pi ux]du \qquad (2.2)$$

Eqs.(2.1) and (2.2), which are a Fourier transform pair, can be shown to exist if $f(x)$ is continuous and integrable and $F(u)$ is integrable. These conditions are almost always satisfied in practice.

Throughout this treatise, function $f(x)$ is normally real. The Fourier transform of a real function, however, is generally complex; that is

$$F(u) = R(u) + jI(u) \qquad (2.3)$$

where $R(u)$ and $I(u)$ are, respectively, the real and imaginary component of $F(u)$. It is often convenient to express Eq.(2.3) in exponential form

$$F(u) = |F(u)|exp[j\Phi(u)] \qquad (2.4)$$

where
$$|F(u)| = [R^2(u) + I^2(u)]^{\frac{1}{2}} \qquad (2.5)$$

and
$$\Phi(u) = tan^{-1}[\frac{I(u)}{R(u)}] \qquad (2.6)$$

The magnitude function $|F(u)|$ is called the Fourier spectrum of $f(x)$, and $\Phi(u)$ is its phase angle. The square of the spectrum

$$P(u) = |F(u)|^2 = R^2(u) + I^2(u) \qquad (2.7)$$

is commonly referred to as the power spectrum of $f(x)$. The term spectral density (intensity) is also commonly used to denote the power spectrum.

The variable u appearing in the Fourier transform is often called the frequency variable. This name arises from the fact that, using Euler's formula, the exponential term, $exp[-j2\pi ux]$, may be expressed in the form

$$exp[-j2\pi ux] = \cos(2\pi ux) - j\sin(2\pi ux) \qquad (2.8)$$

If the integral in Eq.(2.1) is interpreted as a summation of discrete terms, it is evident that $F(u)$ is composed of an infinite sum of sine and cosine terms, and that each value of u determines the frequency of the corresponding sine-cosine pair.

The Fourier transform can be extended to a function $f(x,y)$ of two variables. If $f(x,y)$ is continuous and integrable, and $F(u,v)$ is integrable, the following Fourier transform pair exists

$$\mathcal{F}\{f(x,y)\} = F(u,v) = \int\limits_{-\infty}^{+\infty}\int\limits_{-\infty}^{+\infty} f(x,y)exp[-j2\pi(ux+vy)]dxdy \qquad (2.9)$$

and

$$\mathcal{F}^{-1}\{F(u,v)\} = f(x,y) = \int\limits_{-\infty}^{+\infty}\int\limits_{-\infty}^{+\infty} F(u,v)exp[j2\pi(ux+vy)]dudv \qquad (2.10)$$

where u and v are the frequency variables.

As in the one-dimensional case, the Fourier spectrum, phase and power spectrum are, respectively, given by the relations

$$|F(u,v)| = [R^2(u,v) + I^2(u,v)]^{\frac{1}{2}} \qquad (2.11)$$

$$\Phi(u,v) = tan^{-1}[\frac{I(u,v)}{R(u,v)}] \qquad (2.12)$$

and

$$P(u,v) = |F(u,v)|^2 = R^2(u,v) + I^2(u,v) \qquad (2.13)$$

2.2.2 Discrete Fourier transform

Suppose that a continuous function $f(x)$ is discretised into a sequence $\{f(x_0), f(x_0 + \Delta_x), f(x_0 + 2\Delta_x), \ldots, f(x_0 + [N-1]\Delta_x)\}$ by taking N samples Δx units apart, as shown in Fig.2.1. It will be convenient in subsequent developments to use x as either a discrete or continuous variable, depending on the context of the discussion.

$$f(x) = f(x_0 + x\Delta_x) \tag{2.14}$$

where x now assumes the discrete values $0, 1, 2, \ldots, N - 1$. In other words, the sequence $\{f(0), f(1), \ldots, f(N-1)\}$ will be used to denote any N uniformly spaced samples from a corresponding continuous function.

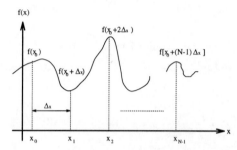

Figure 2.1: *Sampling a continuous function*

With the above notation in mind, the discrete Fourier transform pair that applies to sampled functions is given by

$$F(u) = \frac{1}{N} \sum_{x=0}^{N-1} f(x) exp[-j2\pi ux/N] \tag{2.15}$$

for $u = 0, 1, 2, \ldots, N - 1$, and

$$f(x) = \sum_{u=0}^{N-1} F(u) exp[j2\pi ux/N] \tag{2.16}$$

for $x = 0, 1, 2, \ldots, N - 1$.

The values $u = 0, 1, 2, \ldots, N-1$ in the discrete Fourier transform given by Eq.(2.15) correspond to samples of the continuous transform at values $0, \Delta_u, 2\Delta_u, \ldots, (N-1)\Delta_u$. In other words, $F(u)$ represents $F(u\Delta_u)$. This notation is similar to that used for the discrete $f(x)$, with the exception that the samples of $F(u)$ start at the origin of the frequency axis. It can be shown that Δ_u and Δ_x are related by the expression

$$\Delta_u = \frac{1}{N\Delta_x}. \tag{2.17}$$

In the two-variable case the discrete Fourier transform pair is given by the equations

$$F(u,v) = \frac{1}{MN} \sum_{x=0}^{M-1} \sum_{y=0}^{N-1} f(x,y) exp[-j2\pi(ux/M + vy/N)] \qquad (2.18)$$

for $u = 0, 1, 2, \ldots, M - 1$, $v = 0, 1, 2, \ldots, N - 1$, and

$$f(x,y) = \sum_{u=0}^{M-1} \sum_{v=0}^{N-1} F(u,v) exp[j2\pi(ux/M + vy/N)] \qquad (2.19)$$

for $x = 0, 1, 2, \ldots, M - 1$, $y = 0, 1, 2, \ldots, N - 1$.

Sampling of a continuous function is now a two-dimensional grid with divisions of width Δ_x and Δ_y in the x and y axis, respectively. As in the one-dimensional case, the discrete function $f(x,y)$ represents samples of the function $f(x_0 + x\Delta_x, y_0 + y\Delta_y)$ for $x = 0, 1, 2, \ldots, M - 1$, $y = 0, 1, 2, \ldots, N - 1$. Similar comments hold for $F(u,v)$. The sampling increments in the spatial and frequency domains are related by

$$\Delta_u = \frac{1}{M\Delta_x} \qquad (2.20)$$

and

$$\Delta_v = \frac{1}{N\Delta_y}. \qquad (2.21)$$

When images are sampled in a square array in which $M = N$,

$$F(u,v) = \frac{1}{N} \sum_{x=0}^{N-1} \sum_{y=0}^{N-1} f(x,y) exp[-j2\pi(ux + vy)/N] \qquad (2.22)$$

for $u, v = 0, 1, 2, \ldots, N - 1$, and

$$f(x,y) = \frac{1}{N} \sum_{u=0}^{N-1} \sum_{v=0}^{N-1} F(u,v) exp[j2\pi(ux + vy)/N] \qquad (2.23)$$

for $x, y = 0, 1, 2, \ldots, N - 1$. Note that in this case a $1/N$ term is included in both expressions. Since $F(u,v)$ and $f(x,y)$ are a Fourier transform pair, the grouping of these constant multiplicative terms is arbitrary. In practice, images are typically digitised in square arrays, so the Fourier transform pair given in Eqs.(2.22) and (2.23) is of particular significance.

The Fourier spectrum, phase and power spectrum of one- and two-dimensional discrete functions are also given by Eqs.(2.5) through (2.7) and Eqs.(2.11) through

(2.13), respectively. The only difference is that the independent variables are discrete.

Unlike the continuous case, we need not be concerned about the existence of the discrete Fourier transform since in the discrete case both $F(u)$ and $F(u, v)$ always exist. In the one-dimensional case, for example, this can be shown by direct substitution of Eq.(2.16) into Eq.(2.15)

$$
\begin{aligned}
F(u) &= \frac{1}{N} \sum_{x=0}^{N-1} \left[\sum_{r=0}^{N-1} F(r) exp[j2\pi rx/N] exp[-j2\pi ux/N] \right] \\
&= \frac{1}{N} \sum_{r=0}^{N-1} F(r) \left[\sum_{x=0}^{N-1} exp[j2\pi rx/N] exp[-j2\pi ux/N] \right] \\
&= F(u).
\end{aligned}
\tag{2.24}
$$

Eq.(2.24) follows from the orthogonality condition

$$
\sum_{x=0}^{N-1} exp[j2\pi rx/N] exp[-j2\pi ux/N] = \begin{cases} N, & \text{if } r = u \\ 0, & \text{otherwise.} \end{cases}
\tag{2.25}
$$

Note that a change of variable from u to r was made in Eq.(2.15) to clarify the notation.

Substitution of Eq.(2.15) into Eq.(2.16) would also yield an identity for $f(x)$, thus indicating that the Fourier transform pair given by these equations always exists. A similar argument holds for the discrete, two-dimensional Fourier transform pair.

2.2.3   Properties of the Fourier transform

In this subsection the properties of the two-dimensional Fourier transform are demonstrated; these properties also hold for the one-dimensional case. Table 2.1 gives a summary of the properties; some of these properties are discussed in what follows.

1. *Uniqueness.* For continuous functions, $f(x, y)$ and $F(u, v)$ are unique with respect to one another. There is no loss of information if instead of preserving the image, its Fourier transform is preserved. This fact has been utilized in an image data compression technique called *transform coding.*

2. *Separability.* By definition, the Fourier transform kernel is separable, so that it can be written as a separable transformation in x and y, i.e.,

$$F(u,v) = \int_{-\infty}^{+\infty} \left[\int_{-\infty}^{+\infty} f(x,y)exp(-j2\pi xu)dx \right] exp(-j2\pi vy)dy \qquad (2.26)$$

This means the two-dimensional transform can be realized by a succession of one-dimensional transforms along each of the spatial co-ordinates.

3. *Frequency response and eigenfunctions of a shift invariant system.* An eigenfunction of a system is defined as an input function that is reproduced at the output with a possible change only in its amplitude. A fundamental property of a linear shift invariant system is that its eigenfunctions are given by the complex exponential $exp[j2\pi(ux + vy)]$. Thus in Fig.2.2, for any fixed (u,v), the output of the linear shift invariant system would be

$$g(x,y) = \int_{-\infty}^{+\infty} \int_{-\infty}^{+\infty} h(x - x', y - y')exp[j2\pi(ux' + vy')]dx'dy' \qquad (2.27)$$

Performing the change of variables $\hat{x} = x - x', \hat{y} = y - y'$ and simplifying the result, yields

$$g(x,y) = H(u,v)exp[j2\pi(ux + vy)] \qquad (2.28)$$

The function $H(u,v)$, which is the Fourier transform of the impulse response, is also called the *frequency response* of the system. It represents the (complex) amplitude of the system response at spatial frequency (u,v).

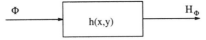

Figure 2.2: *Eigenfunctions of a linear shift invariant system.* $\Phi = exp[j2\pi(ux+vy)]$, $H_\Phi = H(u,v) = Fourier\ transform\ of\ h(x,y)$.

4. *Convolution theorem.* The Fourier transform of the convolution of two functions is the product of their Fourier transforms, i.e.,

$$g(x,y) = h(x,y) \star f(x,y) \Longleftrightarrow G(u,v) = H(u,v)F(u,v) \qquad (2.29)$$

where the symbol $\star$ denotes convolution. This theorem suggests that the convolution of two functions may be evaluated by inverse Fourier transforming the product of their Fourier transforms. The discrete version of this theorem yields a fast transform based convolution algorithm.

The converse of the convolution theorem is that the Fourier transform of the product of two functions is the convolution of their Fourier transforms.

The result of the convolution theorem can also be extended to *spatial cross correlation* between two real functions $h(x, y)$ and $f(x, y)$, which is defined as

$$c(x, y) = h(x, y) \odot f(x, y) = \int\limits_{-\infty}^{+\infty} \int\limits_{-\infty}^{+\infty} h(x', y') f(x + x', y + y') dx' dy' \quad (2.30)$$

where the symbol $\odot$ denotes cross correlation. A change of variables shows that $c(x, y)$ is also the convolution $h(-x, -y) \star f(x, y)$, which yields

$$C(u, v) = H(-u, -v) F(u, v) \quad (2.31)$$

5. *Inner product preservation.* Another important property of the Fourier transform is that the inner product of two functions is equal to the inner product of their Fourier transforms, i.e.,

$$I = \int\limits_{-\infty}^{+\infty} \int\limits_{-\infty}^{+\infty} f(x, y) h^*(x, y) dx dy = \int\limits_{-\infty}^{+\infty} \int\limits_{-\infty}^{+\infty} F(u, v) H^*(u, v) du dv \quad (2.32)$$

Setting $h = f$, we obtain the well-known *Parseval energy conservation formula*

$$\int\limits_{-\infty}^{+\infty} \int\limits_{-\infty}^{+\infty} |f(x, y)|^2 dx dy = \int\limits_{-\infty}^{+\infty} \int\limits_{-\infty}^{+\infty} |F(u, v)|^2 du dv \quad (2.33)$$

i.e., the total energy in the function is the same as in its Fourier transform.

6. *Hankel transform.* The Fourier transform of a circularly symmetric function is also circularly symmetric and is given by what is called the *Hankel transform*.

Table 2.1: *Properties of two-dimensional Fourier transform*

Property	Function $f(x, y)$	Fourier transform $F(u, v)$
Rotation	$f(\pm x, \pm y)$	$F(\pm u, \pm v)$
Linearity	$a_1 f_1(x, y) + a_2 f_2(x, y)$	$a_1 F_1(u, v) + a_2 F_2(u, v)$
Conjugation	$f^*(x, y)$	$F^*(-u, -v)$
Separability	$f_1(x) f_2(y)$	$F_1(u) F_2(v)$
Scaling	$f(ax, by)$	$\frac{F(u/a, v/b)}{\|ab\|}$
Shifting	$f(x \pm x_0, y \pm y_0)$	$exp[\pm j2\pi(x_0 u + y_0 v)] F(u, v)$
Modulation	$exp[\pm j2\pi(\eta x + \xi y)] f(x, y)$	$F(u \mp \eta, v \mp \xi)$
Convolution	$g(x, y) = h(x, y) \star f(x, y)$	$G(u, v) = H(u, v) F(u, v)$
Multiplication	$g(x, y) = h(x, y) f(x, y)$	$G(u, v) = H(u, v) \star F(u, v)$
Cross correlation	$c(x, y) = h(x, y) \odot f(x, y)$	$C(u, v) = H(-u, -v) F(u, v)$
Inner product	$I = \int\limits_{-\infty}^{+\infty} \int\limits_{-\infty}^{+\infty} f(x, y) h^*(x, y) dx dy$	$I = \int\limits_{-\infty}^{+\infty} \int\limits_{-\infty}^{+\infty} F(u, v) H^*(u, v) du dv$

2.3 Fourier Transform Property of a Lens

The optical Fourier transform property (FTP) of a lens is detailed in Refs [1][2], so a rigorous treatment is not given here. The FTP of a lens is easily established from the diffraction integral that describes the propagation of monochromatic light in free space. The diffraction integral is central to the study of Fourier optics, and virtually all optical phenomena can be explained mathematically in terms of it. The diffraction integral can be represented by the angular spectrum of plane waves which is the Fourier transform of the input. The FTP of a lens is usually derived assuming an idealised lens between object and back focal plane (BFP) and the validity of the stationary phase approximation for the Fourier transform configuration. The diffraction integral is applied twice — from the object to the lens and from the lens to the BFP. The light amplitude in the BFP is, apart from a constant and a quadratic phase factor, the classical two-dimensional Fourier transform of the transmittance of the diffracting object.

It is well-known that the diffraction integral takes the form

$$U_z(x, y) = \frac{1}{j\lambda z} \int\limits_{-\infty}^{+\infty} \int\limits_{-\infty}^{+\infty} U_0(\xi, \eta) exp[jk\sqrt{z^2 + r^2}] du dv \qquad (2.34)$$

where $U_z(x, y)$ is the complex amplitude of a plane wave in an xy-plane which is orthogonal to the optical axis z. $U_0(\xi, \eta)$ denotes the object, $U(x, y)$, at the distance $z = 0$. $k = 2\pi/\lambda$ is the propagation number; and $r = \sqrt{(x - \xi)^2 + (y - \eta)^2}$. Using the Fresnel approximation i.e.,

$$
\begin{aligned}
\sqrt{z^2 + r^2} &= \sqrt{z^2 + (x - \xi)^2 + (y - \eta)^2} \\
&= z + (x - \xi)^2/2z + (y - \eta)^2/2z,
\end{aligned} \tag{2.35}
$$

Eq.(2.34) can be written as

$$
U_z(x, y) = \frac{e^{jkz}}{j\lambda z} \int\limits_{-\infty}^{+\infty} \int\limits_{-\infty}^{+\infty} U_0(\xi, \eta) exp\left\{j\frac{\pi}{\lambda z}[(x - \xi)^2 + (y - \eta)^2]\right\} d\xi d\eta, \tag{2.36}
$$

which is a pivotal result and is the form of the diffraction integral most often used in Fourier optics. Its repeated application leads directly to the FTP of a lens. However, the intermediate integrals are rather cumbersome and therefore, for simplicity, the analysis is given in one-dimension. Hence, Eq.(2.36) is written as

$$
U_z(x) = \frac{e^{jkz/2}}{\sqrt{j\lambda z}} \int\limits_{-\infty}^{+\infty} U_0(\xi) exp\left[j\frac{\pi}{\lambda z}(x - \xi)^2\right] du, \tag{2.37}
$$

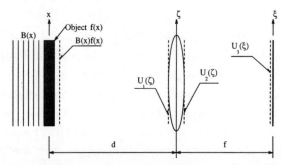

Figure 2.3: *Configuration for analysing the Fourier transform property of a lens. The fields adjacent to the various surfaces are indicated by dashed lines.*

Consider the (one-dimensional) configuration shown in Fig.2.3. The field immediately after the object $f(x)$ is $U_0(x) = B(x)f(x)$, where, for simplicity, $B(x)$ is set to 1, i.e., a unit amplitude plane wave travelling parallel to the z-axis. Just before the lens, a distance d away, the field is

$$
U_1(\zeta) = K_1(d) \int\limits_{-\infty}^{+\infty} f(x) exp\left[j\frac{\pi}{\lambda d}(\zeta - x)^2\right] dx, \tag{2.38}
$$

where Eq.(2.37) is used with $d \equiv z$ and

$$K_1(d) = \left. \frac{e^{jkz/2}}{\sqrt{j\lambda z}} \right|_{z=d} \tag{2.39}$$

The overall lens transmittance is $P(\zeta)exp[-j(\pi/\lambda f)\zeta^2]$, where $P(\zeta)$ is the pupil function associated with the lens aperture and can be generalised to include aberrations. Typically, for an ideal, non-absorbing lens of diameter L,

$$P(\zeta) = rect(\zeta/L), \tag{2.40}$$

where

$$rect\left(\frac{\zeta}{L}\right) = \begin{cases} 1, & \text{when } \zeta < L/2 \\ 0, & \text{otherwise.} \end{cases} \tag{2.41}$$

Right after the lens the field $U_2(\zeta)$ is given by

$$U_2(\zeta) = U_1(\zeta)P(\zeta)exp\left(-j\frac{\pi}{\lambda f}\zeta^2\right), \tag{2.42}$$

and the field in the back focal plane is

$$U_3(\xi) = K_1(f) \int_{-\infty}^{+\infty} U_2(\zeta)exp\left[j\frac{\pi}{\lambda f}(\xi - \zeta)^2\right] d\zeta. \tag{2.43}$$

Substituting Eq.(2.38) into Eq.(2.42) and then inserting Eq.(2.42) into Eq.(2.43) enables us to write, after some manipulation,

$$\begin{aligned} U_3(\xi) = & \ K_1(d)K_1(f)exp\left[j\frac{\pi}{\lambda f}\left(1 - \frac{d}{f}\right)\xi^2\right] \\ & \times \int_{-\infty}^{+\infty} f(x)exp\left(-j\frac{2\pi}{\lambda f}x\xi\right) A(x,\xi)dx, \end{aligned} \tag{2.44}$$

where

$$A(x,\xi) = \int_{-\infty}^{+\infty} P(\zeta)exp\left\{j\frac{\pi}{\lambda d}\left[\zeta - \left(x + \frac{d}{f}\xi\right)\right]^2\right\} d\zeta. \tag{2.45}$$

Because $P(\zeta)$ is a "slowly varying" function, for values of λ that are typical of the optical regime, the integral in Eq.(2.45) can be evaluated by the method of stationary phase ([3], p.234). This gives

$$A(x,\xi) = \sqrt{j\lambda d}P[x + (d/f)\xi]. \tag{2.46}$$

Inserting this result into Eq.(2.44) yields

$$U_3(\xi) = \frac{1}{\sqrt{j\lambda f}} exp\left[j\frac{\pi}{\lambda f}\left(1-\frac{d}{f}\right)\xi^2\right]$$

$$\times \int_{-\infty}^{+\infty} f(x)P\left(x+\frac{d}{f}\xi\right)exp\left(-j\frac{2\pi}{\lambda f}x\xi\right)dx, \qquad (2.47)$$

where the unimportant complex factors $e^{jkd/2}e^{jkf/2}$ are omitted. Eq.(2.47) is the final result. Since ξ can be written in terms of the spatial frequency u according to $\xi = u\lambda f$, we can rewrite Eq.(2.47) as

$$U_3(u\lambda f) \equiv \tilde{U}_3(u) = \frac{1}{\sqrt{j\lambda f}}exp\left[j\pi\left(1-\frac{d}{f}\right)u^2\lambda f\right]$$

$$\times \int_{-\infty}^{+\infty} f(x)P(x+\lambda ud)exp(-j2\pi ux)dx, \qquad (2.48)$$

Thus, based on Eq.(2.48), some interesting conclusions can be drawn:

(1) For $d = f$, i.e., the object in the front focal plane of the lens, the phase factor outside the integral vanishes; thereby an exact Fourier transform relationship exists between the front and back focal planes of a lens. As can be seen from Eq.(2.48), this is only true if the effect of the pupil is ignored.

(2) For $d = 0$, i.e., the object against the lens, the phase factor does not vanish, but the effect of the pupil vanishes if the physical extent of the object is smaller than the lens aperture. Thus, if D is the maximum dimension of the object and $D < L$, then up to a phase factor and a constant, a Fourier transform relation is indeed observed.

(3) For $d \neq 0$, the fidelity of the Fourier transform of the object will depend on the spatial frequency u. For $D < L$, the lens will act as a low-pass filter. From Eq.(2.48) the following can be easily verified

$$\text{for} \qquad |u| < \frac{L-D}{2\lambda d}, \qquad \text{no attenuation of the spectrum;} \qquad (2.49)$$

$$\text{for} \quad \frac{L-D}{2\lambda d} < |u| < \frac{L+D}{2\lambda d}, \quad \text{partial attenuation of the spectrum;} \qquad (2.50)$$

$$\text{for} \qquad |u| > \frac{L+D}{2\lambda d}, \qquad \text{total attenuation of the spectrum.} \qquad (2.51)$$

The attenuation of high frequency components in the Fourier spectrum is known as *vignetting*. As can be seen, vignetting is due to the finite lens aperture and can be minimised by making d small. Although a small d does not eliminate the quadratic phase factor in Eq.(2.48), the presence of the latter is of no consequence in intensity (irradiance) spectrum measurements which only involve $|\tilde{U}_3(u)|^2$. Hence it is preferred practice to place the sample as near to the lens as possible when making spectral measurements; this reduces the low pass bias of the lens.

The two-dimensional form of Eq.(2.48) is,

$$\tilde{U}_3(u) = \frac{1}{j\lambda f} exp\left[j\pi\lambda f\left(1 - \frac{d}{f}\right)(u^2 + v^2)\right] \int\limits_{-\infty}^{+\infty}\int\limits_{-\infty}^{+\infty} t(x,y)$$
$$\times P(x + \lambda du, y + \lambda dv)exp(-j2\pi(ux + vy))dxdy, \qquad (2.52)$$

This assumes illumination by a unit amplitude monochromatic plane wave. If the amplitude of the illumination were C, then this term would appear as a factor in Eq.(2.52). Eq.(2.52) is extremely important for optical information (or pattern recognition) processing, as it can be coded into a computer and used to simulate the performance of such systems, it is thus an extremely useful design tool.

2.4 Complex Spatial Filtering

2.4.1 Coherent Optical Processor

As discussed in the above section, the ease with which a lens can perform the Fourier transform of a two-dimensional distribution is certainly one of the most important assets of coherent optical data processing. Perhaps even more important is the fact that the spectrum of the input is physically accessible and therefore can be manipulated simply by placing masks or optical filters in the Fourier transform plane. The optical processor of Fig.2.4 is typically called a 4-F system. It is one of several possible optical configurations that permit signal processing.

An input transparency of complex amplitude transmittance $f(x,y)$ is placed in the front focal plane of lens 1 and illuminated by a plane parallel beam of uniform intensity and zero phase. The amplitude distribution in the back focal plane of lens

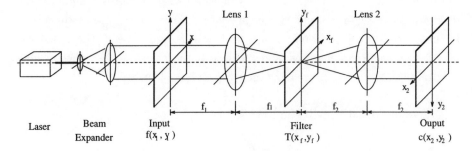

Figure 2.4: *Coherent optical processor.*

1 is represented by the Fourier transform $F(u, v)$ of the input. Neglecting some proportionality factors,

$$
\begin{aligned}
F(u, v) &= \mathcal{F}[f(x, y)] \\
&= \int_{-\infty}^{+\infty} \int_{-\infty}^{+\infty} f(x, y) exp[-j2\pi(ux + vy)]dxdy
\end{aligned}
\tag{2.53}
$$

where (u, v) are the rectangular spatial frequencies of the input. If the wavelength of the illuminating light is λ, the relationship between the coordinates (x_f, y_f), (u, v) and λ in the Fourier plane is given by

$$
u = x_f/\lambda f_1 \qquad and \qquad v = y_f/\lambda f_1
\tag{2.54}
$$

where f_1 is the focal length of lens 1. If a filter transparency of amplitude transmittance $T(x_f, y_f)$ is placed in the back focal plane of lens 1, the amplitude distribution just after the transparency becomes

$$
U_f(x_f, y_f) = F(x_f, y_f)T(x_f, y_f)
\tag{2.55}
$$

The second lens 2 of the processor performs a second Fourier transform of $U_f(x_f, y_f)$, leading to an amplitude distribution in its back focal plane given by

$$
c(x_2, y_2) = \mathcal{F}^{-1}[U_f(u', v')],
\tag{2.56}
$$

where $u' = x_f/\lambda f_2 = u/M$, $v' = y_f/\lambda f_2 = v/M$, and $M = f_2/f_1$ is the lateral magnification of the image system. Use of Eqs.(2.55) and (2.56) leads to the well known relationship between input and output of a linear invariant coherent system.

The output spectrum then becomes the product of the input spectrum with the transfer function $H(u, v)$ which is proportional to the amplitude transmittance of the pupil mask $T(x_f, y_f)$, i.e.,

$$C(u, v) = F(u, v)H(u, v), \qquad H(u, v) = T(\lambda f u, \lambda f v). \qquad (2.57)$$

Equivalently, the output can be represented as the convolution of the input — scaled by a magnification factor M — with a point spread function (impulse response) $h(x_2, y_2)$

$$c(x_2, y_2) = \int\limits_{-\infty}^{+\infty} \int\limits_{-\infty}^{+\infty} f(Mx_1, My_1)h(x_2 - Mx_1, y_2 - My_1)dx_1 dy_1, \qquad (2.58)$$

where

$$h(x_2, y_2) = \mathcal{F}^{-1}[H(u, v)], \qquad (2.59)$$

In abbreviated notation, the convolution product is denoted by the symbol $\star$, thus Eq.(2.58) takes the form

$$c(x, y) = f(x, y) \star h(x, y). \qquad (2.60)$$

2.4.2   Complex spatial filtering

The coherent optical processor of Fig.2.4 is capable of performing a general linear invariant transformation as expressed by Eqs.(2.57) and (2.58). This is possible, of course, as long as the complex-valued filter transmittance $T(x_f, y_f)$ can be constructed. Complex spatial filters have been found to be useful in many applications. Various names have been given to these filters according to the context in which they are used: The terms *holographic filters* and *Fourier holograms* refer to the technique usually involved in filter production. In image enhancement, they might be called inverse filters or deblurring filters, while in pattern recognition, their most common names are VanderLugt filters or matched spatial filters.

An interferometric technique widely used to record any complex filter for which the point spread function is known was introduced by VanderLugt [4]. It consists of recording the interference pattern produced when the desired filter function is mixed with a mutually coherent reference beam. This is essentially a Fourier hologram of the optical system point spread function. The process is similar to the modulation technique in information theory where a complex-valued function (signal) can be recorded as a real valued function on a carrier frequency as long as the sampling theorem is satisfied; i.e., the carrier frequency must be at least twice as large as the signal cut off frequency.

2.4.3 Holographic recording

The most straightforward technique for recording a complex valued holographic filter is shown in Fig.2.5. A transparency of amplitude transmittance proportional to the desired point spread function $h(x, y)$ is placed in the front focal plane of lens L and illuminated by a monochromatic plane wave. The distribution in the back focal plane is made to interfere with a mutually coherent plane parallel reference beam U_R tilted by an angle θ with respect to the z_f-axis. The total complex amplitude U_T in plane P_f is then

$$U_T(x_f, y_f) = U_R(x_f, y_f) + H(x_f, y_f), \qquad (2.61)$$

where

$$U_R(x_f, y_f) = R \; exp(-j2\pi u_0 x_f), \qquad (2.62)$$

R^2 is a measure of the reference-to-object beam energy ratio, and u_0 is the carrier spatial frequency given by

$$u_0 = \sin \theta / \lambda. \qquad (2.63)$$

The plane reference wave can also be regarded as the uniform spectrum of a point source $\delta(x_1 - x'_R, y_1)$ located at the coordinate $(x'_R, 0)$ in the object plane. In the paraxial approximation,

$$x'_R = \lambda f u_0 = f \sin \theta \qquad (2.64)$$

From Eqs.(2.61) and (2.62), the total irradiance in plane P_f is given by

$$
\begin{aligned}
I(x_f, y_f) &= |U_T(x_f, y_f)|^2 \\
&= R^2 + |H(x_f, y_f)|^2 + RH(x_f, y_f) exp(j2\pi u_0 x_f) \\
&\quad + RH^*(x_f, y_f) exp(-j2\pi u_0 x_f) \qquad (2.65)
\end{aligned}
$$

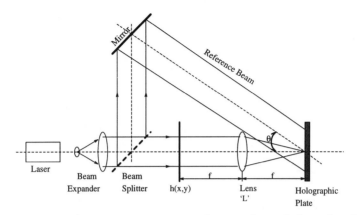

Figure 2.5: *Interferometric arrangement for recording a holographic filter.*

If the complex function $H(x_f, y_f)$ is written as

$$H(x_f, y_f) = |H(x_f, y_f)| exp[j\phi(x_f, y_f)] \tag{2.66}$$

the expression for the irradiance $I(x_f, y_f)$ can be rewritten as

$$
\begin{aligned}
I(x_f, y_f) &= R^2 + |H(x_f, y_f)|^2 \\
&\quad +2RH(x_f, y_f)\cos[2\pi u_0 x_f + \phi(x_f, y_f)].
\end{aligned}
\tag{2.67}
$$

This expression shows explicitly how the phase $\phi(x_f, y_f)$ is encoded as a modulation of the spatial carrier.

At this point, it is customary to assume that this irradiance is recorded linearly on some suitable medium. High resolution photographic emulsions are often used for their high information capacity and relative low cost. Linear recording implies that the amplitude transmittance of the developed plate or film is proportional to the irradiance, i.e.,

$$T(x_f, y_f) \propto I(x_f, y_f). \tag{2.68}$$

Linear recording over an extended dynamic range is extremely difficult to achieve by photographic means. It is, however, useful to perform an analysis of this ideal case.

2.4.4 Coherent optical correlation

If a filter of amplitude transmittance $T(x_f, y_f)$ as described in Eq.(2.68) is placed in the filter plane of a double-diffraction setup such as that shown in Fig.2.4, the resulting system is a processor with a transfer function proportional to Eq.(2.65) or Eq.(2.67). With an amplitude distribution $f(x, y)$ in the input plane, using Eqs.(2.58), (2.68), and (2.65), the amplitude distribution in the output plane is

$$
\begin{aligned}
U_2(x_2, y_2) \;=\; & \mathcal{F}^{-1}[F(u,v)T(u,v)] \\
=\; & \int_{-\infty}^{+\infty}\!\!\int_{-\infty}^{+\infty} R^2 F(u,v) exp[-j2\pi(ux_2 + vy_2)]dudv \\
& + \int_{-\infty}^{+\infty}\!\!\int_{-\infty}^{+\infty} |H(u,v)|^2 F(u,v) exp[-j2\pi(ux_2 + vy_2)]dudv \\
& + \int_{-\infty}^{+\infty}\!\!\int_{-\infty}^{+\infty} RH(u,v)F(u,v) exp(j2\pi u x_R)\, exp[-j2\pi(ux_2 + vy_2)]dudv \\
& + \int_{-\infty}^{+\infty}\!\!\int_{-\infty}^{+\infty} RH^*(u,v)F(u,v) exp(-j2\pi u x_R)\, exp[-j2\pi(ux_2 + vy_2)]dudv
\end{aligned}
$$

$$(2.69)$$

By using elementary properties of the Fourier transform, Eq.(2.69) can also be written as

$$
\begin{aligned}
U_2(x_2, y_2) \;=\; & R^2 f(x_2, y_2) \\
& + \int_{-\infty}^{+\infty}\!\!\int_{-\infty}^{+\infty}\!\!\int_{-\infty}^{+\infty}\!\!\int_{-\infty}^{+\infty} h(\xi, \eta)h^*(\xi + \alpha - x_2, \eta + \beta - y_2)f(\alpha, \beta)d\xi d\eta d\alpha d\beta \\
& + R \int_{-\infty}^{+\infty}\!\!\int_{-\infty}^{+\infty} h(x_2 + x_R - \xi, y_2 - \xi)f(\xi, \eta)d\xi d\eta \\
& + R \int_{-\infty}^{+\infty}\!\!\int_{-\infty}^{+\infty} (\xi - x_2 + x_R, \eta - y_2)f(\xi, \eta)d\xi d\eta
\end{aligned}
$$

$$(2.70)$$

or, in shorthand notation, as

$$
\begin{aligned}
U_2(x_2, y_2) \;=\; & R^2 f(x_2, y_2) \\
& + f(x_2, y_2) \star h(x_2, y_2) \star h^*(-x_2, -y_2)
\end{aligned}
$$

$$+ Rf(x_2, y_2) \star h(x_2, y_2) \star \delta(x_2 + x_R, y_2)$$

$$+ Rf(x_2, y_2) \star h^*(-x_2, -y_2) \star \delta(x_2 - x_R, y_2) \qquad (2.71)$$

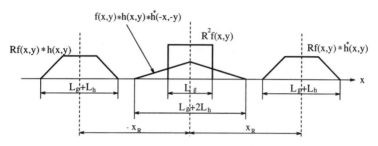

Here '*' means the convolution operation.

Figure 2.6: *Output of an optical processor with a holographic filter.*

In these expressions, $x_R = M x'_R$ is the abscissa of the point in the output plane where the reference beam used to record the holographic filter would come to focus. The different output terms are shown in Fig.2.6. The first two terms of Eq.(2.71) are components centred at the origin of the output plane. The third term is the convolution product of the input $f(x, y)$ with the desired point spread function $h(x_2, y_2)$. The convolution with the delta function shifts the term along the x_2-axis and centres it at $(-x_R, 0)$. The last term is the correlation of the input and the point spread function centred at $(x_R, 0)$ in the output plane. Clearly, if x_R is large enough, the different terms can be separated in the output plane.

2.5 Matched Spatial Filters

According to the above description, correlation and convolution are integral operations that depend on two input functions $f(x, y)$ and $h(x, y)$

$$convolution: \qquad f(x, y) \star h(x, y) = \int \int f(x, y) h(x' - x, y' - y) dx dy \qquad (2.72)$$

$$correlation: \qquad f(x, y) \odot h(x, y) = \int \int f(x, y) h^*(x - x', y - y') dx dy \qquad (2.73)$$

If both inputs are identical, i.e., $f(x, y) = h(x, y)$, the operations are often called autocorrelation (or autoconvolution). Otherwise, they are referred to as cross-correlation (or cross-convolution). For pattern recognition applications, the correlation peak height (at $x' = 0, y' = 0$) is usually measured. In this case the important fact is that the normalised, modulus squared peak (peak intensity) is always higher for an autocorrelation than a cross-correlation. Therefore, the measured intensity peak height in an optical correlation system can be used directly to recognise a specific input signal. The recognition process is, however, sensitive to changes in scale and/or rotation of one or both input functions.

Due to the rapid development of the spatial light modulator, optical materials and filter design techniques, real time pattern recognition exploiting hybrid optical and/or digital correlation offers several interesting solutions to the general problem of object recognition. Thus, much effort has been devoted to designing spatial filters suitable for implementation on currently available spatial light modulators, instead of experimental holographic and/or computer generated holograms implemented in photo-refractive materials or permanent recording media. In the following some fundamental matched spatial filter designs are considered.

2.5.1   Classical matched filter

As is well-known in communication theory, the optimum filter, in the sense of signal-to-noise ratio (SNR), for extracting (recognising) a known signal $s(t)$ from stationary noise $n(t)$, is a matched filter with a transfer function

$$H(u) = kS^*(u)/|N(u)|^2, \qquad (2.74)$$

where $S(u)$ is the signal spectrum, $|N(u)|^2$ is the noise spectral density, and k is a constant. For the optical counterpart of this matched filter, one can simply replace the temporal variables t and u by their spatial equivalents (x, y) and (u, v), respectively. An optical filter matched to the input pattern (image) $f(x, y)$ should have a transfer function proportional to the complex conjugate of the pattern (image) spectrum

$$H(u, v) = kF^*(u, v)/|N(u, v)|^2, \qquad (2.75)$$

If the noise $n(x, y)$ is white, then its power spectrum is a constant, i.e., $|N(u, v)|^2 = N_0^2$. In this case, Eq.(2.75) becomes

$$H(u, v) = kF^*(u, v), \tag{2.76}$$

This filter is called the classical matched filter (CMF) which yields the highest possible output SNR, where SNR is defined as below,

$$SNR = \frac{|E\{c(0, 0)\}|^2}{var\{c(0, 0)\}}, \tag{2.77}$$

where $c(0, 0)$ denotes the correlation output at the origin (in the absence of noise, autocorrelation peak at the origin) and $E\{\ \}$ and $var\{\ \}$ denote the expected value and the variance, respectively.

Although the CMF is optimal from SNR considerations, its optical implementation suffers from several disadvantages. Firstly, because of the complex nature of the filter transmittance, it cannot be conveniently represented by currently available real-time devices. Also, the light throughput efficiency (i.e., Horner efficiency) of the CMF is low, due to the fact that the normalised magnitude in Eq.(2.73) is less than one at most frequencies. These problems led to the introduction of several related spatial filtering schemes such as phase-only filter (POF), binary POF (BPOF), and ternary matched filter (TMF) etc.

2.5.2 Phase-only matched filter

Horner and Gianino [5] suggested a phase-only filter consisting of the phase of the CMF with unity modulus. Writing Eq.(2.76) as

$$H(u, v) = k|F(u, v)|exp[-i\phi(u, v)] \tag{2.78}$$

the POF is defined as

$$H(u, v) = exp[-i\phi(u, v)] \tag{2.79}$$

where $\phi(u, v)$ is the phase of $F(u, v)$. The POF offers the potential of high light efficiency (approaching 100%). It can also yield sharper correlation peaks with higher peak to side lobe ratios than the CMF. This characteristic of the POF is a consequence of the large bandwidths inherent in Eq.(2.79), which can adversely affect the SNR. The POF is implementable on existing spatial light modulators (SLM) such as the liquid crystal television (LCTV).

The importance of the Fourier plane phase information is already well known from image processing. Kinoform elements, which are also phase-only Fourier filters, allow rather general image reconstruction. Therefore, the good performance of phase-only matched filters is not surprising. Besides the improvement of the light efficiency, the output peak structure for the recognition process is also usually enhanced. Obviously the step from the matched filter to the phase-only matched filter can be described in spatial filtering theory as application of a $1/|F(u,v)|$ filter. Since $|F(u,v)|$ usually has a strong peak structure (high amplitude for low spatial frequencies and low amplitude for high spatial frequencies), its inverse can be interpreted as a spatial frequency high-pass filter. The result of the application of the phase-only matched filter is therefore, in general, a conventional high-pass filtered correlation function. For the case of an autocorrelation, the output peak is therefore strongly enhanced. Hence, the peak to sidelobe ratio and the discrimination ability of the filter are improved. On the other hand, this filter is more sensitive to modifications of the input function such as rotation or scale change. Also, it is extremely sensitive to the noise in the input scene, because the all-pass nature of the POF allows unattenuated input noise to pass through the correlator system.

2.5.3 Binary phase-only filter

Binarization of the POF is the 'next step required to develop real time correlation type processors using currently available device technology. Devices such as the magneto-optic spatial light modulator, when operated in the phase mode, have two states: +1 and -1. Two state BPOFs have been shown to produce useful correlation responses in the absence of noise [6][7][8].

Binarization of the phase of the Fourier transform of real functions can be accomplished in several ways. Horner et al. [7] proposed a BPOF defined by

$$H_o(u,v) = \begin{cases} +1, & \text{Im}[F(u,v)] \geq 0 \\ -1, & \text{otherwise.} \end{cases}$$
$$= sgn[-F(u,v)_o] \tag{2.80}$$

where the subscript 'o' is used to emphasise that this filter is effectively matched to the odd part of the object function. Psaltis et al. [9] suggested the algorithm

$$H_o(u,v) = \begin{cases} +1, & \text{Re}[F(u,v)] \geq 0 \\ -1, & \text{otherwise} \end{cases}$$
$$= sgn[-F(u,v)_e] \tag{2.81}$$

where the subscript 'e' corresponds to an effective match with the even part of the object function. Cottrell et al. [8] suggested a binarization based on the Hartley transform of the object function, given by

$$H_H(u,v) = \begin{cases} +1, & H(u,v) \geq 0 \\ -1, & \text{otherwise} \end{cases}$$
$$= sgn[H(u,v)] \tag{2.82}$$

where $H(u,v)$ is the Hartley transform [10]. The Hartley transform of the function $f(x,y)$ is defined by

$$H(u,v) = \int \int f(x,y)[cos(ux+vy) + sin(ux+vy)]dxdy$$
$$= \text{Re}[F(u,v)] - \text{Im}[F(u,v)]$$
$$= F_e(u,v) + F_o(u,v), \tag{2.83}$$

where $F_e(u,v)$ and $F_o(u,v)$ are the even and odd parts of the Fourier transform, respectively.

The Hartley BPOF has the attractive feature that it is, in some sense, matched to both the even and odd parts of the object function. Also, for purely even or odd functions the Hartley BPOF reduces to the BPOF of Eq.(2.80) or (2.81), respectively.

The advantages of using binary techniques are that high fidelity SLMs work well in a binary phase-only mode and can be used to synthesise the threshold filter. Advances in very large scale integration (VLSI) technology offers the possibility for considerable performance improvement in SLM devices; thus large space-bandwidth-product binary filters will give improved performance of BPOFs in terms of correlation peak to sidelobe ratio, diffraction efficiency, and correlation width. Correlation performance is superior to that of the classical matched filter. An example of a binary device operating in the phase-only mode is the magneto-optic SLM, which is electrically addressable and is available with up to 128×128 pixels, with 256×256 pixels about to go into production.

Bibliography

[1] J.W. Goodman, *Introduction to Fourier Optics*, McGraw-Hill, New York (1968).

[2] W.T. Cathey, *Optical Information Processing and Holography*, Wiley (Interscience), New York (1974).

[3] A. Papoulis, *System and transforms with Applications in Optics*, McGraw-Hill, New York (1968).

[4] A. VanderLugt, "Signal detection by complex spatial filtering", *IEEE Trans. Inf. Theory* **IT-10**, 139-145 (1964).

[5] J.L. Horner, and P.D. Gianino, "Phase-only matched filtering", *Appl. Opt.* **23**, 812-816(1984).

[6] J.L. Horner, and J. Leger, "Pattern recognition with binary phase only filters", *Appl. Opt.* **24**, 609-611(1985).

[7] J.L. Horner, and H.O. Bartelt, "Two-bit correlation", *Appl. Opt.* **24**, 2889-2893(1985).

[8] D.M. Cottrell, R.A. Lilly, J.A. Davis and T. Day, "Optical correlator performance of binary phase only filters using Fourier and Hartley transforms", *Appl. Opt.* **26**, 3755-3761(1987).

[9] D. Psaltis, E.G. Paek and S.S. Venkatesh, "Optical image correlation with a binary spatial light modulator", *Opt. Eng.* **23**, 698-704(1984).

[10] R.N. Bracewell, *The Hartley Transform*, Oxford Univ. Press, New York(1986).

Chapter 3

Spatial Frequency Tuning for Pattern Recognition by Correlation

3.1 Introduction

The classical matched filter (CMF) introduced by VanderLugt [1] produces a very broad correlation peak in the output plane resulting in a low discriminatory ability and a low correlation peak detectability. Therefore, it is desirable to modify the filter so that it produces a narrow correlation peak in the output plane when addressed by the desired target. The phase-only filter (POF) [2] which uses the phase information of the reference image and the amplitude-compensated matched filter (ACMF) [3] which uses both phase and amplitude information of the reference image have been successfully exploited to produce a sharp correlation peak in the output plane, but they are extremely sensitive to noise in the input image. This chapter concentrates on techniques which allow varying degrees of edge enhancement to be implemented by the filter; this is shown to improve the discriminatory capability and correlation peak detectability with respect to the classical matched filter. Furthermore, when compared with the phase-only filter, it can give an enhanced output signal-to-noise ratio by optimal tuning of the degree of edge enhancement (i.e. optimal spatial frequency selection).

Since convolution based edge enhancement is equivalent to a bandpass filtering operation in the frequency domain, optical processing exploiting a photorefractive material as a tuneable holographic filter provides a simple and effective method for implementing low noise (low noise in the sense that it does not introduce artefacts in the reciprocal domain) edge enhancement concurrently with correlation. This approach has recently been implemented as part of a matched spatial filter by Young and Chatwin [4]; this method exploits selective erasure of spatial frequencies at the Fourier transform plane in the photorefractive material Bismuth Silicon Oxide (BSO). For want of a better name this will be called the tuneable photorefractive (TPR) filter [5]. The method successfully implements a low noise edge enhancement operation. The POF, in contrast, is an all-pass filter in which the lack of attenuation of the input image spectrum results in an edge enhancement. In this chapter, the TPR filter and its characteristics are first introduced, and then an alternative edge enhancement technique which is called difference of Gaussian (DOG) filtering [5] is discussed; results which compare the TPR and DOG filtering techniques are given. This is followed by an examination of the noise robustness of the TPR filter [6].

3.2 Tuneable Photo-refractive (TPR) Filters

Central to a hybrid scheme is an effective digital to optical interface. Several solutions to this problem are currently being investigated and include: techniques based on direct phase modulation of the coherent processing wavefront by a spatial light modulator [7], the use of high resolution SLMs to act as dynamic holograms [8] and the use of photorefractive materials for a similar purpose [9][10]. The third alternative was chosen for implementation of an up-dateable correlator. This allows both the input and reference to be transferred to the optical system as space domain images via the more readily available amplitude modulating SLMs. The use of the widely available photorefractive material, Bismuth Silicon Oxide has several important consequences for the overall system design. In this section, a brief description of the BSO based up-dateable correlator is given.

3.2.1 TPR filter based correlator

The use of degenerate four wave mixing (DFWM) to implement real time correlation between two images was first proposed by Pepper et al [9]. Much work on
the use of the photorefractive crystal Bismuth Silicon Oxide (BSO) has since been
done by Huignard et al who demonstrated a joint transform correlator configuration
employing non-degenerate four wave mixing in BSO [11]. An alternative NDFWM
configuration that more closely resembles a VanderLugt correlator was proposed
by Cooper et al [10] and further modelled by Nicholson et al [12]. This configuration has certain inherent advantages over the JTC and was therefore adopted for a
hybrid up-dateable correlator demonstrator project: A Hybrid Optical/Electronic
Industrial Inspection System reported by Young and Chatwin in reference [13]. A
system diagram of the NDFWM scheme used to implement the up-dateable correlator is shown in Fig.3.1. The input and reference images are displayed on the
SLMs resulting in the field modulations, $u_1(x, y)$ and $u_2(x, y)$, of the Ar^+ and HeNe
beams respectively. A volume hologram is written to the BSO by the interference of
$U_1(f_x, f_y)$, the Fourier transform (FT) of $u_1(x, y)$, and U_3, a monochromatic plane
wave reference beam of tuneable strength. $U_2(f_x, f_y)$, the FT of $u_2(x, y)$, is diffracted
from the TPR filter, which is the grating formed in the BSO, to yield, after a further
FT, the correlation between $u_1(x, y)$ and $u_2(x, y)$ at the plane P_4.

The system configuration in Fig.3.1 resembles a VanderLugt correlator with the
reference and input image positions transposed. That is, the grating within the
BSO is formed by the input image Fourier transform and plane wave reference
beam rather than the reference image Fourier transform and plane wave. There are
two reasons for this. Firstly, the Bragg phase matching constraints of the volume
hologram formed in the BSO are much less severe for this plane wave reference beam,
allowing a larger effective field of view for a given lens f number. Thus the spatial
invariance property of the correlation algorithm can be exploited since the unknown
image can be located anywhere within this input area. In contrast, the reference
template must be exactly centred in the HeNe beam, any translation resulting in
loss of the correlation signal due to the rapid dephasing that occurs in this beam.
Secondly, there is an asymmetry in the speed requirements between the input and
reference Fourier transforms. In general, many reference templates must be searched

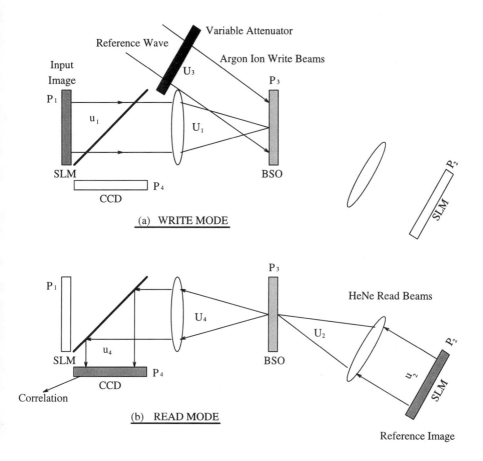

Figure 3.1: *Schematic of up-dateable photorefractive correlator*

to identify the unknown input. In the NDFWM configuration the reference template can be up-dated as rapidly as the SLM and readout CCD can be operated, as the reference Fourier transform simply diffracts from an existing grating in the BSO formed once per input cycle [10]; thus, the relatively slow response time of the BSO can be prevented from degrading the system response time.

As mentioned above, Bragg matching constraints impose a minimum f number on the Fourier transform lenses that can be employed for a given input and reference function spatial bandwidth product. The required f number can be directly related to the magnitude of the e-o effect in the photorefractive material. This is because the resulting change in refractive index, induced in the material, governs how thick the volume hologram must be to achieve the necessary diffraction efficiency.

The use of a HeNe read beam, in addition to having certain practical advantages, simplifies the modelling of the correlator since the non-linear photo-refractive inter-action occurs only with the Ar^+ write beams. The HeNe beam is simply diffracted from the static grating formed by the two Ar^+ beams, rather than writing a further grating as in the case of DFWM. Theoretical estimation of diffraction efficiency, and its deterioration due to Bragg angle mismatch, is complicated by the high degree of optical activity and electric field induced birefringence in BSO [14]. Thus, only rel-ative diffraction efficiencies are accounted for by considering the overall modulation of the grating formed by $U_1(f_x, f_y)$ and $U_3(f_x, f_y)$. This modulation spatially alters the diffracted amplitude of $U_2(f_x, f_y)$, giving rise to spatial filtering effects that may be exploited in the operation of the correlator.

For the steady state and ignoring any beam coupling, the grating may be written as [12]

$$M(f_x, f_y, z) = \frac{2U_1^*(f_x, f_y)exp(\frac{-\alpha_w z}{2})U_3 exp(\frac{-\alpha_r z}{2})}{|U_1(f_x, f_y)|^2 exp(-\alpha_w z) + |U_3|^2 exp(-\alpha_w z) + a|U_2(f_x, f_y)|^2 exp[-\alpha_r(d - z}$$

(3.1)

where α_w and α_r are the absorption coefficients of the write and read beams in BSO.

Since a, the quantum efficiency of the interaction of the HeNe beam with the grating is only about 0.06 of that of the Ar$^+$ beam, Eq.(3.1) reduces to

$$M(f_x, f_y) = \frac{2U_1^*(f_x, f_y)\, U_3}{|U_1(f_x, f_y)|^2 + I_3},$$

(3.2)

where U_3 is a constant plane wave reference beam and I_3 is its irradiance. $U_1(f_x, f_y)$ is the Fourier transform (FT) of the stored input image $u_1(x, y)$ as shown in Fig.3.1.

If the grating modulation is assumed to have a linear relation with the locally generated space charge field in the material, the amplitude of the diffracted field directly behind the grating, $U_4(f_x, f_y)$, will be proportional to $M(f_x, f_y)$ and so can be written

$$U_4(f_x, f_y) = M(f_x, f_y)U_2(f_x, f_y),$$

(3.3)

where $U_2(f_x, f_y)$ is the FT of the stored reference image $u_2(x, y)$. The Fourier transform of $U_4(f_x, f_y)$ gives $u_4(x, y)$, the weighted correlation between $u_1(x, y)$ and $u_2(x, y)$. The spatial frequency weighting of the TPR correlation operation can be tuned by varying the amplitude of the plane wave reference beam U_3 via the attenuator shown in Fig.3.1. The ratio between U_1, at zero spatial frequency, and U_3 is defined as

$$BR = \frac{Amplitude\ of\ U_1(f_x, f_y)\ peak\ (at\ zero\ spatial\ frequency)}{Amplitude\ of\ plane\ wave\ reference\ beam\ U_3}.$$

(3.4)

Note that since any experimentally measured value will be an irradiance, it must be square rooted to give the corresponding beam ratio (BR).

The 2-D Fourier transforms of images have large zero and low frequency components; thus, if the beam ratio is set to unity, values of $|U_1(f_x, f_y)|^2$ for all but the lowest frequencies will be small compared to I_3; consequently, a good approximation to Eq.(3.2) is

$$M(f_x, f_y) \approx kU_1^*(f_x, f_y),$$

(3.5)

When $U_2(f_x, f_y)$ is diffracted from the grating (TPR holographic filter), the field just behind the filter will be

$$U_4(f_x, f_y) = kU_1^*(f_x, f_y)U_2(f_x, f_y),$$

(3.6)

Thus with the BR set to unity the BSO hologram (TPR filter) will act as a classical Matched filter. The correlation peak obtained will be broad and discrimination between in-class and out-of-class images will be poor.

If the beam ratio is set to a much higher value by attenuating the plane wave reference, for low frequencies where $|U_1(f_x, f_y)|^2 \gg |U_3|^2 = I_3$, Eq.(3.2) becomes

$$M(f_x, f_y) \approx \frac{2U_3}{U_1(f_x, f_y)}, \tag{3.7}$$

(BR=32 was the highest value examined, i.e. an intensity ratio of 1000). Under these circumstances there is a small modulation of the grating in the central region of the hologram and thus the low frequency components of $U_1(f_x, f_y)$ are diffracted by the grating with very low efficiency. At higher frequencies, where $|U_1(f_x, f_y)| \approx |U_3|$, the modulation is nearer to unity, which results in the maximum diffraction efficiency attainable from the volume hologram. As will be shown below, these modulation conditions lead to an effect that is very similar to a 2nd differential pre-processing operation on the input image prior to an all-pass correlation. This gives rise to a high discriminatory correlation response but with the possibility of varying the hologram frequency response by direct control from a reference beam attenuator, see Fig.3.1. However, since the amplitude of the Ar^+ write beams is considerably lower for the high frequency modulation conditions, a penalty has to be paid in that the photorefractive response time will be slower and the TPR holographic filter will take longer to write. When the beam ratio approaches infinity (i.e. U_3 approaches zero), Eq.(3.2) actually becomes the inverse filter. This is a limiting case which is not physically implementable.

An equivalent of the 2nd differential operation in the space domain is multiplication of the Fourier transform by $-\omega^2$. Further, make the assumption that the amplitude of the spectrum of the input image $u_1(x, y)$ has a fractal, $1/\omega$, frequency dependence (this is a good approximation for natural images but less so far a more regularly shaped geometric input). When the hologram is illuminated by a plane wave beam, $U_2(f_x, f_y)$, the field emerging directly behind the filter, $U_4(f_x, f_y)$, may then be written

$$U_4(f_x, f_y) = \frac{2U_1^*(f_x, f_y)U_3U_2(f_x, f_y)}{|U_1(f_x, f_y)|^2 + |U_3|^2} = \frac{\frac{2}{\omega}U_3U_2(f_x, f_y)}{\frac{1}{\omega^2} + |U_3|^2}$$

$$= \left[\frac{2U_3 U_2(f_x, f_y)}{1 + |U_3|^2 \omega^2} \right] \omega \qquad (3.8)$$

If the modulus of the bracketed term can be treated as a constant, $U_4(f_x, f_y)$ will have a linear dependence on ω which is equivalent to $\omega^2 \times 1/\omega$ and so its Fourier transform will be the negative of the 2nd differential of $u_1(x, y)$. This approximation obviously depends on the second term in the denominator of Eq.(3.8) being small compared to unity, which will only be true when $|U_3|^2 \ll \omega^2$, i.e. for high values of BR. The higher the frequency content of the image, the lower $|U_3|$ must be set to approximate the 2nd differential operation. In practice $|U_3|$ cannot be set too low, since the areas of the grating in which there is then significant modulation will have a long formation time. Furthermore, it has been found that diminishing returns, in terms of correlation discrimination, are achieved by increasing the value of the BR too far.

Initially, the impulse response of the Fourier transform hologram written to the BSO was calculated for different values of the beam ratio to demonstrate the edge enhancement possible with high values of BR. A simple square block image of size 32×32 pixels in a 128×128 array is used as the input object. The input plane array, P_2, is set to zero apart from an on-axis pixel set to 255 to represent an impulse function. Fourier transformation of this impulse function produces a plane wave that addresses the hologram. Fig.3.2 shows cross-sections through the field values of the reconstructed square block image at plane P_4 for BR = 1.0, BR = 10.0, BR = 20.0 and BR = 32.0. The cross-sections demonstrate that a zero crossing occurs at the location of a step change in the input function, the change becoming progressively more localised the higher the value of BR. The cross-sections resemble the negative of the 2nd differential of the step change, which verifies the explanation given in the previous paragraph. As the BR can be controlled, in real time, from the variable attenuator the TPR filter is tuneable via the selected BR value.

Low pass correlation gives tolerance to in-plane rotation for initial identification purposes; whereas, a high pass correlation yields a sharp and localised response with a high level of discrimination and accurate determination of position. Thus a valuable feature of the up-dateable channel is the ability to vary the bandpass by adjusting the amplitude of the plane wave reference beam writing the Fourier

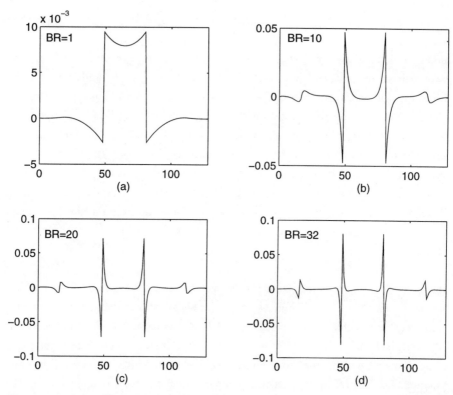

Figure 3.2: *Cross-sections through reconstruction field values of the TPR filter with the BR indicated. These figures were obtained from a square block image that was band pass filtered using the TPR filter with various BR values and then reconstructed.*

transform hologram to the BSO. A range of correlation responses can be generated in this way to increase the flexibility of the technique.

3.2.2   Performance of the TPR filter

The more violently the light distribution varies in the Fourier plane, the broader the correlation peak in the output plane; the flatter the light distribution in the Fourier plane, the sharper the correlation peak. If the filtered Fourier spectrum is a uniform plane wave, the output will be the impulse response of the optical system, i.e. a sharp peak. Thus, in order to produce a narrow localised correlation peak in the output plane, the matched filter should be modified to produce as uniform a field distribution as possible behind the filter plane, depending on sensitivity requirements. For the CMF and POF, the corresponding distributions in the Fourier plane are $A|U_1(f_x, f_y)|^2$ (where A is a constant which ensures a maximum value of unity) and $|U_1(f_x, f_y)|$ respectively.

According to Eq.(3.2), when an image with the same features as the reference is input into the correlator, the light distributions in the Fourier plane of the system may be expressed as

$$U_{4_{TPR}}(f_x, f_y) = \frac{2U_3}{|U_1(f_x, f_y)|^2 + I_3}|U_1(f_x, f_y)|^2 \qquad (3.9)$$

where $U_{4_{TPR}}(f_x, f_y)$ is the light distribution in the Fourier plane of the TPR filter correlation system.

Figure 3.3: *Test image defined on a 128×128 array*

The test image used is shown in Fig.3.3 and defined on a 128×128 pixel array; it is normalised to unit energy. Fig.3.4a, 3.4c, 3.5a and 3.5c show the TPR filter functions in the frequency domain using the test image of Fig.3.3 as a reference image. The filter characteristics with BR set to 5, 10, 20 and 32, respectively, are compared. From these figures, it can be concluded that with the increase of BR, the low frequency components of the TPR filter are progressively more attenuated and the higher frequency components are more enhanced. This illustrates how the band pass filtering performance of the TPR filter can be tuned. Correspondingly, Fig.3.4b, 3.4d, 3.5b and 3.5d show auto-correlation field distributions for the input image of Fig.3.3 directly behind the TPR filter in the Fourier plane. The corresponding

Fourier transforms, i.e. the auto-correlation results (ACR) of test image Fig.3.3, are
shown in Fig.3.6a, 3.6b, 3.6c and 3.6d, respectively. It can be seen that the choice
of beam ratios (BR) greatly affects the light distribution in the Fourier plane which
correspondingly affects the sharpness of the auto-correlation function. These results
illustrate how the TPR filter may be optimised by correct selection of the beam
ratio, BR.

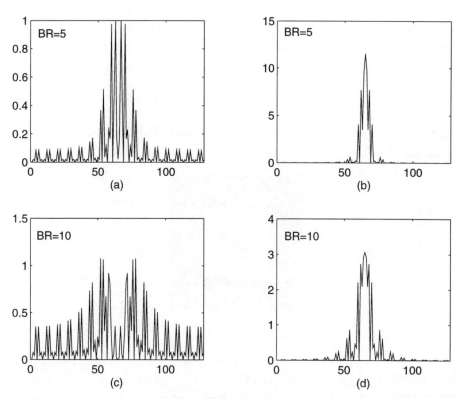

Figure 3.4: *(a) and (c) are the cross-sections through the TPR filter in the frequency
domain with BR set to 5 and 10 respectively. (b) and (d) are corresponding cross-
sections through the field values directly behind the TPR filter.*

It can also be seen from these results that as the TPR filter is biased towards progressively higher spatial frequencies the total correlation plane energy falls. However,
the energy available is concentrated into a progressively more localised correlation

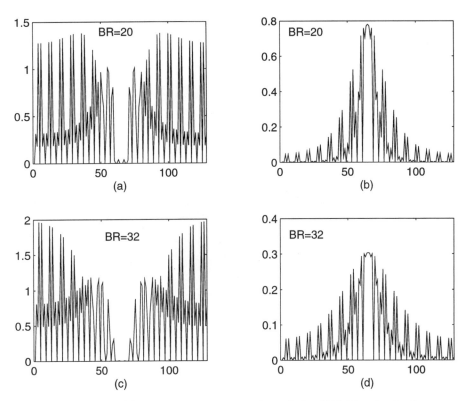

Figure 3.5: *(a) and (c) are the cross-sections through the TPR filter in the frequency domain with BR set to 20 and 32 respectively. (b) and (d) are corresponding cross-sections through the field values directly behind the TPR filter.*

response which results in the peak height increasing with BR.

3.3   Difference of Gaussian (DOG) Filters

For a TPR filter, finer control over the modulation function recorded in the photore-fractive hologram may be required. This could be achieved by adaptively amplitude modulating the reference beam U_3 with an SLM; this would permit closer control of the bandpass characteristics of the recorded hologram. A function particularly suitable for such an implementation is the difference of Gaussian (DOG) filter [15]

Maximum Correlation Peak = 0.0036
Total Output Energy = 0.5549
BR = 5.0

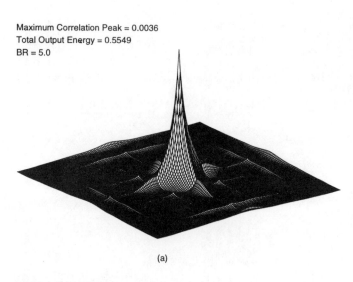

(a)

Maximum Correlation Peak = 0.0042
Total Output Energy = 0.3255
BR = 10.0

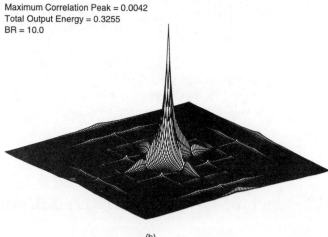

(b)

Figure 3.6: *Autocorrelation results obtained using the input image Fig.3.3 with the BR set to 5, 10, 20 and 32 respectively*

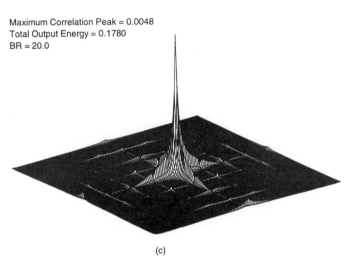

Maximum Correlation Peak = 0.0048
Total Output Energy = 0.1780
BR = 20.0

(c)

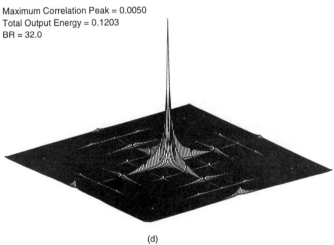

Maximum Correlation Peak = 0.0050
Total Output Energy = 0.1203
BR = 32.0

(d)

Figure 3.6: *Continued*

which has been used previously for the recording of matched spatial filters [15]. In the following section, application of the DOG filtering technique is discussed.

3.3.1 Theoretical aspects

The DOG filter is implemented by convolving a signal $u_1(x,y)$ with a difference of Gaussian function $g(x,y)$

$$m(x,y) = g(x,y) \star u_1(x,y) \qquad (3.10)$$

where the $\star$ denotes the two-dimensional convolution operation. The smooth bandpass DOG function is generated by subtracting two Gaussian functions $g_i(x,y)$ (i=1,2), defined as

$$g_i(x,y) = \frac{1}{2\pi\sigma_i^2} exp\left(-\frac{x^2+y^2}{2\pi\sigma_i^2}\right) \qquad (3.11)$$

Hence, the DOG function is given by

$$g(x,y) = g_1(x,y) - g_2(x,y) \qquad (3.12)$$

where (σ_1,σ_2) are the selected standard deviations. Using the two-dimensional Fourier transform, the DOG function can be expressed in the frequency domain as

$$G(f_x,f_y) = exp\left[-2\pi^3\sigma_1^2(f_x^2+f_y^2)\right] - exp\left[-2\pi^3\sigma_2^2(f_x^2+f_y^2)\right] \qquad (3.13)$$

It can be shown that the DOG function is approximately equivalent to a Laplacian of a Gaussian function (LOG): $g(x,y) \approx \nabla^2 Gaussian(x,y)$ [15]. Fig.3.7 shows a cross-section through a DOG function in the space domain with (σ_1,σ_2) set to (0.1, 0.16), Fig.3.8 illustrates the corresponding function in the frequency domain.

A DOG filter which is matched to the tuning requirements of a stored reference image may be written as

$$
\begin{aligned}
M(f_x,f_y) &= \int_{-\infty}^{\infty}\int_{-\infty}^{\infty} g(x,y) \star u_1(x,y))exp[-i2\pi(f_x x + f_y y)]dxdy \\
&= G(f_x,f_y)U_1(f_x,f_y) \qquad (3.14)
\end{aligned}
$$

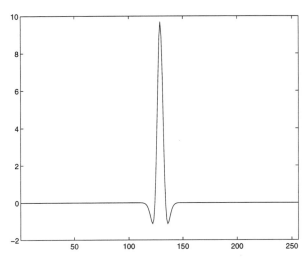

Figure 3.7: *Cross-section through a DOG function in the space domain with (σ_1, σ_2) set to (0.1, 0.16)*

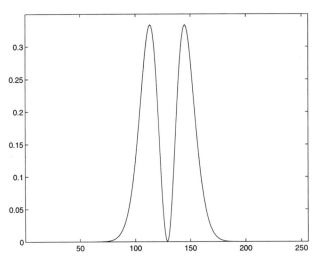

Figure 3.8: *Cross-section through the Fourier transform of the DOG function shown in Fig.3.7*

where $U_1(f_x, f_y)$ is the Fourier transform of the signal $u_1(x, y)$ and $G(f_x, f_y)$ is the Fourier transform of the DOG function $g(x, y)$.

When applied to an image the operation may be thought of as a convolution of the image with a Gaussian blurring function followed by the 2nd differential of the reduced resolution image. The larger the standard deviation of the Gaussian, the greater is the reduction in the intensity gradients within the image leading to a reduction in localisation of the edge information. When combined with a matched filter, it is this property of the DOG filter that is useful in that it provides tolerance to distortions of the target object from that of the reference function stored in the filter.

Fig.3.9 shows cross-sections through the field values of the reconstruction of a square block image for the values of (σ_1, σ_2) indicated. Like the TPR filter, the cross-sections demonstrate that a positive and a negative peak occurs at either side of the edge in the input function, whilst other areas exhibit a zero value. Thus the DOG function enhances the edges of the input function $u_1(x, y)$ by implementing a bandpass filter. From the figure, it can be seen that the bandpass with peak transmission at low frequency, shown in Fig.3.9a, results in the broad edge enhancement shown in Fig.3.9b. Conversely, the higher frequency bandpass, shown in Fig.3.9e, results in the sharp edge enhancement shown in Fig.3.9f. Changing the standard deviations (σ_1, σ_2) of the DOG function changes the bandpass frequency content and thus alters the edge localisation, so tuning the DOG filter to a different spatial resolution.

3.3.2 Performance of the DOG filter

According to Eq.(3.14), when an image with the same features as the reference is input into the DOG filter based correlator, the light distributions in the Fourier plane of the system may be expressed as

$$U_{4_{DOG}}(f_x, f_y) = G^*(f_x, f_y)|U_1(f_x, f_y)|^2 \qquad (3.15)$$

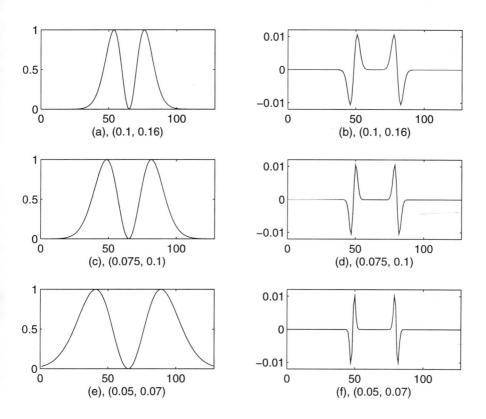

Figure 3.9: *(a), (c) and (e) are cross-sections through the frequency domain DOG function with standard deviations (σ_1, σ_2) set to (0.1, 0.16), (0.075, 0.1) and (0.05, 0.07) respectively. (b), (d) and (f) are cross-sections through the reconstructed square after it has been convolved with the adjacent DOG.*

where $U_{4_{DOG}}(f_x, f_y)$ is the light distribution in the Fourier plane of the DOG filter based correlation system.

The test image used is shown in Fig.3.3 which is the same as that used for the TPR filter. Fig.3.10a, 3.10c, and 3.10e show the DOG filter characteristics in the frequency domain using the test image of Fig.3.3 as a reference image. The standard deviations (σ_1, σ_2) are set to $(0.1, 0.16)$, $(0.075, 0.1)$, and $(0.05, 0.07)$, respectively. From comparing these figures, it can be concluded that the smaller the value of (σ_1, σ_2), the more attenuated the low frequency components of the DOG filter are and the more enhanced are the image high frequency components. This feature of the DOG filter is similar to the TPR filtering operation, thus giving the ability to tune the band pass of the DOG filter via fine control of (σ_1, σ_2). Correspondingly, Fig.3.10b, 3.10d, and 3.10f show auto-correlation field distributions of the input image of Fig.3.3 directly behind the DOG filter in the Fourier plane. Their corresponding Fourier transforms, i.e. the auto-correlation results of test image, Fig.3.3, are shown in Fig.3.11a, 3.11b, and 3.11c, respectively. As with the TPR filter, it can also be seen that the choice of standard deviations (σ_1, σ_2) greatly affects the light distribution in the Fourier plane, which correspondingly affects the sharpness of the auto-correlation function. These results illustrate how the DOG filter can be optimised by correct selection of (σ_1, σ_2).

3.4 Comparison of the TPR Filter with the DOG Filter

It is important to discuss the difference between the POF, DOG and TPR filters. The POF is an all-pass type filter so it does not attenuate the spectrum of the input object; however, compared to the CMF, it biases the response towards high frequencies making it extremely sensitive to image mismatches. In contrast, the DOG and the TPR filter can be tuned to tolerate specific mismatch problems. However, in addition the DOG and TPR filters both attenuate the response of the correlator to low frequency regions of the input object spectrum. This has the important effect of tending to inhibit false cross-correlation, since the matching of

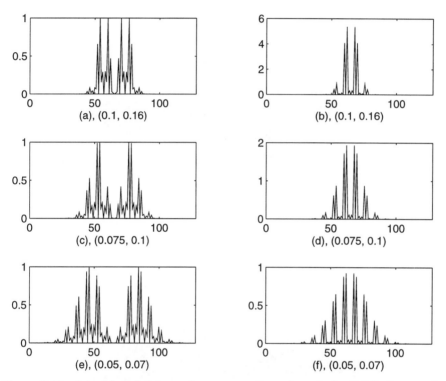

Figure 3.10: *(a), (c) and (e) are the cross-sections through the DOG filter in the frequency domain with (σ_1, σ_2) set to (0.1, 0.16), (0.075, 0.1), and (0.05, 0.07), respectively. (b), (d) and (f) are the corresponding cross-sections through the field values directly behind the DOG filter.*

Maximum Correlation Peak = 0.00089
Total Output Energy = 0.1754
(0.1, 0.16)

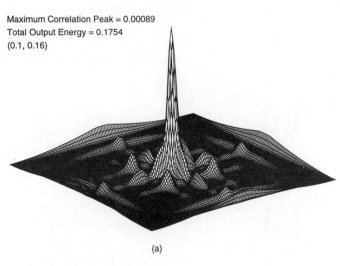

(a)

Maximum Correlation Peak = 0.00069
Total Output Energy = 0.0875
(0.075, 0.1)

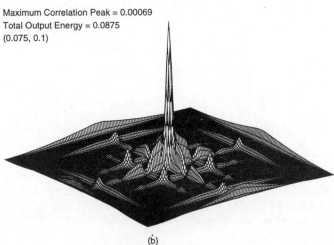

(b)

Figure 3.11: *Autocorrelation results obtained using the input image of Fig.3.3 with* (σ_1, σ_2) *set to (0.1, 0.16), (0.075, 0.1), and (0.05, 0.07), respectively*

Maximum Correlation Peak = 0.00074
Total Output Energy = 0.0603
(0.05, 0.07)

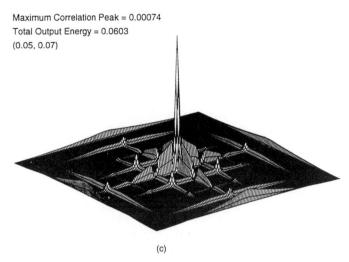

(c)

Figure 3.11: *Continued*

low frequency components from non-target objects is prevented from passing through the filter to the correlation plane, where it can only degrade the signal-to-noise ratio.

For an evaluation of the performance of different matched filters the following criteria are used: correlation peak intensity (CPI), Horner efficiency (ηH), the correlation peak to the root mean square (PRMS) ratio and the number of pixels inside the correlation peak (PNI) at the full width half maximum (FWHM) value. The ηH is defined as the ratio of the correlation peak energy to the energy in the input object, which is a measure of the optical correlation efficiency of the filters. The PRMS is defined as the ratio of the correlation peak response to the rms response outside the FWHM region of the correlation peak, see Eq.(3.18); it gives an indication of the sharpness of the correlation peak. The PNI measure is another important performance measure of the correlation filter because it represents the detectability of the correlation peak and the accuracy with which it may be located.

Table 3.1 shows the simulation results of TPR and DOG filters with appropriate parameter settings selected. For comparison, it also gives the POF and CMF results

Table 3.1: *Filter performance measures*

	$\eta H\%$	PRMS	PNI	CPI
TPR [BR=5.0]	0.358	12.74	129	0.0598
TPR [BR=10.0]	0.421	16.95	49	0.0648
TPR [BR=32.0]	0.494	29.49	13	0.0703
DOG [(σ_1, σ_2)=(0.1, 0.16)]	0.0887	10.01	69	0.0298
DOG [(σ_1, σ_2)=(0.075, 0.1)]	0.0688	12.20	37	0.0262
DOG [(σ_1, σ_2)=(0.05, 0.07)]	0.0739	14.81	13	0.0272
POF	2.124	19.78	13	0.15
CMF	0.033	5.0	581	0.018

Table 3.2: *Comparison of discriminatory abilities for the four filters*

	TPR	DOG	POF	CMF
$\Delta\%$	33.53	28.70	34.58	9.0

listed in the last two rows respectively. The table is arranged in order of the degree of edge enhancement for the DOG and TPR filters. It can be seen from Table 3.1 that the DOG and TPR filters are almost equivalent filtering techniques, thus the TPR filter is an extremely simple method of implementing a DOG like filter.

From Table 3.1, it can be seen that, when exploiting edge enhancement filters, the sharper the edge enhancement the better all the performance measures appear to be. The edge enhancement filters can be tuned by changing the values of (σ_1, σ_2) or BR, subject to the filter performance requirement. Table 3.1 shows that all the edge enhancement results give an improved correlation peak detectability when compared with the CMF. It can be seen from Table 3.1 that the DOG filter has a poorer PRMS than the equivalent TPR filter. From Fig.3.6 and Fig.3.11, it can be seen that the correlation output from DOG filtering has more extensive sidelobes than that of TPR filtering which explains the poorer PRMS. By changing the values of (σ_1, σ_2) and BR to the appropriate values, the modified edge enhancement filter can be tuned to give better PRMS performance than the POF. For example, when (σ_1, σ_2) are set to (0.03,0.045) for the DOG filter and BR = 32.0 for the TPR filter, the PRMSs are 20.71 and 29.49, respectively, which are better than that of the POF, which is 19.78.

Table 3.2 shows the discriminatory capability of TPR and DOG filters compared with the POF and CMF; two very similar images, Fig.3.3 and Fig.3.12, were used in the computer simulation. In the simulation, Fig.3.3 is used as the target image and Fig.3.12 as the non-target image. The values of (σ_1, σ_2) and BR are set to (0.05, 0.07) and 32.0 respectively. Discriminatory ability Δ is defined as

$$\Delta = \frac{|ACPI| - |CCPI|}{|ACPI|} 100\% \qquad (3.16)$$

where ACPI indicates the autocorrelation peak intensity, CCPI denotes the cross-correlation peak intensity. It can be seen that the discriminatory capability of the TPR and DOG filters is better than the CMF but worse than the POF.

Figure 3.12: *Image used for the test of filter discrimination.*

Simple geometric figures have been used to illustrate the useful properties of the TPR filter; however, it is important to show that it also bestows these benefits for recognition of real objects. Fig.3.13a and 3.13b depict the Bradley APC vehicle and Abrams MI tank respectively. The APC vehicle is taken as the target image, and the tank as the non-target image. When the values of (σ_1, σ_2) and BR are set to (0.05, 0.07) and 32.0, respectively, performance is significantly better than that for the simple geometric shapes, proving the general applicability of the TPR filter. Fig.3.14a and 3.14b are the result of correlating the APC vehicle and the tank with the TPR filter respectively; Fig.3.14c and 3.14d are the result of correlating the APC vehicle and tank with the DOG filter respectively. Hence the TPR and DOG filters can effectively discriminate the APC vehicle from the tank; values of Δ are 92.5% and 89.9% respectively. The correlation output using DOG filtering has more extensive sidelobes, which results in a poorer PRMS than that delivered by the TPR filter; this is because a cross-section through the DOG filter (i.e. cross-section orthogonal to the optical axis) is a circular annulus and hence does not provide homogeneous frequency plane modulation. The TPR filter is not compromised by the geometry of Fourier plane frequency distribution; it thus delivers better performance.

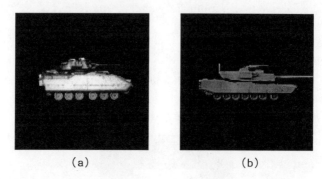

(a)   (b)

Figure 3.13: *Real images encoded at 128×128 pixels: (a) Bradley APC vehicle, (b) Abrams MI tank.*

3.5   Noise Robustness of TPR filters

If it is to recognise realistic targets, a good correlation filter should not only produce sharp correlation peaks at the output plane and give good discrimination ability between similar objects, but also be robust to noise in the input scene. In this section, the noise robustness of the TPR filter is examined.

The influence of the input image noise in the frequency plane of the correlator is greater for higher spatial frequencies. On the other hand, the concentration of most of the energy at low frequencies, for common objects, is responsible for the broad correlation peaks when a classical matched filter is used; that is, it behaves as a low pass filter. The all pass type filter, such as the POF, and high pass type filter, such as the inverse filter (IF) and the amplitude compensated matched filter (ACMF), are very susceptible to noise in the correlator; thus they have a low resistance to input scene noise. The TPR filter has been shown to act as a tuneable bandpass type filter which gives a good compromise between discrimination ability and input scene noise resistance.

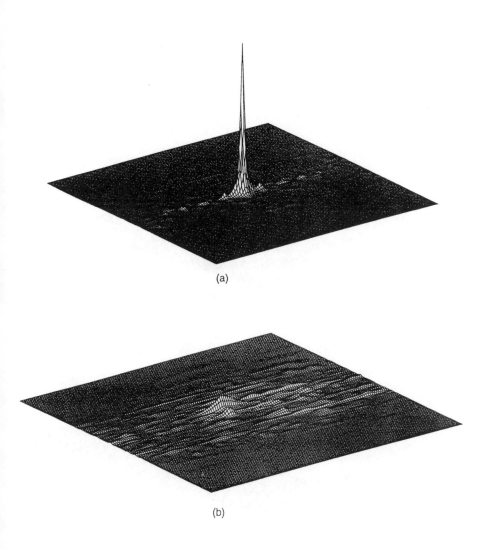

(a)

(b)

Figure 3.14: *Correlation functions: (a) and (b) are from correlating the target and non-target images with the TPR filter (BR set to 32), respectively; (c) and (d) are from correlating the target and non-target images with a DOG filtered version (with (σ_1, σ_2) set to (0.05, 0.07)), respectively*

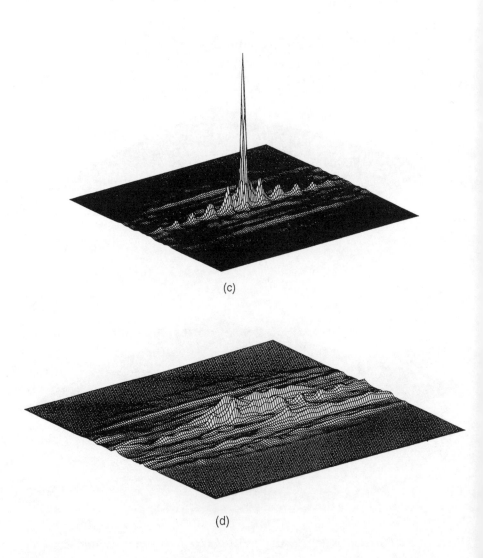

(c)

(d)

Figure 3.14: *Continued*

The performance of the filter's resistance to noise in the input scene is generally examined using the output signal to noise ratio (SNR_o) defined as [16]

$$SNR_o = \frac{|E[c(x_0, y_0)]|^2}{var\{c(x_0, y_0)\}}, \tag{3.17}$$

where E, var and c denote the ensemble average, the variance and correlation output function respectively, and (x_0, y_0) denotes the position of the correlation peak. When the input image is corrupted by noise, a good filter should not only give a high signal-to-noise ratio at the output plane but also a sharp correlation peak with good sidelobe suppression. The peak sharpness is characterised by the ratio of the correlation peak height to the root mean square (PRMS) of the region, A, outside the central correlation area at half its peak intensity, defined as [17]

$$PRMS = \frac{|c(x_o, y_0)|}{\{\frac{1}{N_A} \sum_A |c(x, y)|^2\}^{\frac{1}{2}}}, \tag{3.18}$$

where N_A is the number of pixels of the corresponding area in the correlation plane. The degree of sidelobe suppression is assessed using the peak to secondary peak ratio (PSR) defined as [18]

$$PSR = \frac{Correlation\ Peak}{Secondary\ Peak} = \frac{|c(x_0, y_0)|^2}{MAX_B\{|c(x, y)|^2\}}. \tag{3.19}$$

where MAX denotes the output function maximum and the area B is constrained to $x - x_0 > 3$ pixels and $y - y_0 > 3$ pixels. Noise in the input scene generally is responsible for the production of sidelobes and undesirable peaks at the correlation output plane; hence, the PSR gives an assessment of sidelobe disruption. Thus the filter's ability to accommodate the noise in the input scene, whilst still maintaining good discrimination, is characterised by the three parameters: SNR_o, $PRMS$, and PSR.

The noise resistance performance of the TPR filter with variable BRs is examined using the Bradley APC vehicle shown in Fig.3.15a; the image is encoded at a resolution of 128×128 pixels with grey levels variable from 0 to 255. This image was corrupted using Gaussian white noise with a variable input signal-to-noise-ratio (SNR_I) defined by the ratio of input signal energy to noise energy. Fig.3.15b shows the image corrupted with $20logSNR_I = -17.4dB$. All images, including noisy images, were centred and normalised to unit energy. The maximum BR value used

Table 3.3: *Quantitative comparison of filter performance*

	SNR_o	PRMS	PSR	CPI	PNI	PNO
CMF	52.13	1.51	1.15	2.5×10^{-4}	1618	0
TPR(BR=1.0)	40.96	1.69	1.21	7.1×10^{-4}	1089	0
TPR(BR=5.0)	32.49	1.90	1.86	4.6×10^{-3}	97	0
TPR(BR=10.0)	11.16	2.44	3.19	4.9×10^{-3}	17	0
TPR(BR=20.0)	7.40	5.27	4.89	5.6×10^{-3}	5	0
TPR(BR=32.0)	6.45	8.03	4.32	7.0×10^{-3}	3	0
POF	1.89	1.95	1.01	3.9×10^{-3}	1	8

was 32, because this was the highest experimental value implemented which gives an equivalent irradiance ratio of 1000.

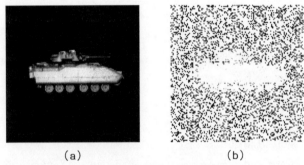

(a)   (b)

Figure 3.15: *(a) The noise free image of the Bradley APC vehicle. (b) The noise corrupted image of the Bradley APC vehicle with* $20 \log SNR_I = -17.4dB$.

Simulation results for the TPR filters with different BR values, together with the POF and the CMF, are summarised in Table 3.3. The severely noise corrupted image of Fig.3.15b was used as the correlator input except when examining the SNR_o measure; the value of SNR_o was obtained from 22 input images corrupted by different levels of noise which varied from noise free to $20 \log SNR_I = -17.4dB$. In the table, CPI denotes the correlation peak intensity, PNI is the number of pixels inside the correlation peak at the full width half maximum (FWHM) value, and PNO is the number of pixels outside the correlation peak that are greater than or equal to the FWHM value.

From the table, it can be seen that as the BR increases, the SNR_o of the TPR filter decreases but the values of the $PRMS$ and PSR increase, except for the PSR value for $BR = 32$; however, the value of $PSR = 4.32$, for $BR = 32$, is large enough to indicate good noise resistance. Although the CMF is robust to noise, indicated by $SNR_o = 52.13$, the other two measures of the $PRMS$ and PSR indicate that it is difficult to precisely locate and recognise the desired image. It can be seen from the table that the POF has the worst performance and is unable to accommodate noise in the input scene. It is concluded from the table that when the BR is tuned within the range from 20.0 to 32.0, the TPR filter gives an excellent compromise between noise resistance and discrimination ability. For this tuning range the SNR_o varies between 7.4 and 6.45 which is clearly adequate to extract the desired signal from the corrupted output function.

Table 3.3 also displays values for CPI, PNI and PNO, these variables further clarify the performance of the TPR filter. The PNI quantifies the detection accuracy, or the ability to accurately locate the spatial position of the object in the input scene. The PNO quantifies the uniqueness of the peak in the correlation plane; if the $PNO > 0$, the target is lost, or at least it can be said to reside at one of several locations. It can be seen from the table that although the POF has just one pixel inside the correlation peak, it also has 8 pixels outside the correlation peak; this is an intolerable ambiguity for any target recognition system. The TPR filters with the BR tuned between 20 and 32.0 give 5 and 3 pixels in the correlation peak respectively, allowing precise location of the input object; as the PNO is zero there is no ambiguity. Thus, the TPR filters, with a relatively high BR, are able to accommodate noise in the input scene and give good discrimination performance; they significantly out-performed both the POF and the CMF.

The correlation functions of the TPR filter with BR=32, POF and CMF using an input image corrupted with: $20logSNR_I = -17.4dB$, are shown in Fig.3.16. The TPR filter yields a sharp correlation peak that is easily isolated by thresholding at 50% of maximum, whereas the POF loses the target. The CMF gives a result similar to the noise free input image autocorrelation, demonstrating excellent noise robustness; however, it has a very broad correlation peak resulting in a poor discrimination performance.

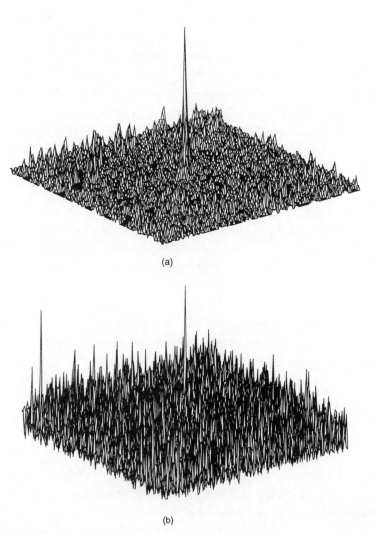

(a)

(b)

Figure 3.16: *Correlation intensity outputs for (a) TPR with BR=32, (b) POF and (c) CMF; correlated with noisy images of the Bradley APC vehicle with* $20logSNR_I = -17.4dB$

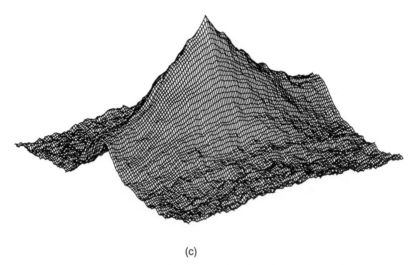

(c)

Figure 3.16: *Continued*

The filter's discrimination ability is tested by comparing correlation performance on a target and non-target object of similar size and shape. This test is performed by comparing the discrimination values of the TPR with BR=20 and 32, CMF and POF for input images of both the Bradley APC vehicle, shown in Fig.3.15, and a similarly scaled and oriented Abrams MI tank shown in Fig.3.17; Fig.3.17a is a noise free tank image and Fig.3.17b is a noise corrupted tank image, with $20logSNR_I = -17.4dB$. The discrimination capability (DC) of the filter is defined as:

$$DC = \frac{P_t}{P_{nt}} , \qquad (3.20)$$

where P_t is the intensity of the correlation peak for the target input and P_{nt} is for the non-target image input. In the simulations, the noise free image of Fig.3.15a was used to construct the three filters; the Bradley APC vehicle was taken as the target input image, and the Abrams MI tank as the non-target input image. The discrimination results are quantified in Table 3.4; where all the correlation peak intensities are normalised to the autocorrelation peak intensity of the TPR filter with BR=20 with the noise free input image of Fig.3.15a. From Table 3.4, it can be seen that when the input images are noise free the TPR filter gives excellent discrimination: DC=9.88 and 13.33 for BR=20 and 32 respectively, values which are intermediate to those of the POF and the CMF. Furthermore, when the input images are buried in noise the TPR filters, with BR=20 and 30, give a discrimination ability of 2.10 and 1.43 respectively; whereas, the POF and CMF lose their discrimination ability.

Table 3.4: *Quantitative comparison of filter discrimination ability*

	Noise Free Case		DC	Noise Level -17.4dB		DC
	target	non-target		target	non-target	
TPR (BR=20)	1.00	0.1012	9.88	0.0512	0.0247	2.10
TPR (BR=32)	1.3318	0.0999	13.33	0.0420	0.0294	1.43
CMF	0.0667	0.0461	1.45	0.0114	0.0158	0.73
POF	7.1730	0.5257	13.65	0.0731	0.0842	0.867

(a)   (b)

Figure 3.17: *Abrams MI tank images used as the non-target object input, (a) noise free, (b) corrupted by noise with $20logSNR_I = -17.4dB$.*

In conclusion, noise robustness of tuneable photo-refractive (TPR) filters, which can be implemented for real time pattern recognition, has been assessed and compared with phase-only and classical matched spatial filters. The bandpass selectivity of the TPR filter results in sharp correlation peaks even when the input scene signal-to-noise ratio is decreased significantly. The filters were found to give a good compromise between correlation peak sharpness and noise robustness. For a BR range between 20 and 32 the TPR filter out-performed both the POF and the CMF. The TPR filter has also been shown to give good discrimination between the target and non-target objects.

Bibliography

[1] A. VanderLugt, "Signal detection by complex spatial filtering", *IEEE Trans. Inf. Theory* **IT-10**, 139-145 (1964).

[2] J.L. Horner, and P.D. Gianino, "Phase-only matched filtering", *Appl. Opt.* **23**, 812-816(1984).

[3] G.G. Mu, X.M. Wang and Z.Q Wang, "Amplitude-Compensated Matched Filtering", *Appl. Opt.* **27**, 3461-3463(1988).

[4] R.C.D. Young and C.R. Chatwin, "Design and Simulations of a Synthetic Discriminant Function Filter for Implementation in an Up-dateable Photorefractive Correlator", *SPIE, Optical Pattern Recognition III*, **1701**, 239-263(1992).

[5] C.R. Chatwin, R.K. Wang and R.C.D. Young, "Tuneable edge enhancement filters for optical correlation", *Optics and Lasers in Engineering* **23**, 75-91(1995).

[6] R.K. Wang, C.R. Chatwin and M.Y. Huang, "Noise robustness of tuneable photo-refractive filters", *Optics and Lasers in Engineering* **21**, 297-306(1994).

[7] D. Psaltis, E.G. Paek and S.S. Venkatesh, "Optical image correlation with a binary spatial light modulator", *Opt. Eng.* **23**, 698-704(1984).

[8] T. Iwaki, Y. Mitsuoka, "Optical pattern recognition of letters by a joint transform correlator using ferroelectric liquid crystal spatial light modulator", *Optics Letters* **15**, 1218-1220(1990).

[9] D. Pepper, J. AuYeung, D. Fekete, A. Yariv, "Spatial Convolution of optical fields via degenerate four wave mixing", *Optics Letters* **3**, 7-9(1978).

[10] I. Cooper, M. Nicholson and C. Petts, "Dynamic Frequency Plane Correlator", *Proc. IEE* **133**, Pt.J. No.1, 70-76(1986).

[11] J.P. Huignard, H. Rajbenbach, Ph. Refregier and L. Solymer, "Wave mixing in photorefractive Bismuth Silicon Oxide crystals and its application", *Opt. Eng.* **26**, 586-592(1985).

[12] M. Nicholson, I. Cooper, M. McCall and C. Petts, "Simple computational model of image correlation by four wave mixing in photorefractive media", *Appl. Opt.* **26**, 278-285(1987).

[13] R.C.D. Young and C.R. Chatwin, "Design and Simulations of a Synthetic Discriminant Function Filter for Implementation in an Up-dateable Photorefractive Correlator",*SPIE, Optical Pattern Recognition III* **1701**, 239-263(1992).

[14] S. Mallick, D. Roude, and A. Apostolidis, "Efficiency and polarisation characteristics of photorefractive diffraction in a $Bi_{12}SiO_{20}$ crystal", *J. Opt. Soc. Am.* **4**, 1247-1253(1987).

[15] D. Marr and E. Hildreth, "Theory of Edge Detection", *Proc. R. Soc. London* **B207**, 187-217(1980).

[16] A. Papoulis, *Probability, Random Variables, and Stochastic Processes* (McGraw-Hill, New York, 1984).

[17] J.L. Horner and H.O. Bartelt, "Two-Bit Correlation", *Appl. Opt.* **24**, 2889-2893 (1985).

[18] B. Javidi, "Nonlinear Joint Power Spectrum Based Optical Correlation", *Appl. Opt.* **28**, 2358-2367 (1989).

Chapter 4

Adaptive Filtering Technique

4.1   Introduction

A good correlation filter should produce sharp correlation peaks at the output plane; be tolerant to noise in the input scene; give good discrimination between similar objects and have a high optical efficiency. As already mentioned in the previous chapter, the classical matched filter [1] (CMF) is optimum for noise robustness but has poor discrimination ability, as it generates very broad output correlation peaks and has a poor optical efficiency. The phase only filter [2] (POF), implemented by setting all the magnitudes to 1.0 and retaining the phase information, exhibits excellent discrimination via very sharp output correlation peaks and a 100% optical efficiency; however, it is extremely sensitive to target distortions and noise in the input scene as it enhances high spatial frequency information. Mu et al [3] proposed including partial magnitude information to produce a filter that is somewhat like an inverse filter because it encodes the low frequencies as a modified inverse filter and the remaining spatial frequencies as a POF. However, Mu's filter is more sensitive to target distortions and noise in the input scene than the POF. These filters – inverse, POF, and CMF – differ only in the manner in which magnitude information is encoded into the filter.

To reduce the sensitivity to noise and target distortions, achieve good discrimination and optical efficiency, a new filter is generated which integrates the phase only filter with the classical matched filter; this is a strategy which attempts to combine the advantages of both filters into a single robust filter [4]. A technique which optimises filter performance to accommodate input scene noise is demonstrated. The results show that the new filter delivers better overall performance than either the phase-only filter or the classical matched filter.

4.2 Filter Synthesis

Let the Fourier transform of the reference object function $f(x,y)$ be denoted by $F(u,v) = |F(u,v)|exp[j\phi(u,v)]$. A filter when introduced at the filter plane is expected to produce the correlation of the target input object at the output plane. The CMF is thus given by the complex conjugate of the reference object Fourier transform

$$F(u,v)_{CMF} = F^*(u,v) = |F(u,v)|exp[-j\phi(u,v)], \qquad (4.1)$$

and the POF is given by

$$F(u,v)_{POF} = \frac{F^*(u,v)}{|F(u,v)|} = exp[-j\phi(u,v)], \qquad (4.2)$$

where the asterisk $*$ denotes the complex conjugate. It is well known that, for common objects, the concentration of most of the energy at low spatial frequencies is responsible for the broad correlation peaks resulting in low filter discrimination when a CMF is used; that is, from Eq.(4.1), it behaves as a low pass filter. On the other hand, the influence of the input scene noise is greater for high spatial frequencies in the filter plane of the correlator; thus, as a low pass filter, the CMF automatically suppresses the higher frequency distortions giving excellent noise robustness.

In contrast the POF effectively attenuates lower frequencies and enhances higher frequencies in the filter plane; thus for distortion free input images it delivers good discrimination ability with sharp output correlation peaks. However, as noise frequently manifests itself as high frequency distortion in the filter plane the POF does not perform well for input images corrupted by noise.

To achieve sharp correlation peaks (i.e. good discrimination and localisation) with good resistance to noise in the input images, it is necessary to attenuate the lower spatial frequencies as well as to retain the higher spatial frequencies of the reference object. To this end, the POF and the CMF may be integrated as

$$
F(u,v) \;=\; \begin{cases} \frac{F^*(u,v)}{|F(u,v)|} \;=\; exp[-j\phi(u,v)] & \text{when } |F(u,v)| > \tau \\[2mm] \frac{F^*(u,v)}{\tau} \;=\; \frac{|F(u,v)|}{\tau} exp[-j\phi(u,v)] & \text{otherwise} \end{cases} \;, \qquad (4.3)
$$

where

$$
\tau \;=\; \varepsilon |F(u,v)|_{max}, \qquad (4.4)
$$

and $0 < \varepsilon \leq 1.0$ and is a pre-set threshold parameter; $|F(u,v)|_{max}$ denotes the maximum magnitude of the Fourier transform of the reference image. Hence, if the amplitude value of the Fourier transform of the reference image $f(x,y)$, at the pixel location (u,v), is greater than the threshold value of τ, only the phase information is recorded onto the filter; otherwise, both the phase and amplitude information, with an amplification factor of $\frac{1}{\tau}$, are encoded onto the filter. Note also that the parameter ε is useful in:

(i)   overcoming the indeterminate condition when the value of $|F(u,v)|$ approaches zero.

(ii) ensuring that the filter gain is less than unity to meet the requirement of the optical implementation.

The parameter ε can be a constant or even a function of u and v. It is used to either suppress the effect of noise or bandlimit the filter or both. For example, an *a priori* knowledge of the noise spectrum in the input scene can be utilized to formulate $\varepsilon(u,v)$ so that part of the filter behaves as a POF and the remainder as a CMF. This filter would then be robust to noise but still give good discrimination via sharp correlation peaks. For convenience, this is called an adaptive discriminant filter (ADF).

The threshold factor τ allows correlator performance to be tuned as a function of the input noise condition. A large threshold value maintains the noise robustness of the ADF as a classical matched filter. If τ is greater than or equal to the maximum value of $|F(u,v)|$, the system would behave as a CMF which has the highest noise resistance. A small value of τ produces a sharp correlation peak at the output plane provided that the input noise level is relatively low. The optimum value of ε (equivalent to finding τ) is based on the balance between adequate sharpness of the correlation peak and filter tolerance to noise.

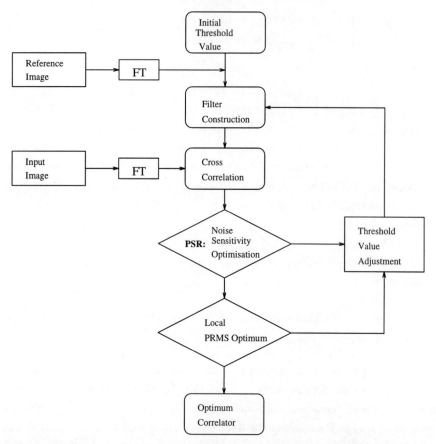

Figure 4.1: *Schematic diagram of iterative procedure for optimum filter construction*

The optimum value of ε depends not only on the degree of noise level in the input image but also on the type of input image. Therefore, the threshold parameter ε in Eq.(4.4) is modified using an iterative scheme to evaluate an optimum value, see Fig.4.1. The reference image is first Fourier transformed. The input image, with known noise level, is also Fourier transformed. The optimum filter construction process is as follows:

(i)   Choose an initial threshold value (i.e. threshold parameter value of ε) to initialise the construction process.

(ii) Construct the filter according to Eq.(4.3).

(iii) Cross-correlate the input image with the filter.

(iv) Measure the peak value and the second highest peak value of the correlation result, calculate the peak to secondary peak ratio (PSR) at the correlation plane.

(v)   Adjust the threshold value and repeat processes (ii) to (iv) to maximise the PSR value.

(vi) Fine-tune the threshold value within the neighbourhood of the previously obtained value and repeat processes (ii) and (iii).

(vii) Measure and calculate the peak sharpness defined as the ratio of peak to root mean square of the output correlation function (PRMS).

(viii) Adjust the threshold value and repeat processes (ii), (iii) and (vii) until the maximum PRMS is obtained.

The corresponding threshold value is the optimum value for the particular image with its particular level of noise.

In the iteration, the PSR is defined by Eq.(3.19). The noise in the input scene results in correlation peak sidelobes and undesired peaks at the correlation output plane; thus, it is reasonable to use the PSR as a measure of the filter resistance to sidelobe disruption. The PRMS is defined by Eq.(3.18), it gives an assessment of the correlation peak sharpness.

4.3   Performance Simulations and Results

Simulations of the ADF are compared with the CMF and POF; the input image was the Bradley APC vehicle, shown in Fig.4.2(a); it was encoded with a resolution of 128×128 pixels with grey levels variable from 0 to 255. This vehicle image was corrupted by Gaussian white noise with a variable input signal-to-noise ratio (SNR_I) defined as the ratio of input signal energy to noise energy. For example, the images corrupted by $20logSNR_I = 0.4dB, -13.6dB$ and $-17.4dB$ are shown in Fig.4.2(b), Fig.4.2(c), and Fig.4.2(d) respectively. All images including noisy images are normalised to unit energy. As is evident from Fig.4.2, these images present a difficult pattern recognition problem.

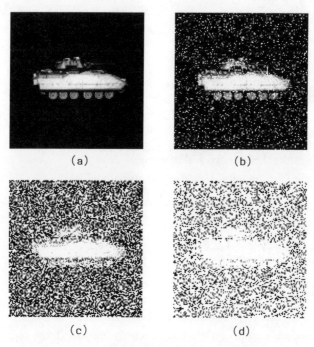

Figure 4.2: *Input images with different noise levels (a) noise free, (b) 0.4dB, (c) -13.6dB and (d) -17.4dB*

The noise free image of Fig.4.2(a) was used as the reference image to construct the filters. In order to construct the ADFs the threshold parameter ε was given initial values of $10^{-2}, 10^{-4}, 10^{-5}$ and 10^{-6}. The real part of the ADFs, in the frequency domain, are displayed in Fig.4.3(a), 4.3(b), 4.3(c) and 4.3(d) respectively. It can be seen that, as the parameter ε decreases, the extent of the ADF phase only region increases; correspondingly, the classical matched filter recedes to the ADF high frequency zones. The different noise levels in the space domain disrupt the filter fidelity requirements, to a greater or lesser extent, in the frequency domain; thus in order to recognise the object buried in noise an optimum value of the parameter ε must be selected. To illustrate the effect of altering the parameter ε, it is useful to inspect the spatial image of the ADFs. Since the spatial image function $r(x, y)$ can be regarded as the impulse response of Eq.(4.3), it can be written as

$$r(x,y) \ = \ \mathcal{F}^{-1}\{F(u,v)_{ADF}\}, \tag{4.5}$$

where $\mathcal{F}^{-1}$ denotes the inverse Fourier transform. Thus the impulse response of the ADFs shown in Fig.4.3 are displayed in Fig.4.4. Hence, the smaller the threshold parameter ε, the greater is the attenuation of low frequency image elements which match the high power reference object features; thus, a type of optimised edge enhancement is implemented.

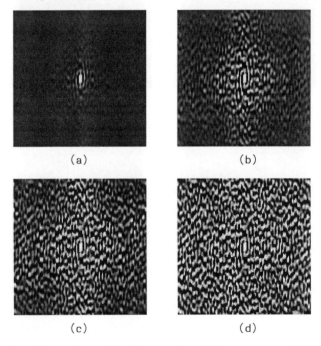

(a)   (b)

(c)   (d)

Figure 4.3: *Correlation filter with different threshold values ε = (a) 0.01, (b) 10^{-4}, (c) 10^{-5} and (d) 10^{-6}*

Next, correlate the filter functions $F(u, v)$ (Fig.4.3) of the ADFs with the input image of Fig.4.2(d), which is severely corrupted by noise. The output correlation

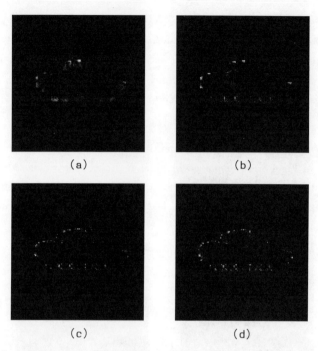

Figure 4.4: *Impulse response of correlation filter with threshold values corresponding to the values in Fig.4.3*

functions obtained are shown in Fig.4.5(a), 4.5(b), 4.5(c) and 4.5(d) respectively. It can be seen that a large threshold parameter ε, for example $\varepsilon = 0.01$ in Fig.4.5(a), gives a robust correlation result that is similar to that of the CMF, but has a very broad correlation peak; a smaller threshold parameter ε, for example $\varepsilon = 10^{-6}$ in Fig.4.5(d), gives a useless correlation result as it loses the target. A more optimum value of ε, for example $\varepsilon = 10^{-4}$ in Fig.4.5(b), not only gives a relatively sharp correlation peak but demonstrates good resistance to severe noise in the input scene. This analysis suggests a strategy to find an optimum threshold parameter ε for different noise levels in the input image; Fig.4.1 illustrates the optimisation strategy.

Exploiting this scheme the optimum threshold parameter ε was found to be 10^{-4} for the noise corrupted image of Fig.4.2(d). For comparison, the real parts of this optimum ADF, POF and CMF are displayed in Fig.4.6(a), 4.6(b) and 4.6(c) re-

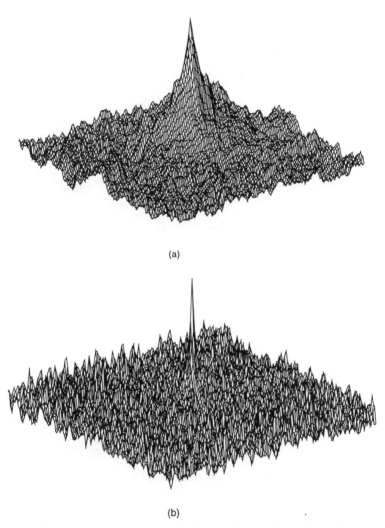

(a)

(b)

Figure 4.5: *Correlation Results from ADF Correlation Filter Using Input Image of Fig4.2(d) with Different Threshold Values* ε = *(a) 0.01, (b)* 10^{-4}*, (c)* 10^{-5} *and (d)* 10^{-6}

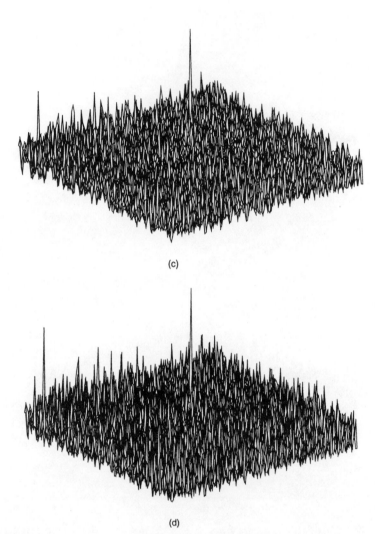

(c)

(d)

Figure 4.5: *Continued*

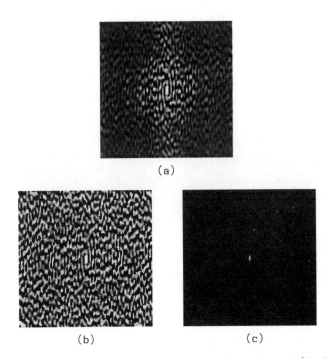

(a)

(b)   (c)

Figure 4.6: *Filters: (a) optimum ADF correlation filter ($\varepsilon = 10^{-4}$), (b) POF and (c) CMF*

Table 4.1: *Quantitative comparision of filter performance*

	SNR_o	PRMS	PSR	ηH	CPI	PNI	PNO
Optimum ADF	14.29	3.51	2.58	70.86%	2.8×10^{-4}	11	0
CMF	52.13	2.56	1.15	7.03%	2.2×10^{-5}	1618	0
POF	1.89	1.97	1.01	100%	4.7×10^{-4}	1	8

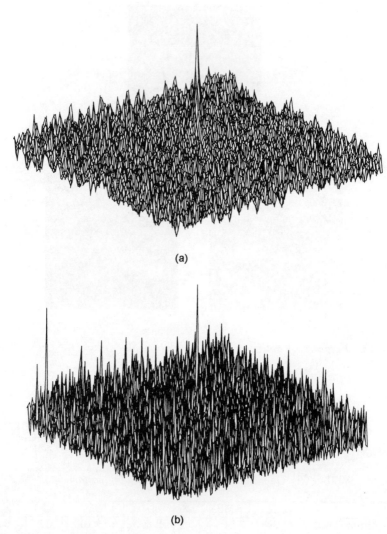

(a)

(b)

Figure 4.7: *Correlatiom results from (a) optimum ADF correlation filter, (b) POF and (c) CMF using the input image of Fig.4.2d*

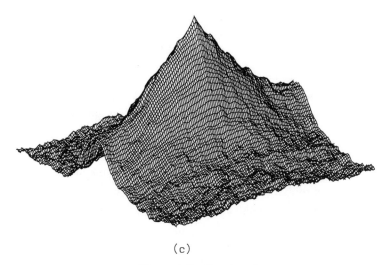

(c)

Figure 4.7: *Continued*

spectively. The correlation outputs obtained with these three filters are illustrated in Fig.4.7(a), 4.7(b) and 4.7(c). It can be seen that the CMF is extremely robust to noise but produces a very broad output correlation peak that is similar to an autocorrelation with a noise free input image; whereas the POF loses its target at the output plane rendering it useless for noisy input images. The optimum ADF delivers excellent overall correlation performance exploiting the advantageous characteristics of the POF and CMF. The performance advantage is quantified by the results tabulated in Table 4.1. The output signal to noise ratio (SNR_o) is defined by Eq.(3.17). ηH is the Horner efficiency, CPI denotes the correlation peak intensity, PNI is the number of pixels inside the correlation peak at the full width half maximum (FWHM) value, and PNO is the pixel numbers outside the correlation peak greater than or equal to the FWHM value.

The SNR_o, defined by Eq.(3.17), gives a good indication of filter noise robustness when the discriminant capability is incorporated. The PSR, defined by Eq.(3.19), gives a further useful indication of noise robustness. The PRMS, defined by Eq.(3.18), gives a good indication of correlation peak sharpness and discriminant capability. A filter's ability to accommodate noise in the input image is quantified by these three metrics.

From Table 4.1, the output SNR_o value of the optimum ADF is 14.29, which is intermediate to those of the POF and the CMF (it should be noted that the SNR_o value herein is obtained according to Eq.(3.17) using 22 different vehicle images, corrupted with different levels of noise); whereas the output ADF $PRMS$ and PSR values are 3.51 and 2.58 respectively, which are greater than either the CMF or the POF. The ηH and CPI values of the optimum ADF are between those for the CMF and POF but nearer to that of the POF, which is useful for energy conservation which is one of the factors determining system bandwidth. The PNI metric indicates the detection accuracy for the correlation peak which may be used to determine the location of the input image. The PNO measure gives the uniqueness of the peak at the correlation plane; if the $PNO > 0$, the object will not be detected without ambiguity. From the table, although the POF has just one pixel inside the correlation peak, the 8 pixels outside the correlation peak result in an ambiguity that makes reliable target detection impossible; the optimum ADF gives a better compromise between the CMF and the POF for the PNI metric, and produces only one peak at the output plane. Thus, the optimum ADF delivers a more useful performance than either the CMF or the POF.

The filter's discrimination ability is tested by comparing correlation performance on a target and nontarget object of similar size and shape. This test is performed by comparing the discrimination values of the optimum ADF, CMF and POF for input images of both the Bradley APC vehicle shown in Fig.4.2 and a similarly scaled and oriented Abrams MI tank shown in Fig.4.8; Fig.4.8(a) is a noise free tank image and Fig.4.8(b) is a noise corrupted tank image, with $20logSNR_I = -17.4dB$. The discrimination capability (DC) of the filter is defined as

$$DC = \frac{P_t}{P_{nt}} \tag{4.6}$$

where P_t is the intensity of the correlation peak for the target input and P_{nt} is the same for the nontarget image input. In the simulations, the noise free image of Fig.4.2(a) was used to construct the three filters; the Bradley APC vehicle was taken as the target input image, and the Abrams MI tank as the nontarget input image.

Table 4.2: *Quantitative comparision of filter's discrimination ability*

	Noise Free Case			Noise Level -17.4dB		
	target	nontarget	DC	target	nontarget	DC
Optimum ADF	1.00	0.1219	8.20	0.127	0.048	2.65
CMF	0.019	0.0131	1.45	0.0033	0.0045	0.73
POF	2.051	0.1503	13.65	0.0209	0.0241	0.867

The discrimination results are quantified in Table 4.2, where all the correlation peak intensities are normalised to the autocorrelation peak intensity of the optimum ADF ($\varepsilon = 10^{-4}$) with the noise free input image of Fig.4.2(a). From Table 4.2, it can be seen that when the input images are noise free the optimum ADF gives excellent discrimination, DC=8.20, which is intermediate to those of the POF and the CMF. Furthermore, when the input images are buried in noise the optimum ADF gives a discrimination ability of 2.56, whereas the POF and CMF lose their discrimination ability.

(a) (b)

Figure 4.8: *Abrams MI tank used as the nontarget image, (a) noise free image, (b) noise corrupted image with $20logSNR_I = -17.4dB$.*

4.4 Implementation

Threshold values for images with the different noise levels used herein were optimised using the procedure illustrated in Fig.4.1. The resulting optimum threshold values

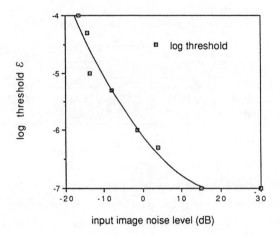

Figure 4.9: *Optimum threshold values vs. input image noise levels. x denotes noise level values in the input scene, and y denotes the logarithm of optimum threshold values. R^2 = residual error square*

are plotted in Fig.4.9; Eq.(4.7) gives the best-fit curve for this data

$$y = -6.1034 - 8.6113exp(-2x) + 1.8817exp(-3x^2) \qquad (4.7)$$

Thus, this equation is used as the embedded model within the hybrid correlation system for this vehicle recognition task. The system diagram is illustrated in Fig.4.10. During the recognition process, the input image is first fed into the adaptive correlation system. When the noise level within the image is known *a priori*, the optimum threshold value is evaluated using Eq.(4.7), thus allowing an optimised filter to be constructed and encoded onto the SLMs. When the noise level is unknown, the input image is entered into the optimum threshold evaluation unit, the detail of which is given in Fig.4.1; an optimum threshold value is determined via feedback from the output correlation plane, the worst case requires five iterations. The reference image is then fed into the adaptive correlation system and an optimum filter threshold value is used to construct an optimised filter which is used to update the SLMs; the system can adapt to change in the input scene noise at video frame rates.

4.5 Conclusion

An optimum adaptive filter which can accommodate noise in the input image has been presented which integrates the phase-only filter with the classical matched filter. A variable amplitude threshold value is set so that, at a particular spatial pixel location, if the amplitude value is greater than the pre-set threshold, only phase information is recorded; otherwise, both the phase and amplitude information are encoded. An iterative procedure to achieve an optimum threshold value to construct the filter is demonstrated. Computer simulation results show that the new filter delivers better overall performance than either the phase only filter or matched spatial filter. When reference images are encoded into the hybrid correlation system the amplitude threshold value is adjusted by an integrated adaptive controller to optimise noise resistance and discrimination ability.

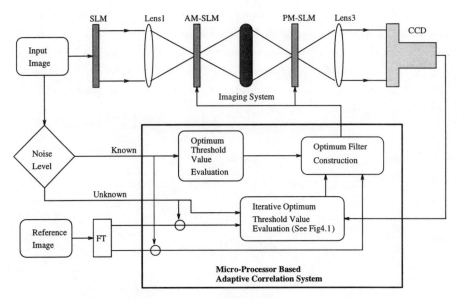

Where ◯ denotes the correlation operation

Figure 4.10: *Hybrid correlation system diagram. AM-SLM denotes the amplitude modulating spatial light modulator, and PM-SLM denotes the phase modulating spatial light modulator.*

Bibliography

[1] A. VanderLugt, "Signal Detection by Complex Spatial Filtering". *IEEE Trans. Inf. Theory* **IT-10**, 139-145(1964).

[2] J.L. Horner and P.D. Gianino, "Phase-Only Matched Filters". *Appl. Opt.* **23**, 812-816(1984).

[3] G.G. Mu, X.M. Wang and Z.Q. Wang, "Amplitude-Compensated Matched Filtering". *Appl. Opt.* **27**, 3461-3463(1992).

[4] R.K. Wang, C.R. Chatwin and M.Y. Huang, "Correlation Filter with a Noise Adaptive Discrimination Capability", *Optik* **99**, 18-24(1995).

[5] B. Javidi, "Nonlinear Joint Power Spectrum Based Optical Correlation". *Appl. Opt.* **28**, 2358-2367(1989).

[6] J.L. Horner and J.R. Leger, "Pattern Recognition with Binary Phase-Only Filters". *Appl. Opt.* **24**, 609-611(1985).

[7] A. Papoulis, *Probability, Random Variables, and Stochastic Processes.* McGraw-Hill, New York, (1984).

Chapter 5

Synthetic Discriminant Functions (SDFs)

5.1 Introduction

Classical matched spatial filters [29] (CMFs) are optimal in the sense that they deliver the maximum output signal-to-noise (SNR) ratio, which is defined by the ratio of the average output peak value to its standard deviation, in detecting a known reference signal in additive (usually assumed to be white) noise [23]. However, the CMF suffers from the following practical difficulties in optical pattern recognition.

(i) The output correlation peak produced by the CMF degrades rapidly with image distortions due to scale mismatch, in-plane rotation, and out-of-plane rotation etc.

(ii) The CMF has a very low optical efficiency, or Horner efficiency.

(iii) Most available spatial light modulators (SLMs) cannot accommodate the full complex frequency response required by CMFs.

(iv) The CMF cannot be used for multi-class pattern recognition.

Optical efficiency can be improved by using phase-only filters [14] (POFs), because the frequency plane filter will then pass all the incident light. Real-time SLMs such as the magneto-optic SLM can be employed in the filter plane if the filters are restricted to be binary phase-only filters [24] (BPOFs). However, they are not capable of providing distortion invariant pattern recognition or multi-class pattern recognition.

To overcome the limitations of the CMF and POF, several new filter synthesis techniques have been proposed. These filters use combinations of training images that are designed to overcome the expected distortions. The intensity at the central position of the cross correlation function can be specified for each training image during synthesis; hence, by multiplexing and applying a variety of algorithms to the filter, several object classes can be handled by the correlation filters. This type of filter is given the generic name: synthetic discriminant function (SDF) filter. In this approach, the filters are computed as linear combinations of the training set reference images to give an equal central correlation amplitude for each training set image. However, the SDFs based on CMFs yield very broad correlation peaks in the correlation plane, which give very poor discrimination between objects that are similar and thus may result in false detection responses. In order to overcome these difficulties, various modifications of the SDF algorithm have been successively tested in the past ten years.

The purpose of this chapter is to present a brief review of the basic concepts of correlation based, distortion invariant pattern recognition algorithms proposed in the literature.

5.2 Historical Background

To appreciate the evolution of distortion invariant filter design, let's consider the problem of recognising the 26 uppercase letters in the English alphabet by using optical correlators. An obvious first approach is to use 26 CMFs, each matched to a different letter. The input image is correlated by using all 26 CMFs, the maximum among these outputs indicates the input class. In practice, this simple method does not work very well because of the great similarity between certain pairs of letters (e.g. E and F, C and O). Caulfield and Maloney [5] suggested that the discrimination between such similar pairs of letters can be improved by processing the resulting correlation outputs. In particular, they suggested using linear combinations of the correlation outputs. For example, the weights of these linear combinations are found so that when E is in the input, only one combination (corresponding to class E) results in output 1, whereas all other combinations (corresponding to the remaining 25 classes) yield zero. This method improves the discrimination capability. However, N correlations are required to recognise an input from a set of N training images. Braunecker et al [2] suggested that this process was redundant and that only K correlations are performed where K is the ceiling of $log_2 N$.

Hester and Casasent [13] suggested that this recognition process could be further simplified by using a linear combination of reference images to create a composite image and then cross correlating the inputs with this one composite image. The weights for the linear combinations are selected so that the cross correlation output at the origin is the same for all images belonging to one class. This technique was termed the synthetic discriminant function (SDF) approach. The SDF approach requires only one cross correlation per input image. Once the linear combination weights are obtained, the required SDF can be synthesised in a digital computer or in an optical laboratory by using multiple exposure holographic techniques. Since its introduction in 1980, the SDF has been the focus of much research in the field of optical pattern recognition.

5.3   Synthetic Discriminant Functions

In this section the technical details for the basic SDF [13] are described. This basic filter is also known as the equal correlation peak (ECP) SDF and also as the projection SDF. Some suggested modifications to this basic idea are then presented.

5.3.1 Frequency plane correlator

Let $t_1(x, y), t_2(x, y), \ldots, t_N(x, y)$ denote N training images representing possible distortions to a reference image $t(x, y)$. Let $T(u, v)$ denote its two dimensional Fourier transform as defined below

$$T(u, v) = \int \int t(x, y) exp[-j2\pi(ux + vy)] dx dy, \qquad (5.1)$$

where u and v denote the spatial frequencies. The limits on all integrals in this chapter are from $-\infty$ to $+\infty$ unless otherwise stated. The objective is to design a composite image $s(x, y)$ such that when $S^*(u, v)$ (the complex conjugate is indicated by the superscript asterisk) is placed in plane P_2 of the frequency plane correlator shown in Figure 5.1, the correlation peak height, in correlation plane P_3, is equal for all N inputs $t_1(x, y), t_2(x, y), \ldots, t_N(x, y)$ placed in plane P_1.

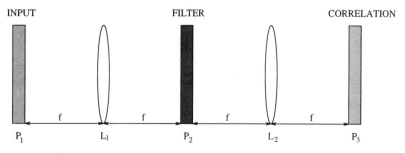

Figure 5.1: *Schematic of the frequency plane correlator*

The optical correlator system shown in Fig.5.1 is well known to researchers in optical processing as the frequency plane correlator. When the input function $f(x, y)$ is placed in plane P_1 and a complex function $S^*(u, v)$ is placed in plane P_2, the resulting correlation output $c(\tau_x, \tau_y)$ in plane P_3 is given by

$$\begin{aligned} c(\tau_x, \tau_y) &= \int \int F(u, v) S^*(u, v) exp[j2\pi(u\tau_x + v\tau_y)] du dv, \\ &= \int \int s^*(x, y) f(x + \tau_x, y + \tau_y) dx dy, \\ &= s(x, y) \odot f(x, y), \qquad (5.2) \end{aligned}$$

where $\odot$ denotes a 2-D cross correlation. In this brief discussion, some important details are omitted, such as holographic methods for synthesising the complex valued filter functions [29], the effect of lens focal length [11], requirements of the light coherence, and other correlator architectures such as the joint-transform correlator [32]. See the books by Goodman [11] and Yu [33] for further information on these topics.

5.3.2 Equal correlation peak SDF

In the ECP SDF design, the objective is to select a filter impulse response $s(x, y)$ so that the resulting cross correlation with all N-input training images is the same. Clearly this is impossible. However, Hester and Casasent [13] suggested that only the central optical axis values of these cross correlations be the same

$$
\begin{aligned}
s(x, y) \odot t_i(x, y)|_{\tau_x=0, \tau_y=0} &= \int \int s^*(x, y) t_i(x, y) dx dy, \\
&= c, \qquad i = 1, 2, 3, \ldots, N,
\end{aligned} \tag{5.3}
$$

where c is a pre-specified constant. Such an $s(x, y)$ would yield the same constant value of c at the origin (the location of the autocorrelation peak) with all N training images, i.e. $t_1(x, y), t_2(x, y), \ldots, t_N(x, y)$. The hope is that when the input is a non-training image, but from the same class, the cross correlation output at the origin will be sufficiently close to this constant c that it can be recognised. The success of this approach depends on selecting the correct training set.

To enable it to be synthesised by multiple exposure techniques, Hester and Casasent [13] assumed that $s(x, y)$ is a linear combination of the N training images

$$
s(x, y) = a_1 t_1(x, y) + a_2 t_2(x, y) + \ldots + a_N t_N(x, y), \tag{5.4}
$$

where the coefficients $a_1, a_2, \ldots, a_N$ have to be determined to satisfy the constraints in Eq.(5.3). Substituting Eq.(5.4) into Eq.(5.3), the following equations are obtained

$$
\sum_{i=1}^{N} a_i^* R_{ij} = c, \qquad j = 1, 2, \ldots, N, \tag{5.5}
$$

where

$$
R_{ij} = \int \int t_i^*(x, y) t_j(x, y) dx dy \tag{5.6}
$$

is the inner product (i.e. the cross correlation at the origin) of the training images $t_i(x, y)$ and $t_j(x, y)$. If the training images are real, there is no need for the conjugate in Eq.(5.6). Eq.(5.5) represents N complex linear equations in N complex unknowns, $a_1, a_2, \ldots, a_N$. When N is of reasonable size these equations can be solved by using standard methods [15], such as Gaussian elimination. When N is large, solving these equations is problematic. The resulting computational considerations will be discussed in Sub-section 5.3.6.

The ECP SDF design does not consider the possibility of noise in the input plane. Thus any random noise can degrade the correlation output severely and can therefore disrupt pattern recognition. Another problem is that $s(x, y)$, which is a linear combination of training images, is not matched to any of the training images exactly. Thus, what is obtained in the correlation plane is always a cross correlation and never an autocorrelation. Only when the phase of the Fourier transform of the input image is completely removed by the phase filter can a correlation peak be guaranteed to appear at the origin. In conventional correlators the output plane is scanned for this peak, and its location indicates the position of the target in the input scene. When the ECP SDF filter is used in the filter plane, the only guarantee is that the cross correlations have a value of c at the origin whenever the input image is one of the N training images. A major problem arising here is that bigger values may occur elsewhere in the output plane because the controlled value c may not correspond to a peak; it may not even be c because of random noise existing in the input scene.

5.3.3   Two class problem

Ideally a filter should be capable of recognising any distorted version of the reference image and reject all others. Unfortunately, this is impossible with a finite number of filters. Therefore, the filter should be made to recognise the training images from one class (called in-class) and reject the training images from another class (called out-of-class). Let $p_1(x, y)$, $p_2(x, y)$, $\ldots$, $p_M(x, y)$ denote the training images which are out-of-class. Then, in addition to the constraints in Eq.(5.3), $s(x, y)$ is chosen to satisfy the following constraints

$$s(x,y) \odot p_i(x,y)|_{\tau_x=0,\tau_y=0} = 0, \qquad i = 1,2,\ldots,M. \tag{5.7}$$

The composite image $s(x,y)$ is now assumed to be a linear combination of the training image set $\{t_1(x,y),\ldots,t_N(x,y),p_1(x,y),\ldots,p_M(x,y)\}$. In order to distinguish between two classes, the expectation is that the output correlation peak will have a value close to the constant c for the in-class non-training images and close to zero for the out-of-class images.

Obviously the above approach can be extended in theory to any number of classes. To maintain a concise notation a single training image set $\{t_1(x,y),\ldots,t_N(x,y)\}$ can be used, with the understanding that these training images can come from any class. The constants c_i for constraints are also used, with the subscript i indicating the constraints corresponding to $t_i(x,y)$. Thus the equation can be rewritten as

$$\sum_{i=1}^{N} a_i^* R_{ij} = c_j, \qquad j = 1,2,\ldots,N. \tag{5.8}$$

This equation can be written compactly if the following matrix vector notation is used. Let $\mathbf{a}$ be an N-dimensional column vector with a_i as the ith entry; similarly, $\mathbf{c}$ is a column of size N with c_i as its ith entry. Let $\mathbf{R}$ be an $N \times N$ square matrix with R_{ij} as the entry in the ith row and the jth column. Then

$$\mathbf{R}\mathbf{a}^* = \mathbf{c} \tag{5.9}$$

If $\mathbf{R}$ is invertible, $\mathbf{a}^*$ is given by $\mathbf{R}^{-1}\mathbf{c}$. It can be shown that $\mathbf{R}$ is invertible if, and only if, the N training vectors are linearly independent. The training image set used must be tested (using the Gram-Schmidt procedure [16] or some other similar method) to ensure this independence. Even when $\mathbf{R}$ is theoretically non-singular its inversion is difficult, especially when the training images are quite similar to each other. This and other issues related to training set selection will be discussed in the next subsection.

5.3.4 Training image set size

The success of the ECP SDF, in fact all composite filter designs, depends critically upon the training image set being used. The training image set must be designed to meet conflicting objectives; because this set must be descriptive of all expected distortions of the target, it must contain many distorted versions of the target. In contrast, N should be kept small so that the matrix size is small (for computational convenience) and so that the matrix is not ill conditioned as a result of training images being too similar to each other. These conflicting requirements are further compounded by the fact that frequently the training set images do not cover the full distortion range and the filter must be constructed using the few images that are available.

Vijaya Kumar and Pochapsky [20] carried out a theoretical analysis to investigate the effects of the training image set size N. They considered the ECP SDF constructed from N in-plane rotated versions of the reference image $t(x, y)$. These rotations are in equal increments of $2\pi/N$ rad. They also assumed that $t(x, y)$ was derived from a Gaussian random process [27] with a specified autocorrelation function (Gaussian shaped or exponential shaped function). They did not use any particular image for $t(x, y)$. Using earlier results derived by Mostafavi and Smith [22], they obtained theoretical expressions which incorporated N, the number of training images, and the space bandwidth product (SBWP) of $t(x, y)$, as parameters.

The theoretical analysis carried out by Vijaya Kumar and Pochapsky [20] shows that when the training set size of N increases, the worst-case signal to noise ratio (SNR) across the entire distortion range increases. Although this analysis provides a clearer understanding of the effects of N on the output SNR, it is not necessarily advantageous to keep increasing N. Vijaya Kumar and Pochapsky [20] also tested the worst case SNR as a function of N for different SBWPs. The SNR initially increases with N and then levels off, indicating no further improvement when a larger training set is used. This method provides a systematic procedure for selecting N for a given SBWP. As far as we are aware, this theoretical analysis has not been generalised to other distortions.

When N becomes large, the ECP SDF will essentially become the average of all rotated versions of $t(x, y)$ to yield the required distortion invariance. However, for large N, the composite image will be saturated with information and will not provide any discrimination ability. The theoretical analysis by Vijaya Kumar and Pochapsky [20] is limited to the problem of detecting an image subject to distortions and additive noise. A similar theoretical analysis must be carried out to assess the discrimination capability. Recently Caelli and Liu [3] used an adaptive approach to invariant pattern recognition to demonstrate that the number of templates needed for efficient pattern recognition is considerably lower than was previously thought.

5.3.5 Selection of training images

Once we have an approximate idea of the optimum number of training images, N, we need to choose the specific training images to be used. One approach is to distribute the N training images uniformly over the range of expected distortions. For example, if in-plane rotation is the expected distortion, the training images can be captured for every $10°$ of target rotation, i.e. 36 training images are used. This has been the popular practice.

For other distortions such as out-of-plane rotations, the procedure of selecting uniformly sampled training images may not be appropriate. For example, more head-on views of an object (such as a tank or aeroplane) may be needed rather than the side views. This leads to the concept of selecting the training images based on a correlation threshold T_c. One procedure for this selection is as follows.

First, all available images are normalised to have unit energy. Then all available images, with the total number of L, are cross correlated with each other. The correlation peak values in these cross correlation outputs are stored in a symmetric matrix $\mathbf{A}$ with the dimensions of $L \times L$. Because all the images are normalised to unit energy, diagonal entries of $\mathbf{A}$ are equal to 1 and off-diagonal entries will be smaller than 1. To start the training set selection process, let us arbitrarily put a new image into the training set. Next find the smallest off-diagonal entry in the first row of $\mathbf{A}$. This entry represents the image that is least correlated with the image in the training set. This new image is added into the training set provided that without its inclusion the cross correlation peak falls below a preset threshold T_c, this ensures that the new training set will give a cross correlation that exceeds T_c. If any of the correlations fall below T_c, the image must be added to the training set. This procedure is continued until all remaining images give a cross correlation peak of T_c, or higher, with at least one image in the training set. The higher the value T_c, the greater the number of images required in the training set.

Another approach proposed by Hassebrook *et al* [12] suggests that the training set be selected so that the resulting correlation matrix **R** is close to a Toeplitz matrix. A Toeplitz [28] matrix is a square matrix with the same values for all entries in any diagonal parallel to the main diagonal. Hassebrook *et al* [12] showed that such a training set would be convenient in the filter design procedure.

5.3.6   Computational issues

As discussed above, the design of an ECP SDF requires the solution of N linear equations in N variables. When N is small, this solution is reasonably straightforward. However, in many realistic cases N can be large. For example, consider the problem of discriminating 10 classes of object where each object may be viewed at any angle and over a range interval. If we sample the range at 10 places, the out-of-plane view angle at 10 angles, and the in-plane rotation every 10°, the resulting N will be $10 \times 10 \times 10 \times 36 = 36,000$. This N is too large for most direct solution techniques and indicates why it is important to keep the training set size small.

One approach suggested by Kumar [17] is to solve Eq.(5.8) iteratively. To simplify our discussion, let us assume that the training images and the weights $a_1, a_2, \ldots, a_N$ are real. Eq.(5.8) gives N linear equations with N unknowns $\{a_1, a_2, \ldots, a_N\}$. Kumar's method represents each equation as a hyperplane in N-dimensional space, with $a_1, a_2, \ldots, a_N$ represented by the N axes. The N equations in Eq.(5.8) represent N hyperplanes in an N dimensional hyper space. If a unique solution exists for this problem, these hyperplanes intersect at a unique point corresponding to that solution. An example of this is shown in Fig.5.2 with $N = 2$.

The iterative solution method is as follows. Let us start with an initial guess $\mathbf{a}_0$ for the solution. This guess is then projected orthogonally onto hyperplane 1 to get the next estimate $\mathbf{a}_1$, this vector $\mathbf{a}_1$ is then projected orthogonally onto hyperplane 2 to yield $\mathbf{a}_2$. This process is continued until $\mathbf{a}_N$ is obtained, which is the projection onto hyperplane N. This projection completes one iteration. Next $\mathbf{a}_N$ becomes the new starting point and the process is repeated. This iterative process is halted when the solution vector $\mathbf{a}$ does not change significantly from one iteration to the next.

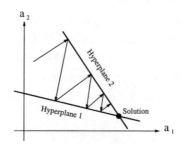

Figure 5.2: *Representation of the SDF equations using hyperplanes. Here the number of training images $N = 2$*

From Fig.5.2 it can be seen that the convergence will be at its fastest when all hyperplanes are orthogonal to each other. When this is not the case, the hyperplanes can be rearranged so that they are mutually orthogonal. The Gram-Schmidt procedure [16] is a possible method for rearranging the hyperplanes. However, it can be shown that rearranging the hyperplanes using the Gram-Schmidt procedure is just as complex as solving Eq.(5.8) directly. Thus this procedure is not recommended.

A computationally simpler procedure is to rearrange the hyperplanes so that hyperplane 1 is orthogonal to hyperplane 2, hyperplane 2 is orthogonal to hyperplane 3, and so on. The last hyperplane N is made orthogonal to the first hyperplane 1. This procedure is much simpler because it requires only N pairwise orthogonalizations instead of the $N^2/2$ pairwise orthogonalizations needed in the general case of forcing all hyperplanes to be orthogonal to each other. Algorithmic details as well as an example of the resulting computational advantages can be found elsewhere [17].

Other methods to deal with large N have also been presented in the literature. Casasent and Chang [7] suggested extracting principal components of training sets from each class to reduce the number of training images. One of the problems with this practice is that forcing the principal components to yield certain cross correlation outputs with a SDF filter is not equivalent to forcing the original training images to yield the same cross correlation values.

5.4 Generalised Synthetic Discriminant Functions

The ECP SDF is designed to produce a value c_i at the origin of the output plane when the ith training image is used as the input. For the two class problem, this constraint value c_i is usually chosen as 1 for training images from one class and as 0 for images from the other class. However, there are some practical problems in using this filter for optical pattern recognition.

The first problem is that the original ECP SDF design does not consider the possibility of random noise in the input. In the presence of noise the output values will not be exactly 1 and 0, even for training images. Thus, composite filters capable of tolerating input noise must be designed. Minimum variance synthetic discriminant functions (MVSDF), proposed by Kumar [18], are designed for this purpose. The difficulty in using the MVSDF is that it generates large sidelobes in the correlation plane. A new technique, proposed by Wang and Chatwin [30][31] and called modified filter synthetic discriminant functions, tolerates input image noise and does not suffer from these difficulties; this is discussed fully in Chapter 6.

The second problem with the ECP SDF is that they are designed to control only one point (the origin) in the correlation output plane. Correlators are attractive because they can not only detect a target, but also locate it. If the input target is shifted by a certain unknown distance from the origin, for a $4f$ system the cross correlation output is also shifted by that distance. The controlled centre values thus move by an unknown amount. Because the other uncontrolled values in the correlation output can be larger than 1, it is impossible to locate the shifted control point in the presence of even a small amount of noise. Thus it is desirable to produce correlation peaks at the origin (when the input is centred) that are sharp. The minimum average correlation energy (MACE) filter, proposed by Mahalanobis *et al*

[21], addresses this problem; this will be reviewed in Section 5.5.

The final problem with the ECP SDF is that its underlying assumption — that $s(x,y)$ is a linear combination of the training images in Eq.(5.4) — is unnecessary. That assumption is useful when the SDF filters are synthesised in the optical laboratory by using multiple exposure techniques. However, the SDF can be synthesised using the digital computer, and thus there is no need for the limiting restriction of Eq.(5.4). To see the limitations this restriction imposes, consider the case of $N = 36$ real images, each with 512^2 pixels in them. If the restriction of Eq.(5.4) is not used, an $s(x,y)$ will be determined to simply satisfy Eq.(5.3). That means that there are 36 equations with 512^2 variables. Thus there are $(512^2 - 36)$ undetermined variables that can be used to achieve other objectives such as noise minimization, peak sharpening, etc. By including the unnecessary restriction of Eq.(5.4), $(512^2 - 36)$ degrees of freedom are thrown away. A general solution that includes all these degrees of freedom is called the generalised synthetic discriminant function.

It is convenient to discretise the images and use vector notation to introduce the generalised SDF. Let's assume that the training images $t_1(x,y)$, ..., $t_N(x,y)$ are sampled to yield arrays with d pixels in them. Let us also assume that they have d-dimensional column vectors — $\mathbf{t_1}, \mathbf{t_2}, \ldots, \mathbf{t_N}$ — by representing the elements in these training images as vectors. We will assume that scanning is from left to right and from top to bottom. Similarly, let us use the d-dimensional column vector $\mathbf{s}$ to denote the composite image $s(x,y)$. Then the constraints in Eq.(5.3) can be rewritten as

$$\mathbf{s^+t_i} = c_i, \qquad i = 1, 2, \ldots, N, \tag{5.10}$$

where the superscript $+$ denotes the conjugate transpose. This equation can be written even more compactly by using the data matrix $\mathbf{T}$. This matrix $\mathbf{T}$ has the vector $\mathbf{t_i}$ as its ith column and is thus a $d \times N$ matrix. We will assume from now on that $d \gg N$ (i.e. the number of pixels in the training images is much larger than the number of training images) and that the columns of this matrix are linearly independent. Using this notation, Eq.(5.10) can be written as

$$\mathbf{T^+s} = \mathbf{c}. \tag{5.11}$$

The ECP SDF assumes that the composite image **s** is of the following form

$$\mathbf{s} = \mathbf{Ta}, \tag{5.12}$$

where **a** is the vector of coefficients defined before. Substituting Eq.(5.12) into Eq.(5.11) and solving for **a** yields

$$\mathbf{a} = (\mathbf{T}^+\mathbf{T})^{-1}\mathbf{c}^*. \tag{5.13}$$

It is easy to verify that Eq.(5.13) is identical to Eq.(5.9) once we realise that $\mathbf{R} = \mathbf{T}^+\mathbf{T}$. Because **R** contains the inner products of various pairs of training images, it is known as the vector inner-product matrix or as the correlation matrix. The filter vector **s** can be obtained by substituting Eq.(5.13) into Eq.(5.12) to get

$$\mathbf{s}_{ECP} = \mathbf{T}(\mathbf{T}^+\mathbf{T})^{-1}\mathbf{c}^*. \tag{5.14}$$

It is trivial to verify that the ECP SDF in Eq.(5.14) satisfies the constraints in Eq.(5.11). However, as discussed previously, the condition in Eq.(5.12) is unnecessary. A general expression for any **s** capable of satisfying Eq.(5.11) is given as follows

$$\mathbf{s} = \mathbf{T}(\mathbf{T}^+\mathbf{T})^{-1}\mathbf{c}^* + [\mathbf{I_d} - \mathbf{T}(\mathbf{T}^+\mathbf{T})^{-1}\mathbf{T}^+]\mathbf{z}, \tag{5.15}$$

where $\mathbf{I_d}$ is the $d \times d$ identity matrix and **z** is any column vector with D complex entries. It can be verified that the **s** in Eq.(5.15) satisfies the constraints in Eq.(5.11). The ECP SDF is obtained when **z**=**0**. Because any vector **z** can be employed, we have a multitude of solution vectors. In fact, the set of vectors of the form $[\mathbf{I_d} - \mathbf{T}(\mathbf{T}^+\mathbf{T})^{-1}\mathbf{T}^+]\mathbf{z}$ (considering all possible **z** vectors) can be shown to be a vector space of dimensionality $(d - N)$. The second term in Eq.(5.15) represents filter vectors that are orthogonal to the data matrix **T**. The set of solution vectors is not a vector space because it does not include the **0** vector. Many details about the properties of this solution set are discussed by Bahri and Kumar [1]. The solution vector in Eq.(5.15) is known as the generalised SDF.

5.5 Minimum Average Correlation Energy Filters

MACE filters are designed for good location accuracy and discrimination capability; they produce sharp correlation peaks in the output plane. Let $t_1(x,y), \ldots, t_N(x,y)$

denote the N training images as before and let $T_1(u,v), \ldots, T_N(u,v)$ denote their two dimensional Fourier transforms. Let $S^*(u,v)$ denote the transmittance of the filter function. Then, the filter is constrained to satisfy the following

$$\int \int T_i(u,v)S^*(u,v)dudv = c_i, \qquad i = 1, 2, \ldots, N \qquad (5.16)$$

In addition, the MACE filter [21] minimizes the following average correlation plane energy

$$\begin{aligned} E_{ave} &= \frac{1}{N} \sum_{i=1}^{N} \int \int |c_i(\tau_x, \tau_y)|^2 d\tau_x d\tau_y, \\ &= \frac{1}{N} \sum_{i=1}^{N} \int \int |T_i(u,v)|^2 |S(u,v)|^2 dudv, \end{aligned} \qquad (5.17)$$

where Parseval's theorem was used in deriving the above equation. By minimizing E_{ave}, it attempts to reduce the sidelobes in the correlation plane. This is essentially an indirect attempt at reducing the problem of correlation sidelobes.

To carry out the minimization of E_{ave}, the usual vector notation is used. Let $\hat{t}_i$ denote the d-dimensional complex column vector obtained by sampling $T_i(u,v)$. Then the constraints in Eq.(5.16) can be rewritten as

$$\hat{T}^+ \hat{s} = c^*, \qquad (5.18)$$

where $\hat{T}$ is a $d \times N$ matrix with $\hat{s}_i$ as its ith column. E_{ave} in Eq.(5.17) can be expressed as

$$E_{ave} = \hat{s}^+ \hat{D} \hat{s}, \qquad (5.19)$$

where $\hat{D}$ is a $d \times d$ diagonal matrix. The entries along the diagonal are obtained by averaging $|S_i(u,v)|^2$, $i = 1, 2, \ldots, N$ and then scanning the average from left to right and from top to bottom.

Minimizing E_{ave} in Eq.(5.19), subject to the constraints in Eq.(5.18), leads to the following filter

$$\hat{s}_{\text{MACE}} = \hat{D}^{-1} \hat{T} (\hat{T}^+ \hat{D}^{-1} \hat{T})^{-1} c^*. \qquad (5.20)$$

The resulting minimum average energy is then given by

$$E_{min} = c^T (\hat{T}^+ \hat{D}^{-1} \hat{T})^{-1} c^* = c^+ (\hat{T}^T \hat{D}^{-1} \hat{T}^*)^{-1} c. \qquad (5.21)$$

In many simulation studies, filters designed using this approach have produced impressively sharp correlation peaks. However, MACE filters appear to have two drawbacks. The first is that there is no noise tolerance built into the filters. The second, and most critical, is that the MACE filter seems to be more sensitive to intra-class variations than other composite filters [9], making it almost useless in practical implementations; it actually approaches the behaviour of the inverse filter.

Recently, Casasent *et al* [10] proposed Gaussian MACE filters to reduce the sensitivity of the MACE filters to intra-class variations. The idea behind Gaussian MACE filters is to reduce the sharpness of the resulting correlation peak and thus improve its noise tolerance. Other recent variations in MACE filter design include the use of circular harmonic components [4][8][25], and the inclusion of input noise considerations [26]. When compared with the original MACE filter, these modifications give improved resistance to noise occurring in the input plane; little has been implemented in practical systems.

In this chapter, only the basic concepts of synthetic discriminant functions and several other important filters, that are frequently referenced in this treatise, have been reviewed. There are numerous other useful variations of SDF filters that are not included in this chapter. For a good introduction to composite filter design for optical correlators, Kumar's paper [19] is extremely useful.

Bibliography

[1] Z. Bahri and B.V.K. Vijaya Kumar, "Generalized synthetic discriminant functions", *J. Opt. Soc. Am.* **A5**, 562-571(1988).

[2] B. Braunecker, R.W. Hauck and A.W. Lohmann, "Optical character recognition based on non-redundant correlation measurements", *Appl. Opt.* **18**, 2746-2753(1979).

[3] T.M. Caelli and Z.Q. Liu, "On the minimum number of templates required for shift, rotation and size invariant pattern recognition", *Patt. Recog.* **21**, 205-216(1988).

[4] J. Campos and H.H. Arsenault, "Optimum sidelobe reducing invariant matched filters for pattern recognition", *Optical Computing '88, Proc. Soc. Photo-Opt. Instrum. Eng.* **963**, P. Chavel and J.W. Goodman and G. Robin eds., 298-303(1988).

[5] H.J. Caulfield and W.T. Maloney, "Improved discrimination in optical character recognition", *Appl. Opt.* **8**, 2354-2356(1969).

[6] D. Casasent, "Unified synthetic discriminant function computation formulation", *Appl. Opt.* **23**, 1620-1627(1984).

[7] D. Casasent and W.T. Chang, "Correlation synthetic discriminant functions", *Appl. Opt.* **25**, 2343-2350(1986).

[8] D. Casasent, A. Iyer and G. Ravichandran, "Circular harmonic function MACE filters", *Appl. Opt.* **30**, 5169-5175(1991).

120

[9] D. Casasent and G. Ravichandran, "Advanced distortion invariant MACE filters", *Appl. Opt.* **31**, 1109-1116(1992).

[10] D. Casasent, G. Ravichandran and S. Bollapraggada, "Gaussian MACE correlation filters", *Appl. Opt.* **30**, 5176-5181(1991).

[11] J.W. Goodman, *Introduction to Fourier Optics*, McGraw-Hill, New York (1968).

[12] L. Hassebrook, B.V.K. Vijiaya Kumar and L. Hostetler, "Linear phase coefficient composite filters for optical pattern recognition", in *Optical Pattern Recognition*, H. Liu ed. *Proc. Soc. Photo-Opt. Instrum. Eng.* **1053**, 218-226(1989).

[13] C.F. Hester and D. Casasent, "Multivariant technique for multiclass pattern recognition", *Appl. Opt.* **19**, 1758-1761(1980).

[14] J.L. Horner and P.D. Gianino, "Phase-only filtering", *Appl. Opt.* **23**, 812-816(1984).

[15] M.L. James, G.M. Smith and J.C. Wolford, *Applied Numerical Methods for Digital Computation*, Harper & Row, New York, (1985).

[16] G.A. Korn and T.M. Korn, *Mathematical Handbook for Scientists and Engineers*, McGraw-Hill, New York, (1968).

[17] B.V.K. Vijaya Kumar, "Efficient approach for designing linear combination filters", *Appl. Opt.* **22**, 1445-1448(1983).

[18] B.V.K. Vijaya Kumar, "Minimum variance synthetic discriminant functions", *J. Opt. Soc. Am.* **A3**, 1679-1584(1986).

[19] B.V.K. Vijaya Kumar, "Tutorial survey of composite filter design from optical correlators", *Appl. Opt.* **23**, 4773-4801(1992).

[20] B.V.K. Vijaya Kumar and E. Pochapsky, "Signal-to-noise ratio considerations in modified matched spatial filters", *J. Opt. Soc. Am.* **A3**, 777-786(1986).

[21] A. Mahalanobis, B.V.K. Vijaya Kumar and L. Hostetler, "Minimum average correlation energy filters", *Appl. Opt* **26**, 3633-3640(1987).

[22] H. Mostafavi and F. Smith, "Image correlation with geometric distortion-part I: acquisition performance", *IEEE Trans. Aerosp. Electron. Sys.* **AES 14**, 487-493(1978).

[23] D.O. North, "An Analysis of the factors which determine signal/noise discriminations in pulsed carrier systems", *Proc. IEEE* **51**, 1016-1027(1963).

[24] D. Psaltis, E.G. Paek and S.S. Venkatesh, "Optical image correlation with binary spatial light modulator", *Opt. Eng.* **23**, 698-704(1984).

[25] G. Ravichandran and D. Casasent, "Generalized in-plane rotation invariant minimum average correlation energy filter", *Opt. Eng.* **30**, 1601-1607(1991).

[26] Ph. Refregier, "Filter design for optical pattern recognition: multicriteria optimization approach", *Opt. Lett.* **15**, 854-856(1990).

[27] K.S. Shanmugan and A.M. Breipohl, *Random Signal Detection, Estimation and Data Analysis*, Wiley, New York (1988).

[28] G.W. Stewart, *Introduction to Matrix Computations*, Academic Press, New York(1973).

[29] A. VanderLugt, "Signal detection by complex spatial filtering", *IEEE Trans. Inf. Theory* **10**, 139-145(1964).

[30] R.K. Wang and C.R. Chatwin, "Modified filter synthetic discriminant functions for improved optical correlator performance", *Appl. Opt.* **33**, 7646-7654(1994).

[31] R.K. Wang and C.R. Chatwin, "Multilevel phase and amplitude modified filter synthetic discriminant function filters ", *Appl. Opt.* **34**, 4094-4104(1995).

[32] C.S. Weaver and J.W. Goodman, "A technique for optically convolving two functions", *Appl. Opt.* **5**, 1248-1249(1966).

[33] F.T.S. Yu, *Optical Information Processing*, Wiley, New York(1983).

Chapter 6

Modified Filter-SDF Filter and its Real Time Implementation

6.1 Introduction

The development of synthetic discriminant function (SDF) filters [1][2][3][4] as distortion tolerant filters was motivated by the sensitivity of the classical matched filter [5] (CMF) to distortions in the input image such as in-plane rotations, out-of-plane rotations, and scale variations. These techniques of designing invariant filters for optical correlators pre-suppose the use of continuous complex valued filters. Since programmable spatial light modulators (SLMs) capable of representing continuous complex functions are only available as research devices that require characterisation before they can be used, the utility of spatially invariant filters with actual device performance requires investigation.

Because the distortion invariant filters must be encoded on the available SLMs, it is important to incorporate device constraints into the filter design. This necessity provided the motivation to design composite phase only filters (POFs) and binary phase only filters (BPOFs). The obvious approach is to design a conventional SDF and simply force it to be a phase-only or binary phase-only function [6]. However, it was quickly realized [7] that phase-only or binary phase-only SDFs do not perform very well; these filters produce very sharp correlation peaks but do not satisfy the equal correlation peaks (ECP) rule in the output plane. Thus, Jared et al [8] [9] recently proposed an iterative relaxation algorithm, which enables the design of phase-only SDFs and binary phase-only SDFs to satisfy the ECP rule. Their idea was to ensure that the filter-encoding constraints are taken into account at the design stage; this was called the filter SDF (fSDF). In contrast to fully complex CMFs and conventional SDFs, fSDF filters can be implemented on commercially available spatial light modulators (SLMs) for use in an optical correlator, and are therefore of particular interest for real-time optical pattern recognition systems employing rapidly updateable SLMs.

It is well known that, for common objects, the concentration of most of the energy in the central zone of the spectrum, i.e. low frequency components, is responsible for the poor correlation performance. However, the fSDF implements the filter modulation constraints (e.g. BPOF) on the conventional SDF, which is a linear combination of the training set images. There is no doubt that the conventional SDF is dominated by the lower frequency components of individual training set images. Thus, this degrades the correlation performance even when the filter modulation constraints are implemented on the composite image. To solve this problem, Wang and Chatwin [11] recently gave further consideration to the filter-encoding constraint applied to the SDF construction. The idea is to synthesize the SDF from the linear combination of a set of training images which are already filter modulated, i.e. pre-processed, so that the constructed SDF is dominated by the higher, not the lower, frequency components of the individual training set image. The filter-encoding constraint is then applied to the SDF. For convenience, this is called the modified fSDF (MfSDF).

This chapter gives a full description of the MfSDF design. In order to implement the MfSDF filter, the constraints imposed by the available SLMs must be incorporated into the MfSDF design. Thus this chapter gives computer simulations of the implementation of the MfSDF filter on high speed binary SLMs. Finally the use of liquid crystal television (LCTV) SLMs to implement the MfSDF filter is simulated. The performance of the MfSDF filter is investigated with various in-plane rotated images from an in-class Bradley APC vehicle and an out-of-class Abrams MI tank.

The evaluation was performed to better understand the image distortion range that can be accommodated by the MfSDF filter with the constraints imposed by available SLMs.

6.2 Background — Filter SDF

The fSDF technique [8] [9] [10] begins with a set of centred training images, $t_n(x,y)$, $n = 0, 1, ..., k$, spanning the desired distortion invariant feature range. This image set is used to construct the fSDF, $s'(x,y)$, for a given filter modulation, $\mathcal{M}$. The desired peak correlation response of $s'(x,y)$ is a constant, c_n, for each training image $t_n(x,y)$

$$\int\int t_n(x,y)s'^*(x,y)dxdy = t_n(x,y) \odot s'(x,y) = c_n \qquad (6.1)$$

where the integral is taken over the area of the input field. The function $s'(x,y)$ includes the filter modulation, $\mathcal{M}$, through the equation

$$s'(x,y) = \mathcal{F}^{-1}\mathcal{M}\mathcal{F}[s(x,y)] \qquad (6.2)$$

where $\mathcal{F}$ is the Fourier transform operator. The purpose of the fSDF procedure is to determine the function $s(x,y)$ which solves Eq.(6.1) when given a particular modulation function, $\mathcal{M}$. The function $s(x,y)$ is chosen to be a linear combination of the training images

$$s(x,y) = \sum_{n=0}^{k} a_n t_n(x,y) \qquad (6.3)$$

A general fSDF synthesis equation results from substituting Eqs.(6.3) and (6.2) into Eq.(6.1)

$$t_n(x,y) \odot \mathcal{F}^{-1}\mathcal{M}\mathcal{F}[\sum_{n=0}^{k} a_n t_n(x,y)] = c_n \qquad (6.4)$$

For the POFs and BPOFs, Eq.(6.4) is a system of nonlinear equations which may be solved using an iterative procedure [12] based on the Newton-Raphson algorithm. The filter coefficients, $\mathbf{a} = [a_0, a_1, \ldots, a_k]^T$, are constrained to be real and are initialised to give the desired response vector, $\mathbf{c} = [c_0, c_1, \ldots, c_k]^T$; the accuracy of the filter coefficients is improved using the iteration formula

$$a_n^{i+1} = a_n^i + \alpha[c_n - c_0(\frac{m_n^i}{m_0^i})] \tag{6.5}$$

where, i is the iteration number, α is a damping constant, and m_n^i is the modulus of the peak correlation response of image $t_n(x,y)$ with the filter constructed with $\mathbf{a}^i$.

6.3   Modified Filter SDF (MfSDF)

When a highpass filter modulation of $\mathcal{M}$ is applied to the composite function $s(x,y)$, the higher frequency components of $s(x,y)$ are enhanced. Unfortunately, these higher frequency components are not optimally related to the high frequencies of individual training set images. As a result this limits correlation performance such as discrimination ability and correlation peak to secondary peak ratio (PSR). To overcome this problem, the filter modulation must be applied to individual training set images, thus the function $s(x,y)$ is modified to be

$$s(x,y) = \sum_{n=0}^{k} a_n t_n'(x,y), \tag{6.6}$$

and

$$t_n'(x,y) = \mathcal{F}^{-1}\mathcal{N}\mathcal{F}[t_n(x,y)] \tag{6.7}$$

where $\mathcal{N}$ denotes filter modulation of individual training set images. The requirements of Eqs.(6.1) and (6.2) are still met.

The general modified fSDF synthesis equation is now rewritten as

$$t_n(x,y) \odot \mathcal{F}^{-1}\mathcal{M}\mathcal{F}\{\sum_{n=0}^{k} a_n \mathcal{F}^{-1}\mathcal{N}\mathcal{F}[t_n(x,y)]\} = c_n \tag{6.8}$$

Using the correlation theorem, a simple form of this equation can be written in the frequency domain as

$$\int\int T_n(u,v)\mathcal{M}\{\sum_{n=0}^{k} a_n \mathcal{N}[T_n(u,v)]\}dudv = c_n \tag{6.9}$$

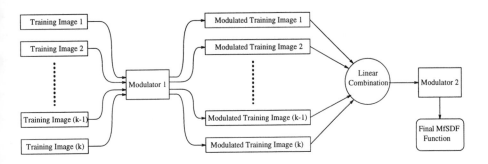

Figure 6.1: *Flow chart of the MfSDF design procedure*

where $T_n(u, v)$ is the Fourier transform of $t_n(x, y)$. Fig.6.1 gives a simple flow chart of this MfSDF filter design procedure.

The filter modulation, $\mathcal{M}$, $\mathcal{N}$, can be specified to take on any desired form. When both $\mathcal{M}$ and $\mathcal{N}$ are the classical matched filter modulation, the MfSDF reduces to the conventional SDF design. When $\mathcal{N}$ is the classical matched filter modulation (i.e. no modulation applied) and $\mathcal{M}$ is free to be defined, the MfSDF reduces to the fSDF design. Thus, the MfSDF is a more generalised filter modulation SDF, where the computational search space is sufficiently constrained to allow an optimal solution to be found in a reasonable time. The MfSDF is a subset of the generalised SDFs presented by Bahri and Kumar [1],

Whether or not the MfSDF produces ECP for all the training set images depends on the choice of the modulation operators $\mathcal{M}$ and $\mathcal{N}$. If the modulation operator, $\mathcal{M}$, is nonlinear, the ECP rule will be broken. For example, if POF or BPOF modulation is implemented as the $\mathcal{M}$ operator the ECP rule will be corrupted and the resulting spread in peak values will significantly lower the lowest correlation peak to secondary peak ratio (worst-case discrimination PSR_w given by Eq.(6.19)) for the training set images.

Consider producing a filter $S'(u,v)$ with a filter modulation operator that can be written as a function of the phase of $S(u,v)$, i.e. $\mathcal{M}$ is governed by phase only modulation

$$S'(u,v) = \mathcal{M}[S(u,v)] = \xi(\theta), \tag{6.10}$$

where the phase,

$$\theta = \frac{S(u,v)}{|S(u,v)|}. \tag{6.11}$$

Assuming $\xi(\theta)$ can be expanded in a Fourier series over the interval $[-\pi, \pi]$, then

$$S'(u,v) = \xi(\theta) = \sum_m f_m exp(im\theta). \tag{6.12}$$

Using Eq.(6.6), Eq.(6.12) can be rewritten as

$$S'(u,v) = \sum_m f_m exp \left[im \frac{\sum_{n=0}^{k} a_n T_n'(u,v)}{\left| \sum_{n=0}^{k} a_n T_n'(u,v) \right|} \right]. \tag{6.13}$$

Given a solution vector $\mathbf{a} = [a_0, a_1, \ldots, a_k]^T$, substitution of $d\mathbf{a}$, where d is an arbitrary constant, into Eq.(6.13) gives

$$S'(u,v) = \sum_m f_m exp \left[im \frac{d \sum_{n=0}^{k} a_n T_n'(u,v)}{|d| \left| \sum_{n=0}^{k} a_n T_n'(u,v) \right|} \right]. \tag{6.14}$$

Thus, if d is chosen to be the inverse of any expansion coefficient (i.e. $d = 1/a_0$) and is restricted to real values, $S'(u,v)$ becomes a function of k coefficients rather than $k+1$ coefficients. This results in a reduction of the dimensionality of Eq.(6.6) by one. Therefore, for filter modulation operators that are solely a function of phase, the filter response is determined not by the individual values of the coefficients but rather the proportionality between the coefficients. As a result, the peak-correlation response cannot be set to an absolute value, rather it is only possible to specify the proportionality between the peak correlation responses for a given set of training images.

To solve the problem of this nonlinear system and determine the parameter vector $\mathbf{a}$, the iterative techniques must be used to find a coefficient vector $\mathbf{a}$ that yields equal correlation peaks for all the training set images. The relaxation algorithm given by

Eq.(6.5) was used with some success herein and by others [8] [9] [10] [13]; whilst there is no theoretical guarantee that this algorithm will converge to a solution, it was successful in nearly all cases studied. An alternative successive algorithm is given by Bahri and Kumar [14].

The iteration procedure followed by the relaxation algorithm is:

(i) Estimate the initial specified weighting coefficient parameter vector i.e. $\mathbf{a}^0 = [a_0^0, a_1^0, \ldots, a_k^0]^T$ and the allowed largest correlation peak modulus variation $|v|$.

(ii) Linear combination to produce the composite image $s(x, y)$ from the $\mathcal{N}$ modulated individual training images.

(iii) Cross correlate the $\mathcal{M}$ modulated function $s(x, y)$ with the individual training images.

(iv) Calculate all correlation peak modulus values, i.e. $\mathbf{c}^i = [c_0^i, c_1^i, \ldots, c_k^i]^T$ for the modulated training images.

(v) Calculate the weighting coefficient vector $\mathbf{a}^i = [a_0^i, a_1^i, \ldots, a_k^i]^T$ according to Eq.(6.5).

(vi) If the largest variation of correlation peak modulus values exceeds the specified value $|v|$, go back to step (ii) and loop. If it does not exceed the specified value $|v|$, the iteration loop is stopped, and the final MfSDF filter, which satisfies the ECP rule, is found.

The simple flow chart of the above iterative procedure is given in Fig.6.2.

6.4   Data Base

The training image set used in the simulations of this chapter consists of in-plane rotated images of the Bradley APC vehicle and Abrams MI tank, each image is centred and normalised to unit energy. The APC vehicle and Abrams MI tank were rotated from $0°$ to 180^0 in increments of $1°$, the images were encoded with a

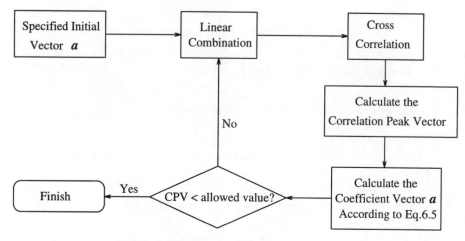

Where CPV = Correlation Peak Variation

Figure 6.2: *Flow chart of the iterative procedure to produce MfSDF function*

resolution of 128×128 pixels. Views of the vehicle and tank at $0°$, $30°$, $60°$ and $90°$ are given in Fig.6.3 and Fig.6.4, respectively. At $0°$ the Bradley APC vehicle is 90 pixels in length and 40 pixels high and the Abrams MI tank is 101 pixels in length and 35 pixels high.

The simulations in this chapter were performed on a SUN Sparc computer. The software automatically detects the resolution of the recorded images. Because the image resolution used in this chapter is 128×128, the resolution of the discrete Fourier transforms (DFT) used in the software is automatically set to 128×128.

6.5 Implementation Study of MfSDF Filters - Using a Binary Spatial Light Modulator

Some filter modulation methods, such as POF, tuneable edge enhancement filters [15] and nonlinear filters [16] etc. pre-suppose the use of continuous amplitude and phase information of the objects in the optical correlator. However, since pro-grammable continuous amplitude and phase spatial light modulators are not cur-

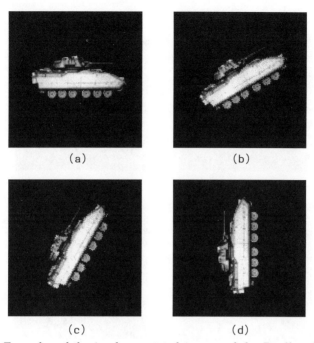

Figure 6.3: *Examples of the in-plane rotated images of the Bradley APC vehicle. (a), (b), (c) and (d) are the vehicle views at 0°, 30°, 60° and 90°, respectively*

rently available and also appear difficult to fabricate, the utility of such correlators is severely limited. However, programmable SLMs limited to binary quantisation of amplitude and/or phase are commercially available. Thus, the MfSDF can be implemented for real time optical correlation with the filter modulator $\mathcal{M}$ set as BPOF. This still leaves the modulation operator $\mathcal{N}$ free to be defined and it can be given any kind of advantageous modulation; hence, this is a big advantage over the fSDF approach. Therefore, it is possible to design a MfSDF with an optimal choice of the modulation operator $\mathcal{N}$ to maximise the overall performance capability of the filter, given the limitations of current SLMs. This approach is aimed at hybrid correlation system arrangements, as suggested by Young *et al* [17]. Their recently proposed high-speed hybrid optical/digital correlator system will employ the MfSDF, with the $\mathcal{M}$ operator selected to be BPOF and the $\mathcal{N}$ operator free to be defined.

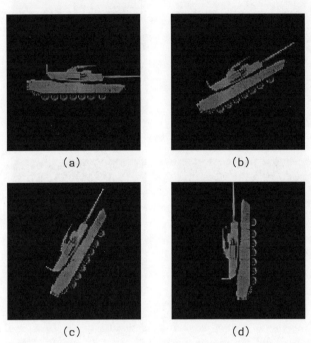

(a)   (b)

(c)   (d)

Figure 6.4: *Examples of the in-plane rotated images of the Abrams MI tank. (a), (b), (c) and (d) are the tank views at 0°, 30°, 60° and 90°, respectively*

6.5.1   Simulation considerations

In general, it is possible to optimise the individual image filter performance for the MfSDF by tuning the band-pass implemented by the modulation operator $\mathcal{N}$ on each image. As this is an extremely large simulation task it was decided to choose the POF as the modulation operator $\mathcal{N}$, as the POF has many of the desirable features required of $\mathcal{N}$. This choice of operator gives a good indication of the relative merits of the MfSDF over the fSDF. Thus, the SDF was constructed using POF modulation of the individual training set images; hence, this gives a higher weighting to image high frequency components. The modulation operator $\mathcal{M}$ was specified to be a BPOF, as this may be implemented in real time on commercially available SLMs. Thus the MfSDF was constructed from the POF-SDF by using the relaxation algorithm, Eq.(6.5), to satisfy the ECP rule at the output plane.

Table 6.1: *Final coefficient parameters for BPOF/MfSDF*

a_0	a_1	a_2	a_3	a_4	a_5	a_6	a_7	a_8	a_9
0.50	0.4086	0.3468	0.4360	0.4289	0.3787	0.4067	0.3510	0.4220	0.4891

In this work, the performance of the filter distortion invariant range is considered. As the extent of the distortion range increases, the number of training images necessary to cover the distortion range increases. Generally, the PSR (i.e. peak to secondary peak ratio) of a filter decreases as the filter is made increasingly more distortion invariant. This behaviour has a direct impact on the design and applicability of optical pattern recognition systems. It is advantageous to design a distortion invariant filter with training images spaced as widely as possible, whilst still maintaining an effective correlation peak to secondary peak ratio at the output plane. This ensures successful system performance whilst minimizing the amount of redundant information encoded into the SDFs. Furthermore, the computational effort expended during the design process is directly reduced with fewer training images.

6.5.2 Filter construction

Fig.6.5 shows the stages in the filter design procedure for the BPOF/MfSDF constructed from the phase-only modulated individual training set images, in which ten in-plane rotated vehicle training set images are encoded, i.e. one image every 5°, from 0° to 45°. A coefficient vector $\mathbf{a} = [a_0, a_1, \ldots, a_k]^T$, that gives equal correlation peaks for all training set images, was determined by using the iteration algorithm given by Fig.6.2. The final weighting coefficient parameters for the ten training images are listed in Table 6.1.

Fig.6.5(a) shows the composite image $S(u, v)$ in the frequency domain; it was constructed from the linear combination of the phase-only modulated training set im-

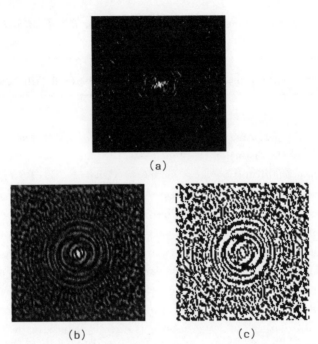

(a)

(b)   (c)

Figure 6.5: *Stages in the filter design procedure for the MfSDF-BPOF made from the phase-only training set images in the frequency domain. (a), (b) and (c) are the composite image S(u,v), real part of the composite image S(u,v) and final binary version of MfSDF, respectively*

ages

$$S(u,v) = \sum_{n=0}^{k} a_n \mathcal{N}_{POF}[T_n(u,v)] \tag{6.15}$$

From Fig.6.5(a), it is obvious that the higher frequency information is enhanced and the lower frequency data is attenuated. Thus the higher frequencies of individual training set images give a greater contribution to the composite image.

In order to produce the binary version of the MfSDF, the BPOF modulation constraint is applied to the above composite image. In this work, BPOF was chosen to be [18]

$$S_b(u,v) = \begin{cases} +1, & \text{Re}[S(u,v)] > 0 \\ -1, & \text{otherwise} \end{cases} \tag{6.16}$$

According to Eq.(6.16), there is a mapping between the complex values of $S(u,v)$

to the set of values allowed by the binary spatial light modulator $(0, \pi)$ to produce the filter $S'(u, v)$ (i.e. $S_b(u, v)$ herein). This mapping is illustrated by Fig.6.6.

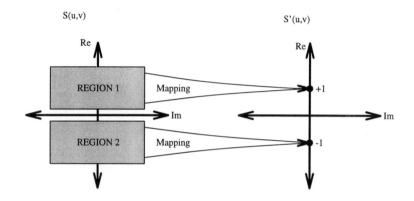

Figure 6.6: *Mapping procedure from complex values of $S(u,v)$ to the binary values of (+1,-1)*

The generalised BPOFs derived by Flannery et al [19] include the angle of a thresholding line in the complex plane and the offset from a centre reference point of the pattern transformed in constructing the filter, which may be used to optimally select the thresholding line angle of the BPOF in the MfSDF construction. Eq.(6.16) was selected for convenience; it is only one point of a continuum of threshold line angles, i.e. line angle $\theta = 0°$.

According to Eq.(6.16), the real part of the composite image $S(u, v)$ is of interest to produce the BPOF/MfSDF. Fig.6.5(b) shows the real part of the composite image in the frequency domain, which is clearly dominated by the higher frequencies of individual training set images. Furthermore, after the iteration to achieve ECPs for all the training set images, it can be seen from Fig.6.5(a) and Fig.6.5(b) that the composite image $S(u, v)$ is a band-pass type image. Finally, the BPOF/MfSDF is shown in Fig.6.5(c); this can be encoded onto a BPOF-SLM to implement reprogrammable correlation at video frame rates.

For comparison, when the procedure is used to construct a BPOF/fSDF, for the same ten training set images, the results are shown in Fig.6.7. The final coefficient

Table 6.2: *Final coefficient parameters for BPOF/fSDF*

a_0	a_1	a_2	a_3	a_4	a_5	a_6	a_7	a_8	a_9
0.50	0.4011	0.3399	0.3631	0.3772	0.3456	0.3636	0.3287	0.3556	0.4226

parameters are listed in Table 6.2. Fig.6.7(a) and Fig.6.7(b) are the composite image $S(u, v)$, which is a linear combination of the ten training set images, and the real part of the composite image $S(u, v)$, respectively. The comparison illustrates that the composite image $S(u, v)$, of the fSDF, is dominated by the very low frequency content of the individual training set images and has little energy at high frequencies. The binary version of the fSDF is shown in Fig.6.7(c). From Fig.6.5(c) and Fig.6.7(c), it can be seen that the mid-band frequencies (between low and high frequency) in the BPOF/MfSDF are richer and more complicated than that of BPOF/fSDF, which undoubtedly results from the bandpass type composite image $S(u, v)$ shown in Fig.6.5(b); other than the mid-band frequency differences the two filters are similar. This characteristic of the BPOF/MfSDF improves correlation performance.

Fig.6.8(a) and Fig.6.8(b) illustrate the impulse responses of the BPOF/MfSDF and BPOF/fSDF filters (i.e. Fig.6.5(c) and Fig.6.7(c)), respectively. From the impulse responses, although both filters reject the low frequencies resulting in edge enhancement, it can be seen that the BPOF/MfSDF filter encodes more detailed information from the training images than does the BPOF/fSDF filter.

6.5.3 Distortion range of filters

Filters designed to be invariant to in-plane rotation, over distortion ranges up to 90°, are constructed using training images of the Bradley APC vehicle separated by a rotation increment of 5°. For example, the BPOF/MfSDF and BPOF/fSDF designed for invariance to in-plane rotation over a distortion range of 45° are constructed from ten training set images. After construction, filters are correlated with images, spanning their entire design range, at every 1° interval. The peak corre-

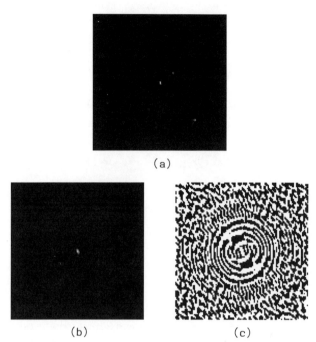

Figure 6.7: *Stages in the filter design procedure for the fSDF-BPOF made directly from training set images in the frequency domain. (a), (b) and (c) are the composite image S(u,v), real part of the composite image S(u,v) and final binary version of fSDF, respectively*

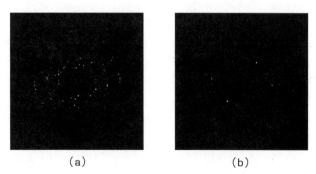

Figure 6.8: *Impulse responses of the (a) BPOF/MfSDF and (b) BPOF/fSDF functions*

lation intensity is measured for each input image, along with the peak clutter, or secondary peak intensity. The peak response is defined to be the intensity of the maximum correlation peak occurring at the output plane

$$CPI = Max\{|c(x,y)|^2\} = |c(x_0,y_0)|^2 \qquad (6.17)$$

where (x_0, y_0) is the position of the maximum correlation peak at the correlator output plane. The secondary peak was defined to be the highest intensity point in the correlation plane at points at least 3 pixels away from the correlation peak P; with the additional condition that $c(x,y)$ must be a local maximum at the secondary peak

$$C = Max\{|c(x,y)|^2\},$$
$$such\ that\ \ |x - x_0| > 3,\ \ |y - y_0| > 3,\ \ and\ \ \frac{\partial c}{\partial x} = \frac{\partial c}{\partial y} = 0. \qquad (6.18)$$

This guarantees that a smooth primary peak base will not be counted as clutter. The peak correlation and peak clutter responses (secondary peaks) were measured over the specified distortion range for a given SDF. Fig.6.9(a) shows the peak correlation and peak clutter responses for a BPOF/MfSDF constructed from in-plane rotated training images with a distortion range from $0°$ to $45°$. The training images used are $5°$ apart. BPOF filters are extremely sensitive to distortion of the image; experience has shown that a training set image separation of $5°$ is probably the maximum that can be used for the cases studied. The $5°$ interval is adequate to ensure that for the MfSDF the correlation peak intensity is adequately separated from the maximum clutter peak. A similar graph for BPOF/fSDF is shown in Fig.6.9(b). From Fig.6.9, it is clear that the BPOF/MfSDF filter is invariant to distortion over the range from $0°$ to $45°$, whereas the BPOF/fSDF does not give complete invariance as one of the peak clutter responses exceeds the minimum correlation peak response. In order to further illustrate this, Fig.6.10 gives 3D plots of correlation functions most likely to cause false alarms; Fig.6.10(a) and Fig.6.10(b) are the cases with the lowest correlation peak and highest secondary peak, respectively, which occurred over the range from 0^0 to 45^0 for the BPOF/MfSDF, and Fig.6.10(c) and Fig.6.10(d) are the same cases for the BPOF/fSDF, respectively.

The ratio CPI/C, Eq.(3.19), defines the correlation peak to secondary peak ratio

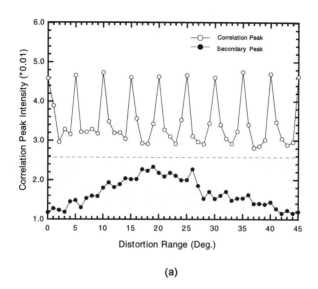

(a)

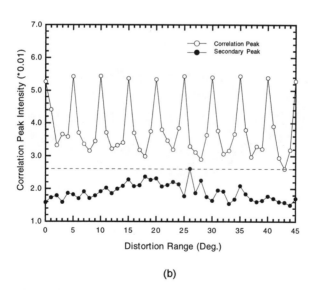

(b)

Figure 6.9: *Peak correlation and peak clutter responses with a distortion range from 0° to 45°: (a) binary phase-only MfSDF and (b) binary phase-only fSDF*

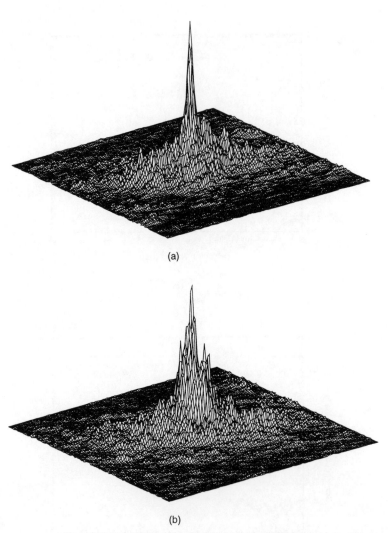

(a)

(b)

Figure 6.10: *The 3-D representations of the correlation functions which present the highest possibility of erroneous correlation peak detection over the range from 0^0 to 45^0; (a) and (b) are the cases of lowest correlation peak and highest second peak for the BPOF/MfSDF respectively; (c) and (d) are the same cases for the BPOF/fSDF respectively*

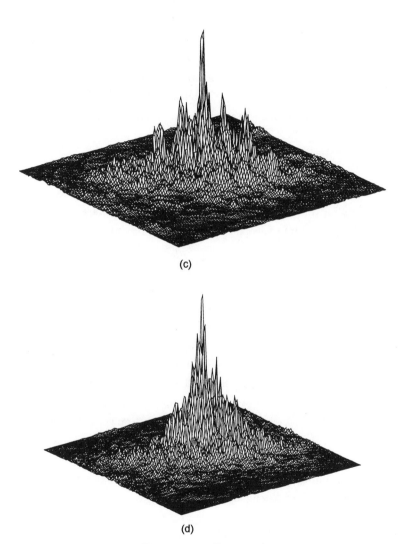

(c)

(d)

Figure 6.10: *Continued*

(PSR) [20]. The worst-case ratio of PSR across the distortion range is

$$PSR_w = \frac{CPI_{min}}{C_{max}}, \tag{6.19}$$

this is used to qualify the rotation invariance of an SDF, where CPI_{min} is the lowest correlation peak value and C_{max} denotes the highest secondary peak value across the distortion range. If $PSR_w > 1$ for an SDF, there will be no ambiguity in extracting the correlation peaks from clutter anywhere over the distortion range; hence, a simple thresholder may be used to evaluate the correlation response to an input image.

The PSR_w data for the BPOF/MfSDF and BPOF/fSDF with distortion ranges up to 90° are displayed by Fig.6.11 and Fig.6.12 respectively. These results were obtained by making a filter from the 0° and 5° training set images and testing it on images from 0°-5° at 1° intervals and finding the PSR_w value, then making a filter from the 0°, 5° and 10° training set images and testing it on images from 0°-10° at 1° intervals and finding the PSR_w value, then continuing this process up to 90°. From Fig.6.11, it can be seen that the value of PSR_w drops below 1 for a distortion range of approximately 65°-70° for the BPOF/MfSDF; whereas, Fig.6.12 shows that this occurs at about 45° for the BPOF/fSDF. Therefore, it can be concluded that a BPOF/MfSDF with $\mathcal{N}$ set to phase-only modulation gives distortion invariance for in-plane rotations up to at least 65°; whereas, a BPOF/fSDF only achieves 45° of rotation invariance. Thus, the MfSDF method can be designed to be a distortion invariant filter with training images spaced at greater intervals than the fSDF. To achieve the distortion invariance over a 180° range, with the information content minimised, the BPOF/MfSDF needs three filters; whereas, four filters are necessary for the fSDF. Thus, the binary phase-only filter constructed utilising the MfSDF method is more suitable than the fSDF method for high-speed hybrid optical correlation as proposed by Young and Chatwin [17].

To better understand the behaviour of the two filters, the average modulus of the correlation peak and average SNR (i.e. average over the distortion range) are plotted in Fig.6.13 and Fig.6.14, respectively, as functions of the distortion ranges. A range value of 0° corresponds to a filter matched to a single image. The SNR (signal to noise ratio) is defined as the ratio of the correlation peak response to the rms response

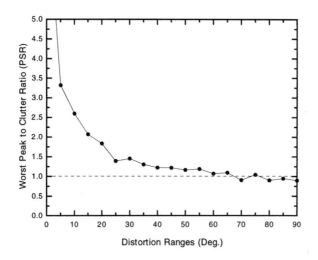

Figure 6.11: *The worst correlation peak to secondary peak ratio (PSR$_w$) over distortion ranges from 0° to 90° for the MfSDF method*

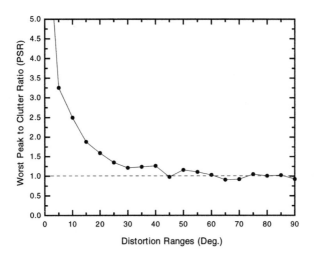

Figure 6.12: *The worst correlation peak to secondary peak ratio (PSR$_w$) over distortion ranges from 0° to 90° for the fSDF method*

outside the 50% correlation peak intensity [21]. It can be seen from Fig.6.13 that the BPOF/fSDF filters produce the higher peaks for every distortion range. However, the loss in correlation peak height, of the BPOF/MfSDF, is more than compensated for by the increased sharpness of the correlation peaks, which can be seen from Fig.6.14 to give a better SNR for every distortion range.

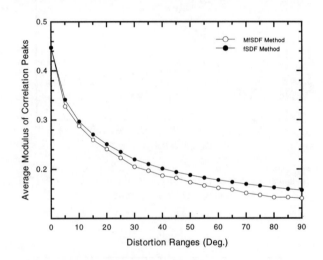

Figure 6.13: *Average modulus of the correlation peaks over distortion ranges up to 90°*

6.5.4 Target discrimination

The fine structure of the target object image translates into high frequency components in the frequency domain which contribute greatly to the discrimination ability of the filter. The MfSDF design places a greater weighting on the higher frequencies of individual training set images incorporated into the filter than does the fSDF. Thus, it is important to verify that the MfSDF filters give better discrimination between the target and a non-target object, of similar size and shape, than do the fSDF filters. This test is performed by comparing the discrimination values of the BPOF/MfSDF and BPOF/fSDF to the input images of both Bradley APC vehicle shown in Fig.6.3 and a similarly scaled and oriented Abrams MI tank shown in

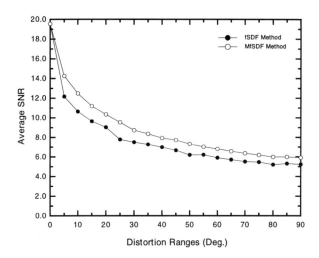

Figure 6.14: *Average values of the signal to noise ratio (SNR) over distortion ranges up to 90°.*

Fig.6.4. The discrimination capability of the filter is defined by Eq.(3.20). In the simulations, the Bradley APC vehicle is taken as the target input image and the Abrams MI tank as the non-target input image. The correlation peak responses of the target and non-target images are evaluated from 0° to 90° at 5° increments of rotation for both the BPOF/MfSDFs and BPOF/fSDFs, the average values of the filter discrimination metric are illustrated by Fig.6.15(a). For instance, the discrimination value at 10° is obtained by making a filter from the 0°, 5° and 10° training set images and testing it on 0°, 5° and 10° input images (target and non-target) and then finding the average value of these three discrimination values. It can be seen from Fig.6.15(a) that, with the exception of one marginal point at 30°, the MfSDF delivers superior discrimination performance. However, the inputs at 5° intervals are only representative of the training set images, and not the full distortion range. Thus, the filter discrimination ability was also tested at 1° intervals; the results from averaging discrimination values are plotted in Fig.6.15(b). Hence, the discrimination value at 10° was obtained by making a filter from the 0°, 5° and 10° training set images and testing it on input images (target and non-target) from 0° to 10° at 1° intervals and then finding the average value of these discrimination values. Fig.6.15(b) shows that the MfSDF still delivers slightly better discrimination performance over the whole distortion range than does the fSDF. If the training set included images at $1°$ intervals, better discrimination would result.

The correlation functions of target image and non-target image at a rotation angle of $40°$ for both the BPOF/MfSDF and BPOF/fSDF, designed for $40°$ in-plane vehicle rotation invariance, are shown in Fig.6.16. These correlation functions give an excellent illustration of filter discrimination performance. In order to clearly show the discrimination ability of the filters, all non-target correlation functions are normalised to the target auto-correlation peak height.

6.5.5 Conclusions

An initial investigation to compare the MfSDF filter's performance, with modulators $\mathcal{M}$ and $\mathcal{N}$ being chosen to be BPOF and POF respectively, with that of the fSDF filter has been completed. Computer simulations show that the BPOF/MfSDF filter can achieve distortion invariance to in-plane rotations up to at least $65°$, whereas the BPOF/fSDF filter only attains 45^0, in the case studied. Therefore, the BPOF/MfSDF method can be designed to be a distortion invariant filter with training images spaced at larger distortion increments than the BPOF/fSDF method. Hence, the BPOF/MfSDF method needs less filters to cover a distortion invariant range of $180°$ than does the BPOF/fSDF method. For the case studied, the computer simulations also show that the BPOF/MfSDF filter has a better signal to noise ratio and target discrimination ability when compared with the BPOF/fSDF filter. The slightly lower correlation peaks achieved with the MfSDF filter correlations do not cause any detection difficulty due to the good peak sharpness. The MfSDF demonstrates better discrimination ability between target and non-target objects. Thus overall, its performance is better than that of the fSDF.

The choice of the modulator $\mathcal{N}$ to be POF was made to allow an initial investigation of the MfSDF design, it is not the optimal choice. Further research is required to obtain optimal performance from the MfSDF filter.

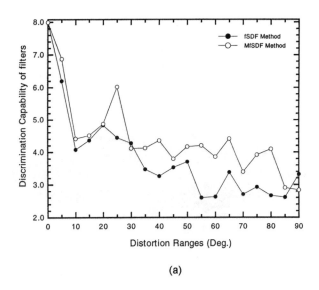

(a)

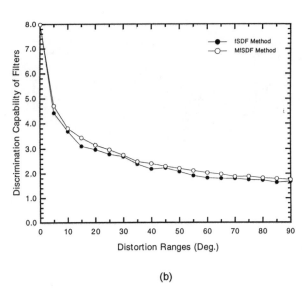

(b)

Figure 6.15: *Discrimination capability of filters over distortion ranges up to 90°; the target and non-target inputs are at the same rotation angle. (a) average value of inputs at 5° increments, (b) average value of inputs at 1° intervals*

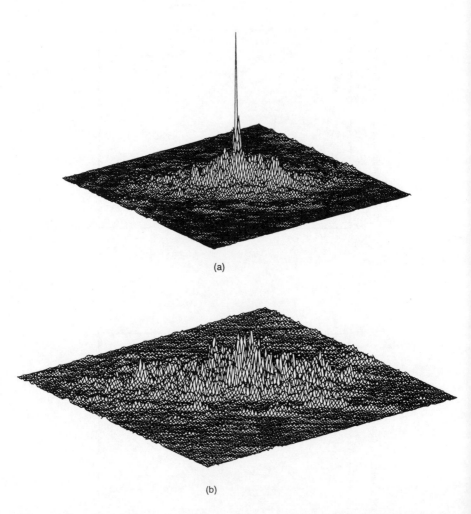

(a)

(b)

Figure 6.16: *The 3-D representations of the correlation functions obtained from correlating the target image and non-target image at the rotation angle of 40° with both MfSDF and fSDF designed for 40° in-plane vehicle rotation invariance. (a) and (b) are the results from the MfSDF filter for the target and nontarget input images respectively; (c) and (d) are the results from the fSDF filter*

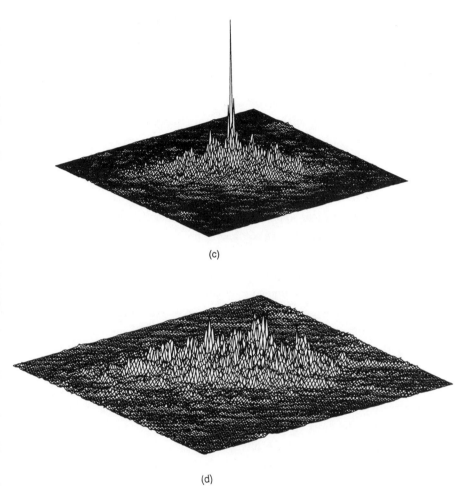

(c)

(d)

Figure 6.16: *Continued*

6.6 Implementation Study of MfSDF Filters Using a Liquid Crystal Television as a Modulator

The use of commercially available programmable SLMs limited to binary quantization of amplitude and/or phase has been an attractive approach in the past ten years. The last section demonstrated that it is possible to construct a MfSDF filter limited to binary phase only modulation that will achieve a specified correlation peak for a set of training images; significantly, this is very easy to implement using binary SLMs. However, this approach only partially exploits the finesse of filters designed for processing images with continuous phase and amplitude information.

Current spatial light modulator performance and spatial filter encoding with limited modulation levels have been combined to create an implementable real-time optical pattern recognition system concept. The binary phase-only filter (BPOF) is a good example of a discrete-valued spatial filter that has been successfully implemented in real-time optical correlators using commercially available SLMs [22][23]. Recently, the use of the liquid crystal television (LCTV) — for example the Epson LCTV panels, which are part of a commercially available video projector — as SLMs in optical correlator systems has become an increasingly common approach [24][25][26][27]. One of the salient features of this device is that it can encode multilevel spatial phase and amplitude. Thus, if the filter includes the constraints imposed by the LCTV design, the performance predicted from simulation will more closely represent the optical correlator performance.

Thus, Wang and Chatwin [28] very recently suggested that, in order to implement the designed filter accurately, the multilevel constraints of the LCTVs should be incorporated into the MfSDF filter design; furthermore, the filter may then be optimised to take account of the SLM limitations. The purpose of this section is to quantify the performance of multilevel phase and amplitude (MLAP) encoded MfSDF filters.

6.6.1 Consideration of multilevel LCTV constraint

Recently, it has been reported that LCTV SLMs can encode multi-level discrete amplitude and/or phase information, given a coding domain. The Seiko Epson LCTV works quite well in the amplitude mode if the attached film polarizers are removed and replaced with high quality external polarizers [29]. When the usual polarizers are removed the phase mode of operation can be operated over the range of $0°$ to $360°$ [25]. Thus, the combined use of phase and amplitude modes of the LCTVs can approach near-true continuous conditions for the MfSDF filter. For implementation of an MfSDF the available SLM discretisation resolution N must be quantified. The phase and amplitude information of the pre-designed filter function is then represented, and constrained by, the N discrete levels — which to some extent restricts the functional complexity of $\mathcal{M}$.

The method for taking account of the constraints imposed by the LCTV SLM is to apply an algorithm to the composite image from the linear combination of modulated training images, $S(u,v)$, to produce a filter $S'(u,v)$; where: $S'(u,v) \in (\mathcal{A}, \mathcal{P})$ and $\mathcal{A}$ and $\mathcal{P}$ are defined by the specific characteristics of the amplitude and phase coding domains allowed by the LCTV. There is a mapping between the continuous complex values of $S(u,v)$ to the set of quantified values allowed by $(\mathcal{A}, \mathcal{P})$ to produce the filter $S'(u,v)$. The filter is implemented using two LCTVs; one is for the quantified amplitude encoding and the other is for the quantified phase encoding. Fig.6.17 gives a simplified flow chart for this encoding procedure.

When mapping the continuous complex values of $S(u,v)$ to the set of quantified values to produce the filter $S'(u,v)$, the phase $(0, 2\pi)$ and amplitude are divided into N equal intervals respectively. Assume that $S(u,v)$ has the form

$$S(u,v) = |S(u,v)| \, exp[j\phi(u,v)] \qquad (6.20)$$

Thus, when $\phi(u,v)$ falls into a particular k'th interval, $\phi(u,v)$ is assigned to be a constant value ϕ_k, so that

$$\phi_k = \frac{k2\pi}{N} \qquad when \qquad \frac{(2k-1)\pi}{N} \leq \phi(u,v) < \frac{(2k+1)\pi}{N} \qquad (6.21)$$

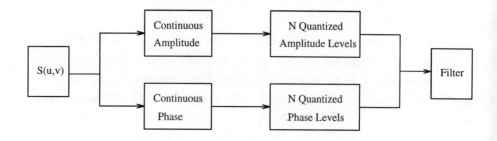

Figure 6.17: *Flow chart of the filter coding procedure*

Likewise,

$$S_l = \frac{lAS_{max}}{N} \quad when \quad \frac{lAS_{max}}{N} \le |S(u,v)| < \frac{(l+1)AS_{max}}{N} \qquad (6.22)$$

where A is a scaling factor and S_{max} is the maximum amplitude of $S(u,v)$. Thus, at the particular position (u,v), the discrete value of the filter becomes

$$S'(u,v) = S_l \, exp[j\phi_k] \qquad (6.23)$$

However, the procedure for mapping $S(u,v)$ to $S'(u,v)$ is not so easy because the computed filter values can not be guaranteed to fall into the dynamic range of the modulator. To solve this problem, Juday [30] proposed that the filter values are encoded onto the modulator so as to minimise the Euclidean distance, in the complex plane, between the computed filter values and the modulator's realizable values. Therefore, according to the characteristics of the LCTV SLMs, Eq.(6.23) must be changed to

$$S'(u,v) = \varepsilon_l S_l \, exp[j\varepsilon_k \phi_k] \qquad (6.24)$$

so that

$$\varepsilon_k \phi_k \in \mathcal{P}, \quad \varepsilon_l S_l \in \mathcal{A} \qquad (6.25)$$

where ε_k and ε_l are the mapping factors when the computed filter values are encoded onto the SLM employing the minimum Euclidean distance principle. An alternative algorithm, to map the filter onto constrained modulation SLMs, is given by Laude *et al* [31].

It should be noted that although the modulation operator $\mathcal{M}$ is chosen to be the constraint imposed by the LCTV SLM, the other modulation operator $\mathcal{N}$ in the MfSDF filter design is still free to be defined. It can be given any type of advantageous modulation; hence, the flexibility of the MfSDF filter design is not compromised. Therefore, it is possible to find a MfSDF with an optimal choice of the modulation operator $\mathcal{N}$ to maximise the overall performance capabilities of the filter, when given the limitations of current LCTV SLMs.

This approach is aimed at hybrid correlation system arrangements, as suggested by Young *et al* [17]. Their recently proposed high-speed hybrid optical/digital correlator system will utilise the MfSDF, with the $\mathcal{M}$ operator selected to be the constraint imposed by the LCTV SLMs and the $\mathcal{N}$ operator selected to be an optimal modulator.

6.6.2 Simulation considerations

In order to compare the performance of the filter, when applying the LCTV constraint, with that of the filter with the modulation $\mathcal{M}$ specified as BPOF, the modulation operator $\mathcal{N}$ was selected to be phase-only which is the same as the last section and a previous paper [11]. Thus, the SDF function $s(x, y)$ was constructed using POF modulation of the individual training set images. The modulation operator $\mathcal{M}$ was specified to give phase and amplitude modulation within the performance limitations of the LCTV, as this may be implemented in real time on the commercially available Epson LCTV SLM. Consistent with SLM performance, the multilevel, N discrete levels of phase and amplitude (MLAP) information for the designed filter was chosen to be 16 levels, i.e. $N = 16$, in the simulations. Thus, the MfSDF was constructed from the POF-SDF by limiting the phase and amplitude information to 16 discrete levels and using the relaxation algorithm to satisfy the ECP rule for each training image.

In this work, the following filter performance criteria are considered: distortion invariant range, discrimination sensitivity between in-class and out-of-class images, training image spacing, and ability to accommodate the input image noise. Greater distortion invariant range with 100% discrimination capability designed into a single filter (i.e. SDF filter) translates into fewer filters required to achieve object recognition over the specified range. Generally speaking, when the extent of the distortion range increases, the number of training images necessary to cover the distortion range increases, and the correlation peak height decreases as the filter needs more information from the training set images to be encoded in order to satisfy the ECP rule for each training image. It is advantageous to design a distortion invariant filter with training images spaced as widely as possible, whilst still maintaining an effective correlation peak height and 100% discrimination capability. This ensures successful system performance whilst minimizing the amount of redundant information encoded into the SDF filter. Furthermore, the computational effort expended during the design process is reduced directly with fewer training images.

6.6.3 Distortion range of filters

Filters designed to be invariant to in-plane rotation, over distortion ranges up to 180°, are constructed using training images of the in-class Bradley APC vehicle and out-of-class Abram MI tank separated by a rotation increment of 5°. The correlation peaks are specified to give a constant value of c for the in-class training set images and zero for the out-of-class training set images at the central position in the output plane. For example, the MfSDF designed for invariance to in-plane rotation over a distortion range of 45° are constructed from ten in-class and ten out-of-class training set images. After construction, filters are correlated with images at every 1° interval, spanning the entire design range of 45°. Fig.6.18(a) shows the peak correlation and secondary peak responses for a MLAP/MfSDF constructed from in-plane rotated training images with a distortion range from 0° to 90°. The training images used are 5° apart. A similar graph for BPOF/MfSDF is shown in Fig.6.18(b). From Fig.6.18, it is clear that the MLAP/MfSDF filter is invariant to distortion over the range from 0° to 90°; whereas, the BPOF/MfSDF does not give complete invariance as a few secondary peak responses exceed the minimum correlation peak response. In order to clearly show the correlation functions, Fig.6.19(a) and Fig.6.19(b) give the best-case and worst-case correlation functions for the MLAP/MfSDF, which occur at 0° and 67° respectively. For comparison, the best-case and worst-case correlation functions from the BPOF/MfSDF are given in Fig.6.19(c) and Fig.6.19(d), respectively.

The PSR_w data for the MLAP/MfSDF and BPOF/MfSDF with distortion ranges up to 130° are displayed by Fig.6.20. These results were obtained by making a filter from the 0° and 5° training set images and testing it on images from $0^o \sim 5^o$ at 1° intervals and finding the PSR_w value, then making a filter from the 0°, 5° and 10° training set images and testing it on images from $0^o \sim 10^o$ at 1° intervals and finding the PSR_w value, then continuing this process up to 130°. From Fig.6.20, it can be seen that the value of PSR_w drops below 1 for a distortion range of approximately $65^o \sim 70^o$ for the BPOF/MfSDF; whereas, for the MLAP/MfSDF it happens at $120^o \sim 125^o$, almost twice that of the BPOF/MfSDF. Therefore, it can be concluded that a MLAP/MfSDF with $\mathcal{N}$ set to phase-only modulation gives distortion invariance for in-plane rotations up to at least 120°; whereas, a BPOF/MfSDF only achieves approximately 65° of rotation invariance. Thus, the MfSDF with a multilevel LCTV implementation can be designed to be a distortion invariant filter with training images spaced at greater intervals than that with binary encoding onto a binary SLM. To achieve distortion invariance over a 360° range, with the information content minimised, the MLAP/MfSDF needs at most three filters; whereas, six filters are necessary for the BPOF/MfSDF. Thus, the effective use of the phase and amplitude information in a filter constructed utilising the MfSDF method gives a more useful result than that using only phase information.

To better understand the behaviour of the two filters, the average moduli of the correlation peak (i.e. average over the distortion range) are plotted in Fig.6.21 as a function of the distortion ranges. A range value of 0° corresponds to a filter matched to a single image. It can be seen from Fig.6.21 that the BPOF/MfSDF filter produces higher peaks for distortion ranges greater than 20°. This is because the MLAP/MfSDF has to encode much more information (includes phase and amplitude information) from the training set images into a single filter than does the BPOF/MfSDF when the distortion range is more than 20°; this leads to a predictable loss in correlation peak height. However, this loss in correlation peak height is compensated for by greatly increased distortion invariant ranges.

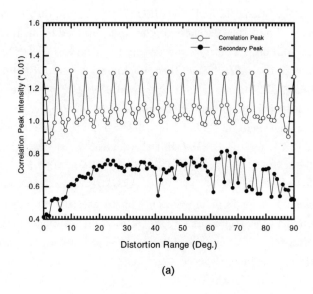

(a)

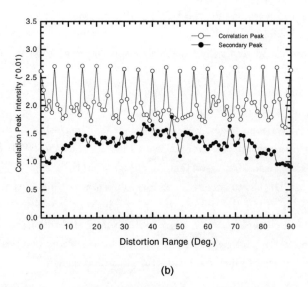

(b)

Figure 6.18: *Peak correlation and secondary correlation peak responses over a distortion range of 90°: (a) MLAP/MfSDF and (b) BPOF/MfSDF*

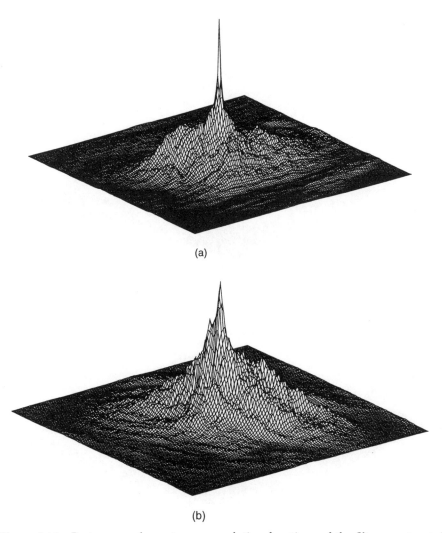

(a)

(b)

Figure 6.19: *Best-case and worst-case correlation functions of the filter constructed for a distortion range from 0° to 90° with the input images at 1° intervals, (a) and (b) are the best-case and worst-case for MLAP/MfSDF respectively, (c) and (d) are the best-case and worst-case for BPOF/MfSDF respectively*

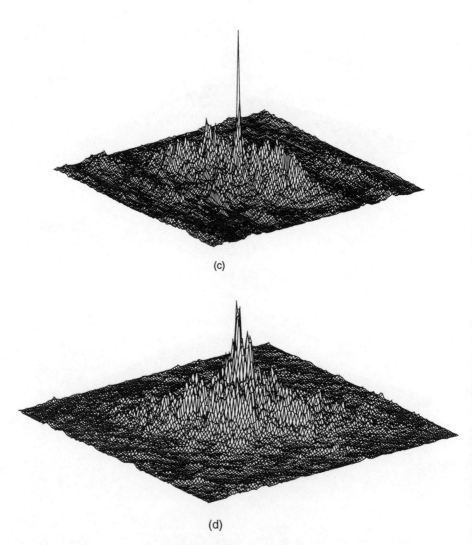

(c)

(d)

Figure 6.19: *Continued*

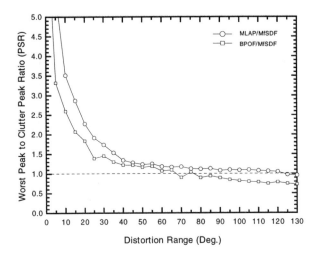

Figure 6.20: *The worst correlation peak response to secondary peak response ratio (PSR_w) over the distortion ranges from $0°$ to $130°$*

6.6.4   Discrimination capability of filters

Although a filter may be distortion invariant over a certain distortion range, this does not guarantee that it can discriminate the in-class images at any angle from the out-of-class images with 100% reliability. As mentioned in the last section, the fine structure of the in-class training set images translate into high frequency components in the frequency domain which contribute greatly to the discrimination ability of filters. The BPOF/MfSDF considers only the binary phase information from the training set images; whereas the MLAP/MfSDF applies the complex weighting of the frequencies (i.e. both phase and amplitude information from the training set images) to the filter, which is expected to give a better discrimination ability. Therefore, it is important to verify that the MLAP/MfSDF delivers better discrimination between the in-class and out-of-class images over the distortion invariant range of the filter. This test is performed by comparing the discrimination values of MLAP/MfSDF and BPOF/MfSDF using the input images of both the in-class

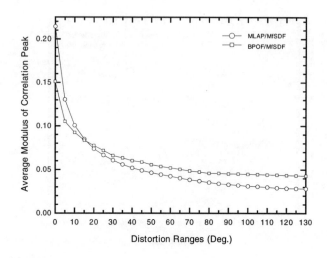

Figure 6.21: *Average modulus of the correlation peak responses over the distortion ranges up to* 130°

Bradley APC vehicle and out-of-class Abram MI tank, shown in Fig.6.3 and Fig.6.4 respectively. Fig.6.22(a) shows the peak correlations for the in-class image inputs and out-of-class image inputs for a MLAP/MfSDF constructed from in-plane rotated training set images with a distortion range from 0° to 90°, in which the training set images used are 5° apart. A similar graph for BPOF/MfSDF is given in Fig.6.22(b). It is clear from Fig.6.22 that the MLAP/MfSDF filter delivers 100% discrimination ability between the distorted in-class and out-of-class images, at any angle over the distortion invariant filter range 0° to 90°; whereas, the BPOF/MfSDF filter does not achieve 100% discrimination.

In order to clearly show the discrimination correlation functions, Fig.6.23(a) and Fig.6.23(b) give the worst-case correlation functions for the MLAP/MfSDF, which occur at 2° for the in-class input and 60° for the out-of-class input respectively. For comparison, the worst-case correlation functions from the BPOF/MfSDF are given in Fig.6.23(c) for the in-class input and Fig.6.23(d) for the out-of-class input,

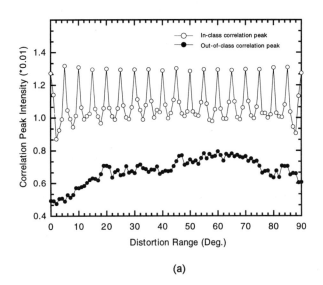

(a)

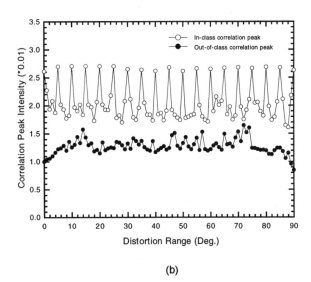

(b)

Figure 6.22: *In-class correlation peak and out-of-class correlation peak responses over a distortion range of 90°: (a) MLAP/MfSDF and (b) BPOF/MfSDF*

respectively.

The filter discrimination capability is defined by Eq.(3.20) as

$$DC = \frac{P_t}{P_{nt}} \qquad (6.26)$$

A more conservative evaluation of the 100% discrimination ability of a SDF filter is to consider the worst-case DC values across the distortion range,

$$DC_w = \frac{(P_t)_{min}}{(P_{nt})_{max}} \qquad (6.27)$$

where the critical DC_w is found from the ratio of the lowest in-class correlation peak to the highest out-of-class correlation peak measured at any angle (i.e. every $1°$ interval in this case) over the distortion ranges. If $DC_w > 1$ for an SDF there will be no ambiguity in discriminating in-class images from out-of-class images when a simple thresholder is applied to evaluate the 100% discrimination ability of the filter.

Fig.6.24 shows the worst-case discrimination values DC_w of MLAP/MfSDF measured at any angle within each distortion range up to $130°$. For example, the data point at $60°$ in Fig.6.24 is obtained from finding the minimized in-class correlation peak, $(P_t)_{min}$, for all sixty-one in-class images and the maximized out-of-class correlation peak, $(P_{nt})_{max}$, for all sixty-one out-of-class images, and then taking the ratio of $(P_t)_{min}$ to $(P_{nt})_{max}$. It can be seen from Fig.6.24 that, for the MLAP/MfSDF, the value of DC_w drops below one for a distortion range of $120° \sim 125°$; hence, the MLAP/MfSDF can be designed for an invariant distortion range of at least $120°$ whilst still maintaining 100% discrimination against the out-of-class targets with training images spaced at $5°$, whereas, for the BPOF/MfSDF, the DC_w value drops below one at a $60°$ distortion range, just half the value achieved by the MLAP/MfSDF method. It should be noted that although the BPOF/MfSDF can achieve an invariant distortion range of $65°$, from the conclusion of the previous subsection, it does not guarantee 100% discrimination capability between the in-class and out-of-class images; thus its effective invariant distortion range is $60°$. This is an issue frequently not addressed by other authors. Therefore, the MLAP/MfSDF delivers much better discrimination capability between in-class and out-of-class images than does the BPOF/MfSDF in the case studied.

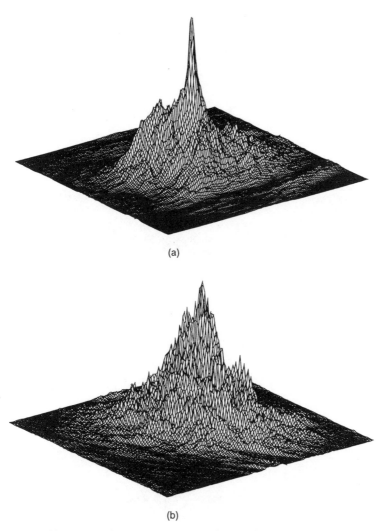

(a)

(b)

Figure 6.23: *Worst-case discrimination correlation functions of the filter over the range from 0^0 to 90^0, (a) and (b) are from correlating the MLAP/MfSDF with the in-class input at 2^0 orientation and the out-of-class input at 60^0 orientation respectively, (c) and (d) are from correlating the BPOF/MfSDF with the in-class input at 88^0 orientation and the out-of-class input at 72^0 orientation respectively*

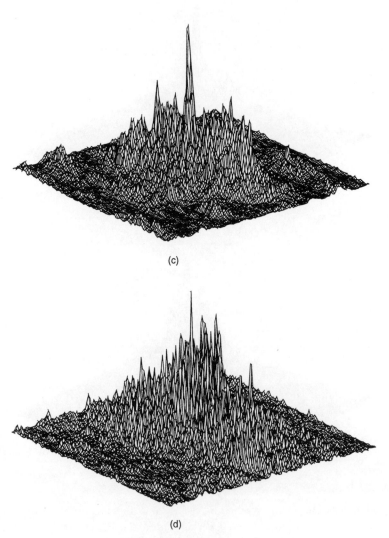

(c)

(d)

Figure 6.23: *Continued*

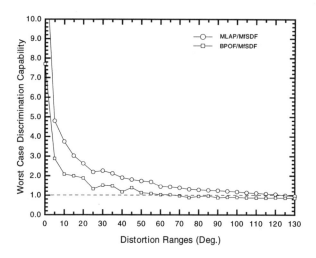

Figure 6.24: *The worst discrimination capability (DC$_w$) of filters between in-class and out-of-class images over the distortion ranges up to 130°*

6.6.5 Training image spacing

Selection of the in-class training image spacing is important for overall system performance. The training image spacing used in the design of a synthetic discriminant function primarily depends on the distortion range required of the filter, and the sensitivity of the filter to the slight distortions of the in-class images between the training images. The primary objective is to design an SDF with training images spaced as widely as possible, whilst still satisfying the invariance to distortion requirement and the 100% discrimination capability between in-class and out-of-class images. This ensures that redundant information, from the training set images, encoded into the SDFs is minimized. Another practical consideration is that fewer training set images translate into a more efficient design and construction process.

This test is performed by selecting several different training image spacings to discover which is optimum. The training image spacings used herein are 3°, 5° and

$8°$. The data resulting from these three different training image spacings are tabulated in Table 6.3. From Table 6.3, it can be seen that the smaller the training image spacing, the greater the invariant distortion range the MLAP/MfSDF can accommodate. For the training image spacing of $8°$, the MLAP/MfSDF can only achieve an invariant distortion range of $72°$. Furthermore, it is very sensitive to slight distortions of the in-class images, as the highest and lowest correlation peak responses are 0.0235 and 0.0115 respectively; that is, a variation of 51% over the image distortion range, which is significantly greater than that for a $5°$ and $3°$ image spacing. Except for the lower average correlation peak responses, the training image spacings of $5°$ and $3°$ give better performance than that with an $8°$ spacing, see Table 6.3. Significantly, the MLAP/MfSDF constructed with a $5°$ separation between training set images requires the same number of filters, to cover the full range of $360°$ object distortion, as the one constructed with training set images spaced at $3°$; furthermore, it delivers a higher average correlation peak than that for $3°$.

The optimal angular training image spacing was taken to be the maximum value that did not allow the peak correlation response to drop below the Rayleigh criterion [32] ($\sim40\%$) for the images between training set images. This is similar to the method suggested by Gregory [32] and Jared [9]. This criterion places a constraint on the minimum number of the training set images required (or the maximum spacing between training images in distortion space) to construct the filter. From Table 6.3, this criterion suggests a spacing of $5°$ between training images as the peak correlation response only drops by a maximum of 30% for images between the training set images; 51% for an $8°$ spacing does not satisfy this criterion. A 14% fall for a $3°$ spacing means that there is less variation over the distortion range, but this over satisfies the Rayleigh criterion and does not give such a high ACPi.

Therefore, it can be concluded that training set images spaced at $5°$ are the optimal choice in this case. To further check this conclusion the MLAP/MfSDFs, designed to cover the same distortion range, with a training image spacing of $5°$ and $3°$ were also compared; the average peak correlation response for training images $3°$ and $5°$ apart were very similar. The advantage of using training images spaced at $3°$ is that the filter exhibits less variation in the peak correlation responses over the distortion range than when using training images spaced $5°$ apart. However, this

Table 6.3: *Comparision of different training image spacings*

TIS	IDR	100% DC	FER	TIR	LFR	ACPi	GV	ASPi	ACPo
3°	171°	165°	165°	55	3	$0.65_{0.59}^{0.69}$	14%	$0.47^{0.56}$	$0.45^{0.58}$
5°	120°	120°	120°	24	3	$0.89_{0.75}^{1.07}$	30%	$0.58^{0.71}$	$0.59^{0.70}$
8°	72°	80°	72°	9	5	$1.42_{1.15}^{2.35}$	51%	$0.82^{1.03}$	$0.81^{0.94}$

Legend:
TIS – Training image spacing
IDR – Largest invariant distortion range of filter
100% DC – Largest distortion range over which the filter can achieve 100% discrimination
FER – Final effective range of filter when accounting for out-of-class target cross correlation
TIR – Number of training images required to encode filter
LFR – Least number of filters required to cover full range of 360° target distortion
ACPi – Average correlation peak from in-class images tested at every 1°, where the subscript value is the minimum correlation peak response and the superscript value is the maximum correlation peak response
GV – Greatest variation of correlation peak responses for images at any angle over the distortion range. $GV = (maximum\ peak - minimum\ peak)/maximum\ peak$
ASPi – Average secondary peak from in-class images tested at every 1°, where the superscript value is the maximum secondary correlation peak
ACPo – Average correlation peak from out-of-class images tested at every 1°, where the superscript value is the maximum correlation peak
Note: all values given in the columns of ACPi, ASPi and ACPo are multiplied by 100.0 compared with the actual values.

increase in filter performance must be weighed against the increased computational requirements of constructing a MLAP/MfSDF with more training images.

6.6.6 Noise resistance of filter

A good SDF filter should not only deliver a large distortion invariant range, with 100% discrimination between the in-class and out-of-class images, but also be robust to noise appearing in the input image. In this sub-section, an examination of the noise resistance of the MLAP/MfSDF is given by comparing it with that of the

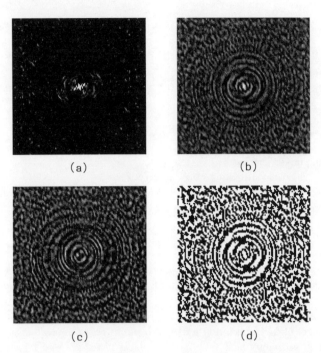

Figure 6.25: *(a) The intensity distribution of the MLAP/MfSDF filter constructed for a distortion range from 0° to 60° with training images spaced at 5°; (b) and (c) are its real and imaginary parts respectively, where the grey levels vary from 0 to 255. (d) is the BPOF/MfSDF constructed from the same training images but in which the white pixels denote the values of 1 and black pixels denote the values of -1*

BPOF/MfSDF, and the BPOF/fSDF suggested by Jared *et al* [8][9].

The noise resistance of the filter primarily depends on the type of filter. It is well known that the influence of the input image noise in the frequency plane of the correlator is greatest for the higher frequencies. Thus the low pass type of filters, such as the CMF and classical SDF filter, are not greatly affected by the input image noise but produce a very broad correlation peak at the output plane; whereas the all pass type of filters, such as the BPOF and BPOF/SDF, are very susceptible to noise in the correlator as they enhance the high frequencies and attenuate the low frequencies of the input image. Fig.6.25(a) shows the intensity distribution of the MLAP/MfSDF filter, in the frequency domain, designed for the invariant distortion range of 60° with training images spaced at 5° intervals, i.e. twelve in-plane rotated Bradley APC vehicle in-class images and twelve in-plane rotated Abram MI tank out-of-class images are encoded into the filter. Its real and imaginary parts are given in Fig.6.25(b) and Fig.6.25(c), respectively; these figures clearly illustrate that the MLAP/MfSDF filter is a band-pass type filter; it enhances the higher frequencies and attenuates the lower frequencies, the information content is very rich in the filter midband. From inspection there is no doubt that this filter, with a band-pass characteristic, will possess relatively good noise resistance. For comparison, the BPOF/MfSDF is given in Fig.6.25(d) in which the white pixels denote values of 1 and black pixels denote the values of -1. As the amplitude of the BPOF/MfSDF is unity everywhere, the energy is distributed equally over the whole filter plane; hence, it is very sensitive to noise in the input image. Fig.6.26(a) and Fig.6.26(b) illustrate the impulse responses of the MLAP/MfSDF and BPOF/MfSDF filters (i.e. Fig.6.25(a) and Fig.6.25(d)), respectively.

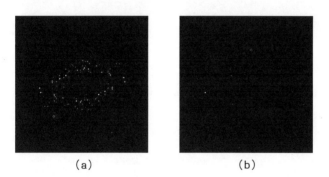

(a) (b)

Figure 6.26: *Impulse responses of the (a) MLAP/MfSDF and (b) BPOF/MfSDF functions*

The filter noise resistance performance is examined by using the in-plane rotated images of the noise corrupted in-class Bradley APC vehicle and out-of-class Abram MI tank; the ratio of image energy to noise energy is equal to 0.5 which means that the images are severely corrupted by noise. The noise corrupted APC vehicle and MI tank images were rotated from 0° to 90° in 1° steps. Views of the noise corrupted APC vehicle and MI tank at 0° are given in Fig.6.27 and have the same resolution as the noise free images shown in Fig.6.3 and Fig.6.4. When the noise corrupted in-class image Fig.6.27(a) is correlated with the above constructed MLAP/MfSDF and BPOF/MfSDF filter, i.e. Fig.6.25(a) and Fig.6.25(d), the resulting correlation functions are given in Fig.6.28(a) and Fig.6.28(c) respectively. For comparison, the correlation functions for noise free input are correspondingly given in Fig.6.28(b) and Fig.6.28(d) respectively. It can be seen from these correlation functions that the MLAP/MfSDF filter delivers much better noise resistance performance than that of the BPOF/MfSDF filter, the MLAP/MfSDF filter still yields a sharp correlation peak at the central position that is easily isolated by a simple thresholding procedure; whereas, the BPOF/MfSDF filter loses the target within the noise.

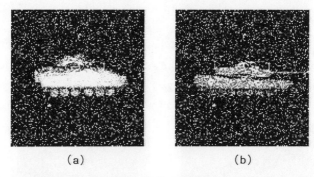

(a)   (b)

Figure 6.27: *Views of (a) Bradley APC vehicle and (b) Abram MI tank at the orientation angle of 0°, corrupted by noise with an image energy to noise energy ratio of 0.5*

Fig.6.29(a) shows the in-class and out-of-class peak correlation responses, using the noise corrupted in-class and out-of-class images as the input images, for a MLAP/MfSDF constructed from the noise free in-plane rotated training images with a distortion range from 0° to 40°. The training images used are 5° apart. A similar graph for the BPOF/MfSDF is shown in Fig.6.29(b). From Fig.6.29, it is clear that the MLAP/MfSDF filter is invariant to the distortion range of 40° whilst delivering a superior discrimination capability (the value of $DC > 1.6$ everywhere) between the in-class and out-of-class images in this noise corrupted case; whereas, the BPOF/MfSDF does not give complete invariant distortion over this range as several secondary correlation peaks and out-of-class correlation peaks exceed the lowest in-class correlation peaks.

Fig.6.30 illustrates the representative correlation functions from this test. Fig.6.30(a)

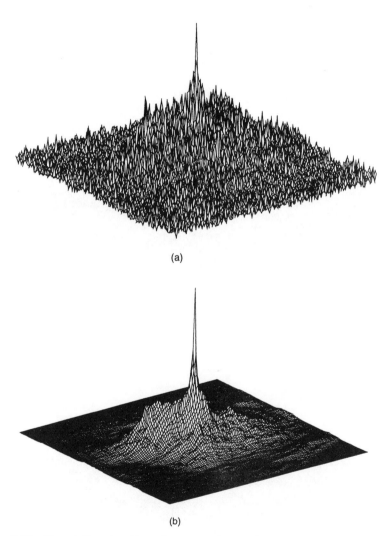

(a)

(b)

Figure 6.28: *Correlation functions from correlating the input images of Fig6-27(a)
and Fig6-3(a) with the filters of Fig6-25(a) and Fig6-25(d) respectively. (a) and (b)
are the results from correlating the filter Fig6-25(a) with the inputs of Fig6-27(a)
and Fig6-3(a) respectively; (c) and (d) are the results from correlating the filter
Fig6-25(d) with the inputs of Fig6-27(a) and Fig6-3(a) respectively*

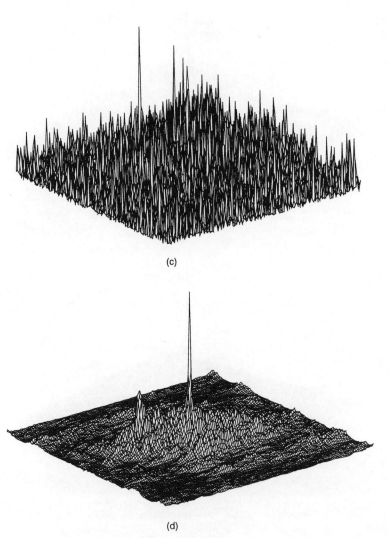

(c)

(d)

Figure 6.28: *Continued*

and Fig.6.30(b) are from correlating the MLAP/MfSDF with the inputs of in-class image and out-of-class image at a 35^0 orientation, respectively; Fig.6.30(c) and Fig.6.30(d) are from correlating the BPOF/MfSDF with the inputs of in-class image and out-of-class image at a 35^0 orientation, respectively; clearly, the performance of the BPOF/MfSDF filter is inadequate.

The PSR_w data for the MLAP/MfSDF and BPOF/MfSDF, with distortion ranges up to 60°, are displayed by Fig.6.31; the resulting graphs are similar to those in Fig.6.20, except that the input images used are the noise corrupted images shown in Fig.6.27. From Fig.6.31, for the noise corrupted image inputs, the MLAP/MfSDF still delivers distortion invariance, with 100% discrimination capability between the in-class and out-of-class images, up to at least 45°; whereas, the BPOF/MfSDF achieves less than 15°. The noise resistance performance of the BPOF/fSDF filter suggested by Jared *et al*[8][9] was also tested; it delivers an even worse performance than the BPOF/MfSDF. Thus overall, the MLAP/MfSDF filter has superior noise resistance performance to either the BPOF/MfSDF or BPOF/fSDF filters; it can be concluded that the performance of the MLAP/MfSDF filter benefits significantly from its band-pass characteristic, shown in Fig.6.25(a).

6.6.7 Conclusions

The commercially available liquid crystal television, which is able to encode the multilevel discrete amplitude and/or phase information, may be exploited to implement the modified filter synthetic discriminant function design. The filter modulation operator $\mathcal{M}$ is governed by the constraints imposed by the LCTV, the other modulation operator $\mathcal{N}$ is still free to be defined; hence, the flexibility of the MfSDF filter design is not compromised. Therefore, it is possible to find a MfSDF with an optimal choice of the modulation operator $\mathcal{N}$ to maximise the overall performance capabilities of the filter when given the limitations of the current LCTV SLMs.

With the modulation operator $\mathcal{N}$ set to POF, the performance of the MLAP/-MfSDF with the multilevel constraint $N = 16$ has been studied via simulation. The image sets studied were chosen to be practical objects, i.e. the Bradley APC vehicle

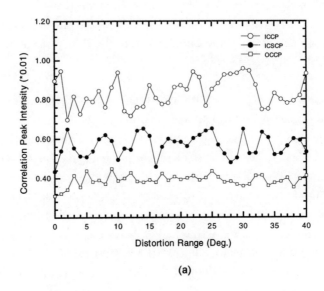

(a)

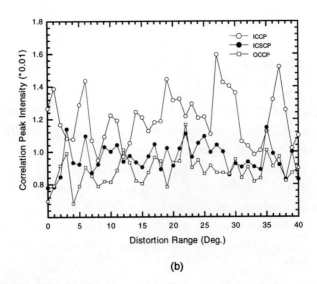

(b)

Figure 6.29: *Correlation peak, secondary peak and out-of-class correlation peak responses with a distortion range from 0° to 40°, where ICCP means the in-class correlation peak, ICSCP is in-class secondary correlation peak and OCCP is out-of-class correlation peak. (a) MLAP/MfSDF and (b) BPOF/MfSDF*

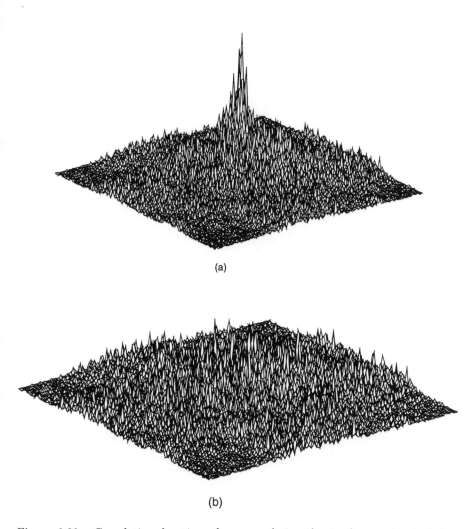

(a)

(b)

Figure 6.30: *Correlation functions from correlating the in-class and out-of-class input images of the APC vehicle and MI tank, at a 35^0 orientation, with the filters of MLAP/MfSDF and BPOF/MfSDF respectively*

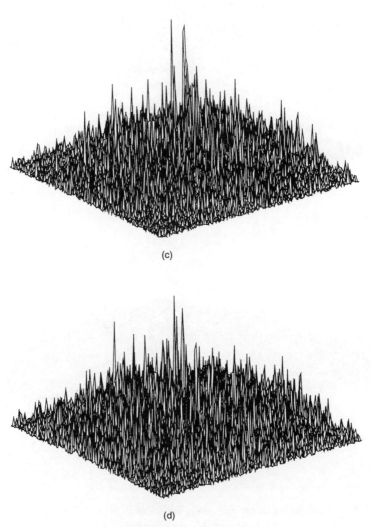

(c)

(d)

Figure 6.30: *Continued*

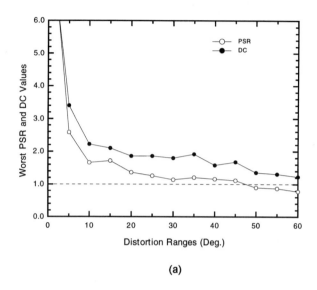

(a)

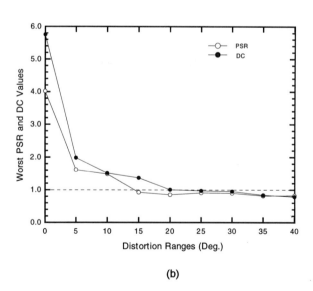

(b)

Figure 6.31: *The worst correlation peak response to secondary peak response ratio (PSR_w) and the worst discrimination capability (DC_w) of filter between in-class and out-of-class images over the distortion ranges from $0°$ to $60°$: (a) MLAP/MfSDF and (b) BPOF/MfSDF*

and Abram MI tank, to provide a challenging design test. The evaluation was performed to better understand the distortion range that can be effectively covered by the MLAP/MfSDFs. With the training image spacing of 5°, the MLAP/MfSDF filters can achieve distortion invariance to in-plane rotation up to at least 120° whilst still maintaining the 100% discrimination capability between in-class and out-of-class images; whereas, the BPOF/MfSDF filters only attain 60°, almost half the range of the MLAP/MfSDF, in the case studied. Thus the MLAP/MfSDF filters can greatly improve the correlator system speed as larger distortion range filters translate into fewer correlations required to perform image identification. Based on the constraint that a minimum number of training images will be required to assure that the peak correlation response over the distortion range does not drop below the Rayleigh criterion, a relatively good choice of training image spacing was shown to be about 5° for the case studied. The ability of the filter to resist noise in the input images has also been investigated. The band-pass type characteristic of the MLAP/MfSDF filters gives a much better ability to resist noise in the input images than does the BPOF/MfSDF or BPOF/fSDF filter. When the input images were buried in a noise background with the ratio of the object energy to noise energy equal to 0.5, the MLAP/MfSDF filters still achieved an invariant distortion range of at least 45°, whilst maintaining a superior discrimination capability between the noise corrupted in-class and out-of-class images; whereas, only one-third of this range, i.e. 15°, was attained by the BPOF/MfSDF filters. Thus overall, the MLAP/MfSDF filters deliver much better performance than either the BPOF/MfSDF or BPOF/fSDF; the MLAP/MfSDF benefits from its relatively richer phase and amplitude information. The MLAP/MfSDF filter can dynamically track a vehicle or tank as it moves along a random trajectory in the input field by using a hybrid optical/digital correlator system. Views of the object intermediate to those of the training set images are also recognized when training images are sufficiently close, i.e. 5° apart.

Bibliography

[1] Z. Bahri and B.V.K.Vijaya Kumar, "Generalized Synthetic Discriminant Functions", *J.Opt.Soc.Am.* **A5**, 562-571(1988).

[2] C.F. Hester and D. Casasent, "Multivariant Technique for Multiclass Pattern Recognition", *Appl. Opt.* **19**, 1758-1761(1980).

[3] D. Casasent, "Unified Synthetic Discriminant Function Computational Formulation", *Appl. Opt.* **23**, 1620-1627(1984).

[4] D. Casasent and W.-T. Chang, "Correlation Synthetic Discriminant Functions", *Appl. Opt.* **25**, 2343-2350(1986).

[5] A. VanderLugt, "Signal Detection by Complex Spatial Filtering", *IEEE Trans. Inf. Theory*, **IT-10**, 139-145(1964).

[6] J.L. Horner and P.D. Gianino, "Applying the Phase-only Filter Concept to the Synthetic Discriminant Function Correlation Filter", *Appl. Opt.* **24**, 851-855(1985).

[7] D. Casasent and W. Rozzi, "Computer Generated and Phase-Only SDF Filters", *Appl. Opt.* **25**, 3767–3772 (1986).

[8] D. Jared and D. Ennis, "Inclusion of Filter Modulation in the Synthetic Discriminant Function Construction", *Appl. Opt.* **28**, 232-239(1989).

[9] D. Jared, "Distortion Range of Filter Synthetic Discriminant Function Binary Phase-only Filters", *Appl. Opt.* **28**, 4335-4339(1989).

179

[10] M.B. Reid, P.W. Ma, J.D. Downie and E. O. Choa, "Experimental Verification of Modified Synthetic Discriminant Function Filters for Rotation Invariance", *Appl. Opt.* **29**, 1209-1214(1990).

[11] R.K. Wang, C.R. Chatwin and M.Y. Huang, "Modified Filter Synthetic Discriminant Functions for Improved Optical Correlator Performance", *Appl. Opt.* **33**, 7646-7654(1994).

[12] G.F. Schils and D.W. Sweeney, "Iterative Technique for the Synthesis of Optical-correlator Filters", *J. Opt. Soc. Am.* **A3** 1433-1442(1986).

[13] J.D. Downie, "Case Study of Binary and Ternary Synthetic Discriminant Function Filters with Similar In-class and Out-of-class Images" *Opt. Eng.* **32**, 561-570(1993).

[14] Z. Bahri and B.V.K.Vijaya Kumar, "Binary Phase-only Synthetic Discriminant Functions Designed Using the Successive Forcing Algorithm", in *Hybrid Image and Signal Processing II, Proc. SPIE* **1297**, 188-193(1990).

[15] C.R. Chatwin, R.K. Wang and R.C.D Young, "Tuneable Edge Enhancement Filtering", *Optics and Lasers in Engineering* **23**, 75-91(1995).

[16] O.K. Ersoy, Y. Yoon, N. Keshava and D. Zimmerman, "Nonlinear Matched Filtering", *Opt. Eng.* **29**, 1002-1012(1990).

[17] R.C.D. Young, C.R. Chatwin and B.F. Scott, "High-speed Hybrid Optical/Digital Correlator System", *Opt. Eng.* **32**, 2609-2615(1993).

[18] D. Psaltis, E. Paek, and S. Venkatesh, "Optical Image Correlation with a Binary Spatial Light Modulator", *Opt. Eng.* **23**, 698-704(1984).

[19] D.L. Flannery, J.S. Loomis, and M.E. Milkovich, "Design Elements of Binary Phase-Only Correlation Filter", *Appl. Opt.* **27**, 4231-4235(1988).

[20] M.A. Flavin and J.L.Horner, "Amplitude Encoded Phase-only Filters", *Appl. Opt.* **28**, 1692-1696(1989).

[21] J.L. Horner and H.O. Bartelt, "Two-bit Correlation", *Appl. Opt.* **24**, 2889-2893(1985).

[22] D.L. Flannery, J.S. Loomis, M.E. Milkovich and P.E. Keller, "Application of Binary Phase-only Correlation to Machine Vision", *Opt. Eng.* **27**, 309-320(1988).

[23] S. Mills, and W. Ross, "Dynamic Magneto-Optic Correlator: Real-Time Operation", in *Acousto-Optic, Electro-Optic, and Magneto-Optic Devices and Applications*, J. Lucero ed., *Proc. SPIE* **753**, 54-63(1987).

[24] H.-K. Liu, and T.-H Chao,"Liquid Crystal Television Spatial Light Modulators", *Appl. Opt.* **28**, 4772-4780(1989).

[25] D.A. Gregory, J.A. Loudin, J.C. Kirsch, E.C. Tam, and F.T.S. Yu, "Using Properties of Liquid Crystal Television", *Appl. Opt.* **30**, 1374-1378(1991).

[26] T.H. Barnes, T. Eiju, K. Matsuda, and N. Ooyawa, "Phase-Only Modulation Using a Twisted Nematic Liquid Crystal Television", *Appl. Opt.* **28**, 4845-4852(1989).

[27] V. Laude, S. Maze, P. Chavel, and Ph. Refregier, "Amplitude and Phase Coding Measurements of a Liquid Crystal Television", *Optics Comm.* **103**, 33-38(1993).

[28] R.K. Wang, and C.R. Chatwin, "Multilevel Phase and Amplitude Encoded Modified Filter Synthetic Discriminant Function Filters", *Appl. Opt.* **34**, 4094-4104(1995).

[29] G.A. Gregory, "Real-Time Pattern Recognition Using a Modified Liquid Crystal Television in a Coherent Optical Correlator", *Appl. Opt.* **25**, 467-469(1986).

[30] R.D. Juday, "Optimal Realizable Filters and the Minimum Euclidean Distance Principle", *Appl. Opt.* **32**, 5100-5111(1993).

[31] V. Laude and Ph. Refregier, "Multicriteria Characterization of Coding Domains with Optimal Fourier Spatial Light Modulator Filters", *Appl. Opt.* **33**, 4465-4471(1994).

[32] D.A. Gregory, "Rayleigh Criteria Separation of Optical Correlation Signals", *Appl. Opt.* **26**, 3170-3171 (1987).

Chapter 7

The Wiener Filter and Its Application to Optical Correlation

7.1 Introduction

The classical matched spatial filter[1] (CMF) is optimal for the recognition of objects in additive noise but produces a broad correlation peak in the output plane resulting in a low discriminatory capability between an object of the class to be detected and an out-of-class object which is to be rejected. In order to overcome this performance limitation, numerous methods[2]-[9] have been proposed. The phase-only filter[2] (POF) which uses the phase information of the reference image, and the amplitude-compensated matched filter[3][4] (ACMF), which uses both phase and amplitude information of the reference image, have successfully produced a sharp correlation peak in the output plane of a correlation system; furthermore, when compared with the CMF, they give good discriminatory capability between an in-class image, to be detected, and an out-of-class image, to be rejected. An optimal filter, which maximises the discrimination capability, was reported by Yaroslavsky[10][11] and gives better performance than the POF.

The common factor in this research is the implementation of spatial filters by recording all or part of the information contained in a set of patterns which are to be discriminated from noise or from each other. A more exact statement of this approach is that a filter should be designed to be matched to one or more of the possible input patterns and thus produce a suitable correlation function at the output plane of a correlation system.

An extremely useful approach to filter design is to start from the correlation plane and define the desired output distribution; the synthetic discriminant function (SDF) [12]-[15] may be implemented in this manner. To achieve the required output distribution a suitable spatial filter is generated by using numerical methods. The initial results for conventional SDFs[16] indicated that their pattern classification performance is inadequate because they produce a very broad correlation peak at the output plane and as a result they do not achieve a 100% success rate in discriminating one class of images from another. To solve this problem, Horner et al[17] extended phase-only filtering to SDF design; these filters do produce very sharp correlation peaks but do not satisfy the equal correlation peaks (ECP) rule in the output plane. Another popular approach is the minimum average correlation energy[15] (MACE) filter; this produces a sharp output correlation peak and maximizes the ratio of the squared peak value of the correlation function to the average correlation plane energy. However, the MACE filter is similar to the inverse filter which is difficult to realise physically; furthermore, it is very sensitive to intra-class variations[18].

In this chapter, the Wiener filter is applied to optical pattern recognition [24]; previously the Wiener filter has been successfully implemented for image restoration and signal processing[11][19]. In this implementation the Wiener filter is formulated so as to incorporate the out-of-class image, to be rejected, as the Wiener filter noise term. The proposed Wiener filter has much better discriminatory capability for the inter-class images than the POF and CMF. Furthermore, when an SDF is constructed from the proposed Wiener filter it is less sensitive to image distortions (e.g. out-of-plane rotation in this case) whilst still providing good performance in the output plane and achieving a 100% discrimination in detecting one class of images from another.

7.2 Wiener Filter Based Correlation

7.2.1 Wiener filter formulation

The general model of an image formation system in which the point spread function is random can be written as

$$g(x,y) = \int\limits_{-\infty}^{+\infty}\int\limits_{-\infty}^{+\infty} p(x-x_1, y-y_1)f(x_1, y_1)dx_1 dy_1 + n(x,y)$$
$$= p(x,y) \star f(x,y) + n(x,y) \qquad (7.1)$$

where $p(x,y)$ is the random point spread function, $f(x,y)$ is the object image function, $n(x,y)$ denotes the detection noise which will include the out-of-class image; $g(x,y)$ is the recorded image, and the sign $\star$ signifies the convolution operation. In Eq.(7.1) it is assumed that the optical system is linear and shift-invariant.

Suppose that an estimate for $f(x,y)$ denoted by $\widehat{f}(x,y)$ is of the form

$$\widehat{f}(x,y) = w(x,y) \star g(x,y) \qquad (7.2)$$

Clearly, the problem is to find $w(x,y)$ or equivalently its Fourier transform $W(f_x, f_y)$. The Wiener filter[19] is based on utilizing the least squares principle to find $w(x,y)$. Thus $w(x,y)$ is found in such a way that the error

$$\varepsilon = \left| f(x,y) - \widehat{f}(x,y) \right|^2 \qquad (7.3)$$

is a minimum. Using the orthogonality principle, this error is a minimum when

$$[f(x,y) - (w(x,y) \star g(x,y))] \odot g^*(x,y) = 0 \qquad (7.4)$$

Hence, using the correlation and convolution theorems, in Fourier space, the following equations can be obtained

$$F(f_x, f_y)G^*(f_x, f_y) = W(f_x, f_y)G(f_x, f_y)G^*(f_x, f_y) \qquad (7.5)$$

or

$$W(f_x, f_y) = \frac{G^*(f_x, f_y)}{|G(f_x, f_y)|^2} F(f_x, f_y) \qquad (7.6)$$

Since

$$G(f_x, f_y) = P(f_x, f_y)F(f_x, f_y) + N(f_x, f_y) \qquad (7.7)$$

Therefore, the Wiener filter $W(f_x, f_y)$ with correlated noise can be written as

$$W(f_x, f_y) = \frac{P^*(f_x, f_y)\,|F(f_x, f_y)|^2 + N^*(f_x, f_y)F(f_x, f_y)}{|P(f_x, f_y)|^2\,|F(f_x, f_y)|^2 + |N(f_x, f_y)|^2 + D(f_x, f_y)} \qquad (7.8)$$

where,

$$D(f_x, f_y) = P(f_x, f_y)F(f_x, f_y)N^*(f_x, f_y) + N(f_x, f_y)P^*(f_x, f_y)F^*(f_x, f_y) \qquad (7.9)$$

where P, F and N are the Fourier transforms of the point spread function $p(x,y)$, the object image function $f(x,y)$ and the noise image $n(x,y)$, respectively. The asterisk $*$ means complex conjugate.

Eq.(7.8) is derived incorporating the correlated noise. For this pattern recognition application the correlated noise is excluded. However, the uncorrelated noise, i.e. independent noise, is included in the filter, hence the correlation of the noise with the object function $f(x,y)$ is zero and vice versa,

$$n^*(x,y) \odot f(x,y) = 0 \qquad (7.10)$$

and

$$f^*(x,y) \odot n(x,y) = 0 \qquad (7.11)$$

where $\odot$ denotes the correlation operation. In the Fourier space, it follows that

$$N^*(f_x, f_y)F(f_x, f_y) = 0 \qquad (7.12)$$

and

$$F^*(f_x, f_y)N(f_x, f_y) = 0 \qquad (7.13)$$

Hence, $D(f_x, f_y) = 0$ and the Wiener filter $W(f_x, f_y)$ reduces to

$$W(f_x, f_y) = \frac{P^*(f_x, f_y)}{|P(f_x, f_y)|^2 + |N(f_x, f_y)|^2 / |F(f_x, f_y)|^2} \qquad (7.14)$$

Eq.(7.14) is the well-known Wiener filter transfer function. It has been used frequently for image restoration[11][19]. It has the following properties:

(i) As the noise tends to zero and so $|N(f_x, f_y)| \longrightarrow 0$, it reduces to the inverse filter. Hence with minimal noise, the Wiener filter behaves like the inverse filter.

(ii) As the power of the object goes to zero (ie. as $|F(f_x, f_y)| \longrightarrow 0$) the Wiener filter produces zero modulation. This alleviates problems associated with the zeros of $|F(f_x, f_y)|$ and results in the Wiener filter being well conditioned.

7.2.2 Application to the optical correlation

The objective of this chapter is to apply this filter to optical pattern recognition. The Wiener filter for optical pattern recognition is constructed by substituting the object function $f(x, y)$ for the point spread function $p(x, y)$. Hence, for optical correlation, the Wiener filter is written as

$$W(f_x, f_y) = \frac{F^*(f_x, f_y)}{|F(f_x, f_y)|^2 + |N(f_x, f_y)|^2 / |F(f_x, f_y)|^2} \qquad (7.15)$$

where $F^*(f_x, f_y)$ is the complex conjugate spectrum of the object to be detected (in-class image), and $|N(f_x, f_y)|^2$ is the power spectrum of the object to be rejected (out-of-class image). Eq.(7.15) requires that the correlation filter based on the Wiener approach is constructed by incorporating the out-of-class object into the filter. This is significantly different from the POF and CMF in that a one step formulation simultaneously encodes the in-class and out-of-class images into the filter. A further advantage of a WF produced in this manner is that it is not indeterminate when the function passes through zero.

When the input image $u(x, y)$, in-class or out-of-class, is input into the Wiener filter based correlator, the amplitude of the diffracted field directly behind the filter, U_{out}, will be proportional to $W(f_x, f_y)$ and so can be written as

$$U_{out}(f_x, f_y) = W(f_x, f_y) \, U(f_x, f_y) \qquad (7.16)$$

where $U(f_x, f_y)$ is the Fourier transform of the input image $u(x, y)$. The Fourier transform of U_{out} gives u_{out}, the weighted correlation function of $u(x, y)$ with $n(x, y)$ and $f(x, y)$.

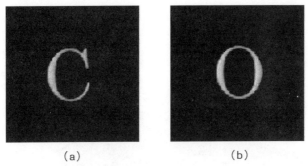

(a)   (b)

Figure 7.1: *Characters used to produce the Wiener filter, (a) in-class image, (b) out-of-class image*

To test the performance of the Wiener filter for optical pattern recognition, two similar characters "C" and "O", shown in Fig.7.1, were used for an initial simulation. In order to assess its relative usefulness, the WF's performance is compared with the CMF and POF. In the simulation, the character "C" is taken as the in-class image and "O" is the out-of-class image. After the Wiener filter $W(f_x, f_y)$ is produced, it is correlated with the input image given in Fig.7.2; Fig.7.3 gives the computed intensities at the correlation output plane. Fig.7.3a, Fig.7.3b and Fig.7.3c are the correlation results using the Wiener filter, CMF and POF respectively. Fig.7.3 clearly illustrates that the Wiener filter has much better discriminatory capability than the POF whilst the CMF cannot discriminate between these two similar characters at all.

Figure 7.2: *Input image used in correlation*

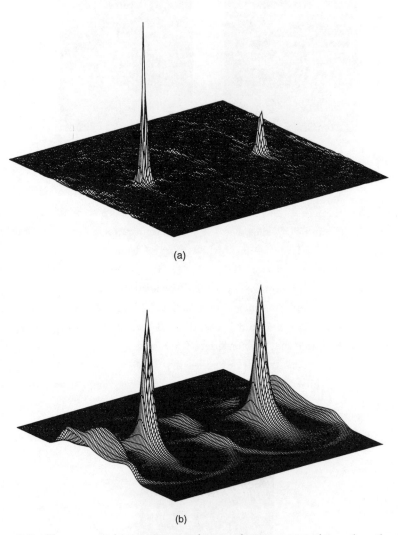

(a)

(b)

Figure 7.3: *The computed intensities at the correlation output plane when the scene shown in Fig7.2 is input into the correlator; (a), (b) and (c) are the correlation results using the Wiener filter, CMF and POF, respectively*

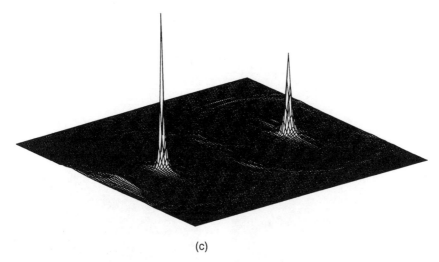

(c)

Figure 7.3: *Continued*

Table 7.1 gives a quantitative comparison of the relative performance of the Wiener filter, POF and CMF respectively. DR denotes the discrimination ratio of the filter which is defined as the ratio of the in-class correlation peak intensity to the out-of-class correlation peak intensity; PNI is the number of pixels inside the correlation peak at full width half maximum (FWHM); ηH is the Horner efficiency and PRMS is defined by Eq.(3.18). From Table 7.1, it can be seen that the discrimination ability of the Wiener filter is almost twice that of the POF and four times that of the CMF. The Wiener filter PRMS is slightly better than that of the POF; however, its energy efficiency is significantly worse than the POF and CMF. The low Horner efficiency does not cause a problem as most of the light passing through the filter is concentrated in the correlation peak.

Fig.7.4a illustrates the form of the Wiener filter in the frequency domain $W(f_x, f_y)$; it is thresholded in order to clearly show the filter's characteristics. From this figure it is clear that the Wiener filter is a highpass-like filter that results in a weighted edge enhancement of the images, Fig.7.4b illustrates the impulse response of the filter, $w(x, y)$. The reason for this can be seen from Eq.(7.15). The Fourier transforms of

Table 7.1: *Quantitative comparison of the filter performance*

	DR	PNI	ηH	PRMS
WF	3.91	4	0.04%	28.05
POF	1.92	2	100%	27.44
CMF	1.04	29	0.23%	7.051

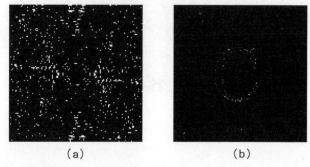

(a)   (b)

Figure 7.4: *(a) The form of the Wiener filter in the Fourier domain $W(f_x, f_y)$; (b) The impulse response of the Wiener filter $w(x, y)$*

the two similar images have large zero and low frequency components. Thus, for low frequencies, $|F(f_x, f_y)|$ is nearly equal to $|N(f_x, f_y)|$; for this condition a good approximation to Eq.(7.15) is

$$W(f_x, f_y) = \frac{F^*(f_x, f_y)}{|F(fx, fy)|^2 + 1} \tag{7.17}$$

Thus there is little modulation in the central region of the Fourier plane; hence, the WF automatically suppresses all the powerful low frequency components of the images, which are virtually identical for images that are similar.

For the higher frequencies, the values of $|F(f_x, f_y)|$ and $|N(f_x, f_y)|$ are much less than one. Thus Eq.(7.15) reduces to

$$W(f_x, f_y) = \frac{|F(f_x, f_y)|^2}{|N(f_x, f_y)|^2} F^*(f_x, f_y) \tag{7.18}$$

Eq.(7.18) shows that all the edge dissimilarities between the two images in the space domain produce high frequency components with different magnitudes in the frequency domain, i.e. the edges that are similar are unaffected whereas the magnitude of the frequency components from the edges that are different are increased for the in-class image and decreased for the out-of-class image. The filter impulse response, Fig.7.4b, illustrates this effect; the right side of the letter "C" — which is the part that is different from the letter "O" — is more enhanced than the left side. Therefore, the out-of-class image is suppressed and the in-class image is emphasised resulting in a very good discriminatory capability.

7.3 Wiener Filter–Synthetic Discriminant Functions

According to the chapter 5, the synthetic discriminant function filter is designed to provide equal central correlation peak values in the output plane for a given training set of centred, in-class images. Suppose that a set of training images, $t_n(x, y)$, $n = 0, 1, ..., k$, with the desired distortion invariant features is used to construct the SDF $s(x, y)$. For each $t_n(x, y)$, the desired correlation response of $s(x, y)$ is a constant c_n, namely,

$$\int \int t_n(x, y) \; s^*(x, y) dx dy) = c_n \qquad (7.19)$$

Typically, $s(x, y)$ is constrained to be a linear combination of the set of training images[12][16],

$$s(x, y) = \sum_{n=0}^{k} a_n \; t_n(x, y) \qquad (7.20)$$

By substituting Eq.(7.20) into Eq.(7.19), the coefficients $\mathbf{a}$ are shown to be

$$\mathbf{a} = \mathbf{R}^{-1} \; \mathbf{C} \qquad (7.21)$$

where $\mathbf{a} = [a_0, a_1, ..., a_n]^T$, $\mathbf{C} = [c_0, c_1, ..., c_n]^T$, and $\mathbf{R}$ is the correlation matrix having elements $R_{ij} = \int \int t_i(x, y) t_j^*(x, y) dx dy$. The SDF $s(x, y)$ is determined by solving Eq.(7.21) and then substituting the coefficients of vector $\mathbf{a}$ back into Eq.(7.20).

7.3.1 Wiener filter SDFs

The above SDF procedure is well known; when producing a Wiener filter synthetic discriminant function (WF SDF), the filter modulation in Eq.(7.15) must be incorporated into the SDF construction process by modifying Eq.(7.19) and Eq.(7.20). The filter must meet the requirement that

$$\int \int t_n(x,y)w^*(x,y)dxdy = c_n \tag{7.22}$$

where $w(x,y)$ is constrained to be a linear combination of the set of individual Wiener filter functions $w_n(x,y)$ of the training image set

$$w(x,y) = \sum_{n=0}^{k} a_n \, w_n(x,y) \tag{7.23}$$

As stated in the above sub-section, a general SDF synthesis equation is provided by substituting Eq.(7.23) into Eq.(7.22). Unfortunately, the WF SDF made from the original WF is not guaranteed to produce equal correlation peaks for all of the in-class training images. The resulting spread in peak values can significantly lower the ratio of the lowest in-class peak to the highest out-of-class peak, which degrades the overall performance capability of the filter. This difficulty — occurring in the WF SDF synthesis — can be solved by iterative techniques [21], which do produce equal correlation peaks for the in-class training images. The following equation was used to iterate trial solution vectors,

$$a_n^{i+1} = a_n^i + \alpha \left[c_n - c_1 \frac{|p_n^i|}{|p_1^i|} \right] \quad n = 0, 1, ...k \tag{7.24}$$

where i is the iteration number, α is a damping constant, and $|p_n^i|$ is the modulus of the central correlation response of training image $t_n(x,y)$ with the filter constructed from vector $\mathbf{a}^i$. There is no theoretical guarantee that this algorithm will converge to a solution, but it has been used with some success [21][22] and has converged in nearly all the cases studied herein.

The initial solution vector is taken to be the solution of the conventional SDF as this may be computed rapidly; this is then iterated to generate the WF SDF. The iteration is stopped when all the peak correlation responses of training images

$t_n(x,y)$ fall within one percent of the mean value of the training set correlation peaks,

$$\left| \frac{Max(p_n^i) - AVE}{AVE} \right| < 1\% \tag{7.25}$$

where

$$AVE = \frac{1}{k} \sum_{n=1}^{k} p_n^i \tag{7.26}$$

This is sufficiently accurate to satisfy the equal correlation peak height criteria.

As the in-class images and the out-of-class images are simultaneously incorporated into the one step Wiener filter formulation, the two class pattern recognition task is achieved very efficiently. For example, if one vehicle needs to be distinguished from another vehicle with an in-plane rotation and each vehicle is sampled at a rotation angle of every $10°$ from $0°$ to $180°$, the necessary number of training set images 'k' is only 18 for the WF SDF, whilst for the previous SDF methods, such as CMF/SDF and POF/SDF etc. k must be 36 to achieve recognition between the two vehicles. Thus the WF SDF requires 18×18 cross-correlation operations to produce correlation matrix **R** whilst 36×36 are necessary for the other methods. Therefore, the computational time, to synthesise the WF SDF, is approximately one quarter of that required for the other methods. For comparison, the MACE filter, which is extremely sensitive to distortions of the in-class images, requires a large increase in the number, k, of training set images. It needs approximately 360 training set images to cope with a two-class pattern recognition task and an object rotation of $90°$.

7.4   Simulations and Results

The main issue studied in these simulations is the performance of the WF SDF as a function of the distortion range: in particular, assessment of whether the WF SDF enhances either discrimination or PRMS in comparison to the conventional SDF and the POF SDF when applied to the same image training set. The greater the allowable spacing in the training image set, the fewer the number of images

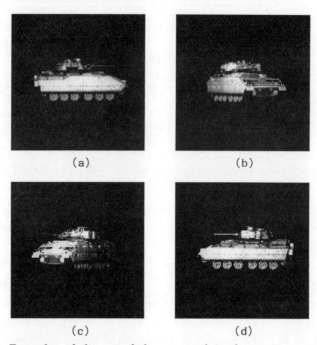

(a)   (b)

(c)   (d)

Figure 7.5: *Examples of the out-of-plane rotated in-class training images of the Bradley APC vehicle. (a), (b), (c) and (d) are at $0°$, $60°$, $120°$ and $180°$ aspect angles respectively*

that need to be encoded into the SDF and hence the lower the construction costs. The measure used to evaluate the correlation output performance in this work is the ability to correctly discriminate between the given in-class set of images and out-of-class set of images.

The training set of images used in the simulations consists of out-of-plane rotated images of the Bradley APC, which are the in-class images to be detected; the Abrams MI tank, provides the out-of-class images to be rejected, over an orientation angle range from $0°$ to $180°$. Each image is centred and normalised to unit energy. A total of 37 images of each in-class and out-of-class vehicle at $5°$ increments from $0°$ to $180°$ were encoded at a resolution of 128×128 pixels. The in-class and out-of-class training images at $0°$, $60°$, $120°$ and $180°$ are shown in Fig.7.5 and Fig.7.6, respectively. As can be seen, each training image is significantly different, presenting a difficult 2–class pattern recognition problem.

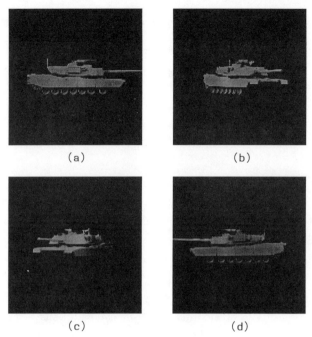

(a) (b)

(c) (d)

Figure 7.6: *Examples of the out-of-plane rotated in-class training images of the Abrams MI tank. (a), (b), (c) and (d) are at $0°$, $60°$, $120°$ and $180°$ aspect angles respectively*

An accepted criterion for expressing the discrimination capability of the SDF filters has not been defined to date. Comparison of the in-class peak correlation responses to the out-of-class peak correlation responses appears to be the best practical measure. In previous literature[22][23], the peak correlation has been termed the intensity of the central correlation response (CCR). In actual experiments, only the peak correlation response (PCR) in the output plane is of interest, and this may not occur at the centre of the correlation plane for all the training set images tested. In the present work, the peak correlation CPI is defined as the intensity of the maximum correlation response at the output plane. As any experimentally measured value must be an intensity,

$$CPI = Max\{|c(i,j)|^2\} \qquad (7.27)$$

In order to determine the discrimination capability of the SDF filter, the threshold value t — for image identification — is chosen as the maximum value of the out-of-class peak correlation intensity,

$$t = \underset{j=0}{\overset{k}{\text{Max}}}\{P_{oc}^{j}\} \tag{7.28}$$

where k is the number of out-of-class training images, P_{oc}^{j} is the out-of-class peak correlation intensity. Correlation peaks measured higher than t are classified as in-class images, whereas those lower than t are classified as out-of-class images.

It is desirable to design an SDF with training images spaced as widely as possible whilst still satisfying the condition of 100% discrimination capability. This ensures successful system performance whilst minimizing the amount of redundant information encoded in the SDFs. In other words, for the case presented herein, the larger the angular increment between training set images, the greater the efficiency.

The training image spacing used in the design of a synthetic discriminant function depends on the sensitivity of the filter to the image distortions — i.e. relative to the training images — of the in-class images and out-of-class images; these images are called intra-in-class (IIC) images and intra-out-of-class (IOC) images. As the images input to the correlator are assumed to be allowed in any orientation (in this case, out-of-plane rotation), the correlation peaks of the IIC images must still be significantly higher than those of the IOC images. To this end, the threshold value t for image recognition must be re-selected as,

$$t = \underset{j=0}{\overset{N}{\text{Max}}}\{P_{oc}^{j}\} \tag{7.29}$$

where N is the total number of the out-of-class images (in this case, $N = 37$). If all in-class correlation peaks are above value t and all out-of-class correlation peaks are below value t, the filter can be said to have a 100% discrimination capability.

To illustrate the relative sensitivity or discrimination ability of the WF SDFs to training image spacing for the set of real tank images, the correlation results for filters covering 180° rotation range are shown in Fig.7.7 and Fig.7.8, with training image spacings of 30° and 15° respectively. The SDF filters, constructed from images taken every 30° and 15° from 0° to 180° respectively, are correlated with in-class and out-of-class images rotated at every 5°. It is very clear from these two figures

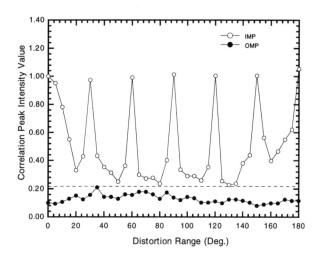

Figure 7.7: *Results of the WF SDF designed with training image spacing of* 30° *for the distortion range* 0° *to* 180°. *IMP and OMP are the in-class and out-of-class maximum correlation peaks, respectively*

that the in-class maximum correlation peaks (IMP) are well above the out-of-class maximum correlation peaks (OMP).

Thus the simple threshold algorithm, Eq.(7.29), can be applied to their correlation planes to extract the peaks so as to determine that the image input to the correlator belongs to the in-class image or the out-of-class image set. The threshold value t is illustrated as the dashed line in Fig.7.7, Fig.7.8, Fig.7.9 and Fig.7.10. Although the WF SDF constructed with a training image spacing of 15° is much better than that of 30°, the latter one can also achieve 100% discrimination. The tolerance range of the WF SDF is greater than that illustrated. Hence, the WF SDF is fairly insensitive to the distortion of images and can be designed with very wide training image spacing.

For comparison, the results for a conventional SDF and SDF/POF are shown in Fig.7.9 and Fig.7.10; these are also made with a 15° spacing between training images.

It should be noted that the conventional SDF is a two-class pattern recognition problem, i.e. assuming the correlation responses of in-class images to be 1 and those

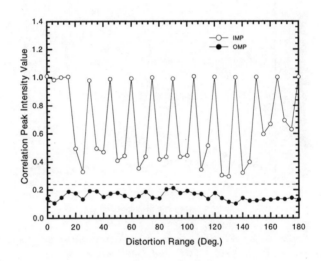

Figure 7.8: *Results of the WF SDF designed with training image spacing of 15° for the distortion range 0° to 180°. IMP and OMP are the in-class and out-of-class maximum correlation peaks, respectively.*

of out-of-class images to be 0. The SDF/POF is constructed from the conventional SDF[17] and then optimised using the iterative technique[21][22] to achieve equal correlation peaks for all training images. In the simulations, all correlation peaks computed are the maximum correlation response values in the correlation plane. As can be seen from Fig.7.9 and Fig.7.10, the problems for the conventional SDF and SDF/POF — made using a 15° training image spacing — are apparent. Some of the IMP peaks fall below the largest OMP peaks, i.e. the threshold value t; this gives erroneous classification of these images. Hence some IIC images will be categorised as out-of-class images, whereas some IOC images will be identified to be in-class images. In contrast, the results from the WF SDF made with 15° training image spacing, shown in Fig.7.8, are clearly separated and will not give any false alarms.

Finally, the 3-D representation of the correlation functions obtained with the 15° training image spacing for the WF SDF, conventional SDF and SDF/POF — for the same in-class and out-of-class tank images — are shown in Fig.7.11. The figures

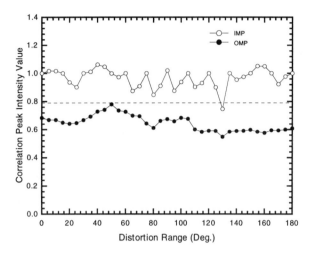

Figure 7.9: *Results of the conventional SDF designed with training image spacing of 15° for the distortion range 0° to 180°. IMP and OMP are the in-class and out-of-class maximum correlation peaks, respectively*

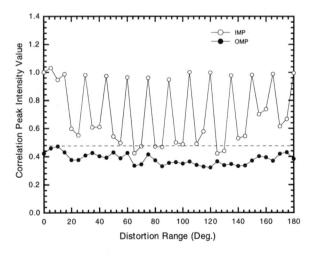

Figure 7.10: *Results of the POF/SDF designed with training image spacing of 15° for the distortion range 0° to 180°. IMP and OMP are the in-class and out-of-class maximum correlation peaks, respectively*

in the left column are the in-class correlations and the figures in the right column
are the out-of-class correlations. These correlation functions give an excellent illustration of filter performance. All out-of-class correlation functions are normalised to
their corresponding in-class training image's correlation peak height to indicate the
discrimination ability of the filters. Fig.7.11 illustrates that the WF SDF gives the
sharpest correlation peak and minimal sidelobe distributions for the in-class training
images, which results in better PRMS performance at the correlation plane. Furthermore, it shows the very broad output distributions for the out-of-class images.

7.5   Wiener Filter Applied to Laser Cutting Process Control

In gas assisted laser cutting, melted and partly vaporised metal liquid rapidly mix
with the assist gas jet and are blown out from the workpiece lower kerf surface.
Characteristic spark cones are formed which are a function of the flow dynamics,
system thermodynamics, kerf geometry, and dross attachment conditions. High
intensity spark cones were produced during a good cut when no dross attachment
was evident on the workpiece lower surface. Sparser spark cones were generated
when dross became attached to the workpiece lower surface and disturbed the flow.
In this cutting process, spark cone images from a good quality cutting process and
a poor quality cutting process are quite similar. They differ only in the scale of the
sparser spark lines; a good cut has few sparse spark lines, whereas a poor cut has
an extensive sparse spark structure. The Wiener filter based correlator, discussed
in this chapter, shows better performance than several traditional filters, especially
in distinguishing similar patterns; thus, it is particularly suitable for assessing the
quality of the laser cutting process through the analysis of its spark cone image.

Fig.7.12 is a typical spark image generated from a gas assisted laser cutting process.
From Fig.7.12, it is found that the spark cone image normally consists of two separated sub-cones. An intense concentrated inner cone, and a lighter sparser outer
cone. The conditions of the dross attachment on the workpiece lower surface alters

(a)

(b)

Figure 7.11: *The 3-D representations of correlation functions obtained with the 15°
training image spacing of WF SDF ((a) and (b)), conventional SDF ((c) and (d)),
and POF/SDF ((e) and (f)) for the same in-class and out-of-class tank images
respectively. The figures (a), (c) and (e) are the in-class correlations; and (b), (d)
and (f) are the out-of-class correlations*

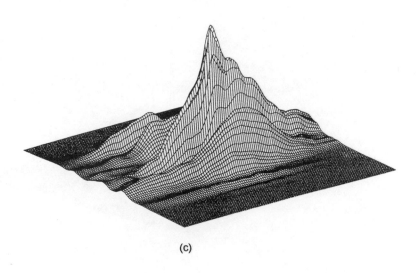

(c)

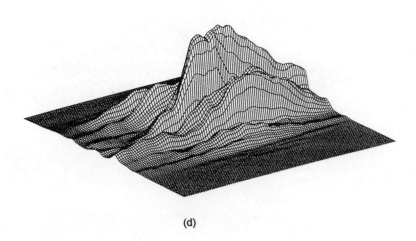

(d)

Figure 7.11: *Continued*

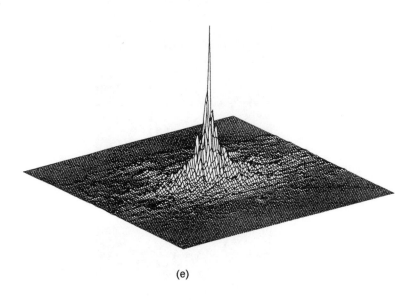

(e)

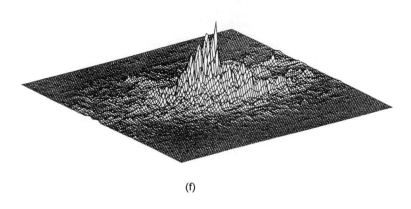

(f)

Figure 7.11: *Continued*

Figure 7.12: *A typical spark cone image from mild steel cutting process*

the relative size of the two sub-cones.

Figure 7.13: *Spark cone image of 2 mm mild steel cutting process — good cut*

Fig.7.13 to Fig.7.17 are spark cone images from good quality cutting processes of mild steel of different thicknesses. There is little or no dross attachment on these workpiece lower surfaces. The figures run from Fig.7.13, "2mm", to Fig.7.17, "6mm". From these figures, it can be seen, that the spark cones are very intense and with nearly no sparse sparks in the outer layer of the cones.

Fig.7.18 to Fig.7.21 are spark cone images for different dross attachment conditions for 4mm mild steel. The figures run from Fig.7.18, dross free, to Fig.7.21, severe dross attachment. From these figures, it can be seen that the smaller the sparse

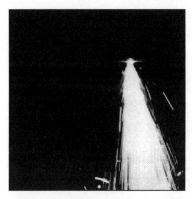

Figure 7.14: *Spark cone image of 3 mm mild steel cutting process — good cut*

Figure 7.15: *Spark cone image of 4 mm mild steel cutting process — good cut*

Figure 7.16: *Spark cone image of 5 mm mild steel cutting process — good cut*

Figure 7.17: *Spark cone image of 6 mm mild steel cutting process — good cut*

spark region the cleaner the cut. There is a high degree of similarity between the images of Fig.7.18 and Fig.7.19; however, one is for a clean cut and the other has dross attached to the workpiece lower surface. It is for these circumstances that the Wiener filter formulation is extremely useful.

Figure 7.18: *Spark cone image of clean cut process — mild steel*

By using the clean cut spark cone image as the in-class image and the low dross cut spark cone image as the out-of-class image, the WF for a specific thickness of mild steel cutting process can be constructed using Eq.(7.15). The quality of the laser cutting process can then be assessed by cross-correlating this filter with the process image. A high correlation peak indicates a quality similar to the good cut. A lower

Figure 7.19: *Spark cone image of low dross cutting process*

Figure 7.20: *Spark cone image of medium dross cutting process*

correlation peak indicates a poor cutting quality. Fig.7.22(a) is the result from a 4 mm mild steel good cutting process, and Fig.7.22(b) results from a poor cutting process.

As mentioned previously, spark cone images generated during poor cutting processes may be similar to those for good cutting processes. Consequently, these images may make it difficult for the filter to distinguish a good cut process from a poor one. A solution to this problem is to combine a greater number of similar images from poor cutting processes into the construction of the WF. Table 7.2 lists the relative output peak heights of the cross-correlation between the process images and various Wiener filters for 4 mm mild steel. In Table 7.2, the various filters were constructed

Figure 7.21: *Spark cone image of heavy dross cutting process*

Table 7.2: *Relative cross-correlation peaks heights*

Filter	GC	PC:1	PC:2	PC:3	PC:4	PC:5	PC:6
WF-n2	1.0	0.058	0.161	0.022	0.175	0.186	0.321
WF-n3	1.0	0.095	0.154	0.118	0.024	0.148	0.302
WF-n4	1.0	0.097	0.166	0.171	0.187	0.021	0.342
WF-n5	1.0	0.101	0.166	0.158	0.171	0.367	0.018

GC = Good Cut; PC = Poor Cut

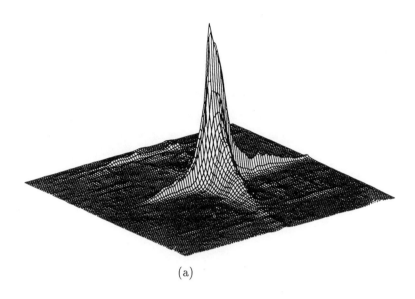

(a)

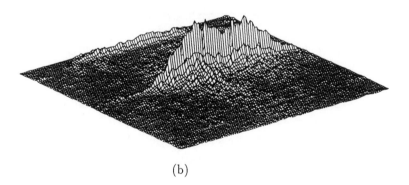

(b)

Figure 7.22: *Cross-correlation result using a WF filter — 4 mm mild steel: (a) from good cutting process, (b) from poor cutting process*

by combining: two similar images from poor cutting processes as the noise image for WF-n2, three similar noise images for WF-n3, and so on. The results are presented graphically in Fig.7.23. The maximum out-of-class image (poor cutting process) cross-correlation resulting from each filter is illustrated in Fig.7.24. By incorporating five similar spark cone images from poor cutting processes into the filter construction, the maximum cross-correlation output peak from the out-of-class image was 37% of that from the in-class image; hence, discrimination is excellent. It was found that the WF-n3 Wiener filter, constructed by incorporating three out-of-class images (poor cut images), gave the best discrimination performance. This indicates that if too many out-of-class images are incorporated into the filter, the information content saturates beyond the optimum discrimination level, and performance deteriorates.

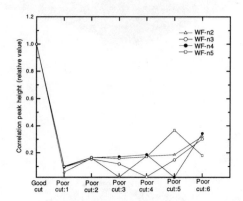

Figure 7.23: *Relative cross-correlation peak heights*

A single WF will only control the cutting process for a single material thickness; thus to produce a general filter capable of being used to control a range of material thicknesses a number of WF filters must be multiplexed together, that is, one for each material thickness. For this purpose, the WF-SDF was constructed from training set images taken from the spark-cones generated by laser cutting of mild steel plate of thickness 1mm, 2mm, 3mm, 4mm, 5mm and 6mm. The good-cut and poor-cut images were integrated into the filter construction as described in Section 7.3. The resulting coefficients obtained for the various mild steel cutting processes are tabulated in Table 7.3. The coefficients were then used to construct the WF based

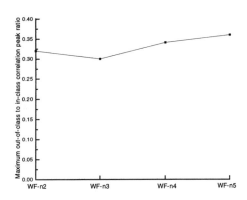

Figure 7.24: *Maximum out-of-class to in-class image cross-correlation peak ratio*

Table 7.3: *WF based SDF filter weighting coefficients*

	a_1	a_2	a_3	a_4	a_5	a_6
WF-SDF coefficient	0.3828	0.7810	0.6430	0.7076	0.4057	0.5220
Mild steel thickness	1mm	2mm	3mm	4mm	5mm	6mm

SDF. The WF based SDF filter can thus be used in an optical correlator, as illustrated in Fig.7.25, to assess the quality of a mild steel laser cutting process [25]. The WF-SDF reference image $u_1(x,y)$ is displayed on the Seiko-Epson-VPJ700-LCTV-SLM. The grabbed process image $u_2(x,y)$ is displayed on the other VPJ700-SLM. Hence the reference and input images are displayed on the SLMs resulting in the field modulations $u_1(x,y)$ and $u_2(x,y)$ of the Ar^+ and HeNe beams respectively. A volume hologram is written to the BSO photo-refractive crystal by the interference of $U_1(u,v)$ (i.e. W(u,v)-SDF), the Fourier transform of $u_1(x,y)$ and U_3, a plane wave reference beam of tuneable strength. $U_2(u,v)$, the Fourier transform of $u_2(x,y)$, is diffracted from the WF-SDF filter, formed in the BSO, to yield, after a further Fourier transform, the correlation between $u_1(x,y)$ and $u_2(x,y)$ at the output, i.e. $u_4(x,y)$. A high cross-correlation output peak, between the process image and the filter, indicates good cut quality; Fig.7.26(a) illustrates the result. A low cross-correlation output peak indicates that the quality of the process is poor; Fig.7.26(b) illustrates the result.

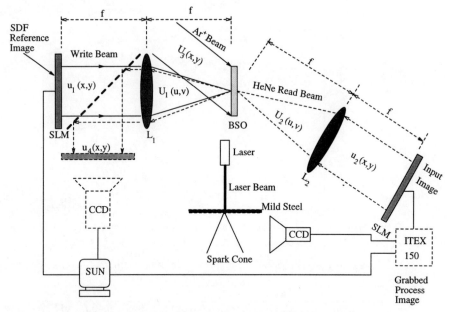

Figure 7.25: *Schematic diagram of updateable correlator*

7.5.1 Experimental result

Mild steel of different thickness was first cut without the SDF filter control system. Fig.7.27 shows the resulting kerf surfaces, which are of poor quality; this is because the power and feedrate were constant for all samples. To avoid the over-heating and consequent dross attachment on the thinner material, the feedrate should be increased; or better still the feedrate should be controlled. Another batch of mild steel was then cut with the SDF filter in place. Figure 7.28 illustrates the improvement in kerf quality when the SDF based spark cone control system was activated. The control system maximises the correlation peak height $u_4(x, y)$ by adjusting the laser cutting feedrate via simple high speed multiple threshold detection algorithms.

7.6   Conclusions

This chapter introduces a new application of the Wiener filter for pattern recognition and classification. The Wiener filter is formulated so as to incorporate the noise image, i.e. the out-of-class image to be rejected, into a one step filter construction. Computer simulations indicate that the Wiener filter delivers superior discrimination performance to that of the POF and CMF.

An SDF incorporating the Wiener filter (WF SDF) has been developed. The computational effort to produce a WF SDF is greatly reduced over that of the CMF/SDF and POF/SDF, only needing approximately one quarter of the CPU time. Filters tolerant to a larger distortion range translate into fewer correlations required to perform image recognition, and this lowers the construction costs. When compared with the conventional SDF and SDF/POF, the WF SDFs were shown to be capable of a larger training image distortion spacing, more than 30°, whilst still satisfying the 100% discrimination capability over the 180° rotation range. This success results from the fact that the WF incorporates the out-of-class image into a one step filter design. It can be concluded that the WF SDF is less sensitive to the distortions of the detected images. The PRMS performance at the correlation plane for the WF SDF is also much better than that for SDF/POF. It has been demonstrated that the WF SDF is very effective in discriminating between images that are quite similar; the filter will thus be efficient in discriminating between highly dissimilar objects and background image noise in the form of a complex background scene.

The major disadvantage of the Wiener filter is its low light efficiency. However, as most of the transmitted energy is concentrated in the correlation peak it should not be difficult to detect the output signal.

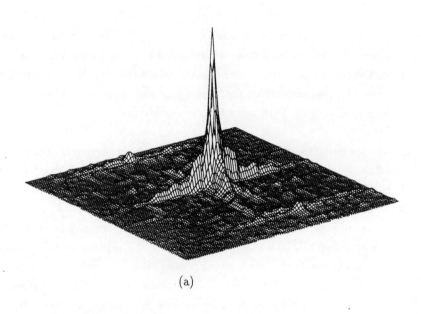

(a)

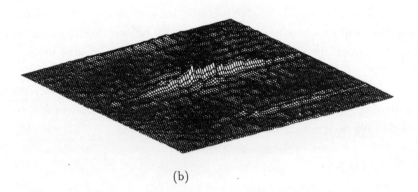

(b)

Figure 7.26: *Cross-correlation result using a WF based SDF filter — 4 mm mild steel: (a) from good cutting process, (b) from poor cutting process*

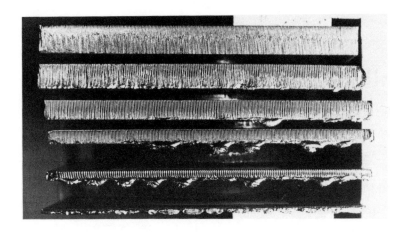

Figure 7.27: *Kerf surfaces of different thickness, mild steel 6mm, 5mm, 4mm, 3mm, 2mm, 1mm (without SDF filter imaging control system)*

Figure 7.28: *Kerf surfaces of different thickness, mild steel 6mm, 5mm, 4mm, 3mm (with SDF filter imaging control system)*

Bibliography

[1] A. VanderLugt, "Signal Detection by Complex Spatial Filtering", *IEEE Trans. Inf. Theory* **IT-10**, 139-145(1964).

[2] J.L. Horner and P.D. Gianino, "Phase-only Matched Filtering", *Appl. Opt.* **23**, 812-816(1984).

[3] G.G. Mu, X.M. Wang & Z.Q. Wang, "Amplitude-compensated Matched Filtering", *Appl. Opt.* **27**, 3461-3463(1988).

[4] A.A.S. Awwal, M.A. Karim and S.R. Jahan, "Improved Correlation Discrimination Using an Amplitude-modulated Phase-only Filter", *Appl. Opt.* **29**, 233-236(1990).

[5] J.L. Horner and J.R. Leger, "Pattern Recognition with Binary Phase-only Filter", *Appl. Opt.* **24**, 609-611(1985).

[6] W.W. Farn and J.W. Goodman, "Optimal Binary Phase-only Matched Filters", *Appl. Opt.* **27**, 4431-4437(1988).

[7] K. Chlanska-Macukow and T. Witka, "Phase-only Filter as Matched Filter with Enhanced Discriminatory capability", *Opt. Commun.* **64**, 224-228(1987).

[8] B.V.K. Vijaya Kumar and Z. Bahri, "Phase-only Filters with improved Signal-to-noise Ratio", *Appl. Opt.* **28**, 250-257(1989).

[9] F.M. Dickey, B.V.K. Vijaya Kumar, L.A. Romero and J.M. Connelly, "Complex Ternary Matched Filters Yielding High Signal to Noise Ratio", *Opt. Eng.* **29**, 994-1001(1990).

[10] L.P. Yaroslavsky, "Is the Phase-only Filter and Its Modifications Optimal in Terms of the Discrimination Capability in Pattern Recognition", *Appl. Opt.* **31**, 1677-1679(1992).

[11] L.P. Yaroslavsky, *Digital Picture Processing: An Introduction*, Springer-Verlag, Berlin, 1985.

[12] D. Casasent and W.-T. Chang, "Correlation Synthetic Discriminant Functions", *Appl. Opt.* **25**, 2343-2350(1986).

[13] D. Casasent, "Unified Synthetic Discriminant Function Computation Formulation", *Appl. Opt.* **23**, 1620-1627(1984).

[14] J. Shamir, H.J. Caulfield and J. Rosen, "Pattern Recognition Using Reduced Information Content filters", *Appl. Opt.* **26**, 2311-2314(1987).

[15] A. Mahalanobis, B.V.K. Viajia Kumar and D.P. Casasent, "Minimum Average Correlation Energy Filters", *Appl. Opt.* **26**, 3633-3640(1987).

[16] C.F. Hester and D. Casasent, "Multivariant Technique for Multiclass Pattern Recognition", *Appl. Opt.* **19**, 1758-1761(1980).

[17] J.L. Horner and P.D. Gianino, "Applying the Phase-only Filter Concept To The Synthetic Discriminant Function Correlation Filter", *Appl. Opt.* **24**, 851-854(1985).

[18] R. Young and C.R. Chatwin, "Design and Simulation of a Synthetic Discriminant Function Filter in an Updateable Photorefractive Correlator", in *Optical Pattern Recognition III*, D.P. Casasent and T.H. Chao. Eds. Proc. SPIE **1701**, 239-263(1992).

[19] H.C. Andrews and B.R. Hunt, *Digital Image Restoration*, Prentice-Hall Inc. Englewood Cliffs, New Jersey, 1977.

[20] J.M. Blackledge, *Quantitative Coherent Imaging*, Academic Press Limited, London, 1989.

[21] G.F. Schils and D.W. Sweeney, "Iterative Technique for the Synthesis of Optical-Correlation Filters", *J.Opt.Soc.Am.* **A3**, 1433(1986).

[22] D.A. Jared and D.J. Ennis, "Inclusion of Filter Modulation in Synthetic-Discriminant-Function Construction", *Appl. Opt.* **28**, 232-239(1989).

[23] M.B. Reid, W. Ma, J.D. Downie and E. Ochoa, "Experimental Verification of Modified Synthetic Discriminant Function Filters for Rotation Invariance", *Appl. Opt.* **29**, 1209-1214(1990).

[24] R.K. Wang, C.R. Chatwin and R.C.D. Young, "Assessment of a Wiener Filter — Synthetic Discriminant Functions for optical Correlation", *Lasers and Optics in Engineering* **22**, 33-51(1995).

[25] M.Y. Huang, C.R. Chatwin and R.K. Wang "Wiener Filter Applied to Laser Cutting Process Control", *Lasers in Engineering* **4**, 1-12(1995).

Chapter 8

Joint Transform Correlation

8.1 Introduction

An alternative architecture to the VanderLugt correlator for optical pattern recognition is the optical joint transform correlator (JTC), proposed several years ago by Weaver and Goodman [1]. In that setup both the reference image and the variable input object are presented simultaneously at the input plane. The joint transform, which is produced at the back focal plane of a lens, is recorded on a square-law-detector (originally a photographic film). Its Fourier transform, generated in a second optical setup, produces the correlation between the reference and input scenes in the first diffraction order. The JTC is advantageous because there is no need for a matched filter to be accurately positioned. Its main disadvantage is the need to share the available space-bandwidth product in the input plane between the input object, the reference image, and a safety band (which ensures separation of the correlation pattern from undesired terms at the output plane).

For practical pattern-recognition applications, real-time square-law detection must be employed. Thus, recent improvements in spatial light modulators (SLMs) have increased the popularity of the JTC. A real-time programmable JTC that uses a magneto-optic device with a liquid crystal light valve (LCLV) was described by Yu and Lu [2]. According to that implementation, input object functions to be correlated are loaded onto a magneto-optic device by using a programmable micro-computer. A LCLV serves as a square-law detector, and at the same time it can be read out with a coherent beam. Correlation between the input objects is obtained by the Fourier transform of this coherent illumination read-out beam.

A real-time JTC scheme that uses a single inexpensive LCTV as a programmable electronically addressed SLM for both the input and the joint transform planes was suggested by Yu *et al* [3]. A microcomputer was employed to generate object and reference patterns simultaneously on the LCTV. A collimated coherent beam was incident upon the LCTV, and after Fourier transforming (using a lens), the joint transform of the input plane was obtained. The joint transform plane was then detected by a CCD camera and recorded onto a video tape, which was then replayed using the same LCTV. The correlation pattern was again detected by the same CCD camera and then displayed on a TV monitor.

Javidi and Horner [4] proposed a joint transform image correlator that uses thresholding at both the input and the Fourier planes. The grey-scale input signal, the reference signal, and the joint Fourier-transform interference intensity are binarized and thresholded to only two values. A single binary SLM with suitable electronics for temporarily storing the joint transform signal was used for both input of the joint image scene and power spectrum encoding.

Javidi and Horner [4] compared, by computer simulation, the performance of this single SLM JTC with that of the classical JTC by assessing: light efficiency, the correlation peak-to-sidelobe ratio, correlation width, and cross correlation sensitivity. Javidi [5] further investigated the nonlinear JTC and provided analytical expressions for the thresholded joint power spectrum. The effects of nonlinearity at the joint transform plane — caused by the nonlinear characteristics of the SLM, as exhibited on the correlation signal at the output plane — were studied.

Javidi and Wang [6] presented a mathematical analysis of the quantization effects of the binarized joint power spectrum on the performance of the hardclipping binary JTC. The relationship between the severity of the Fourier plane quantization and the dynamic range of the joint power spectrum was described. The nonlinear compression followed by the quantization effects of the joint power spectrum on the performance of the hard-clipping binary JTC were investigated. It was shown that nonlinear compression or truncation in the Fourier plane, before quantization, can improve the performance of the hard-clipping binary JTC at low quantization levels. The severity of truncation can be adjusted analytically such that good binary JTC performance is produced in the presence of a finite number of quantization levels.

Fielding and Horner [7] proposed a one-focal-length hard-clipping binary JTC, which uses a Fourier-plane dc block. The use of a dc block relaxes the quantization problem and ensures accurate capture of the joint power spectrum for binarization following quantization with a standard 8-bit detector.

The performance of binary joint transform correlation with realistic input scenes has been studied by Hahn and Flannery [8], who addressed the effects of variations in threshold level, low frequency blocks, and spurious signals caused by regularly spaced groups of multiple (identical) input targets. They introduced a new adaptive thresholding technique that alleviated the problems encountered when constant thresholds are used; it significantly improved performance.

A significant problem with a binary JTC is the substantial computation time required for the determination of the threshold value used for binarizing the joint power spectrum (JPS); this is the main constraint on the system-processing speed. Also the binarization process introduces harmonic correlation peaks in the output plane, and a portion of the correlation plane energy is distributed among these higher order harmonic terms. In addition, the higher order terms may yield false alarms, thereby complicating the target-detection process.

Recently, Alam and Karim [11] introduced a fringe-adjusted-filter (FAF) based joint transform correlator in which the JPS is multiplied by the FAF before applying the inverse Fourier transform to yield the correlation signal output. This technique appears to be particularly attractive as it avoids the problems associated with the other techniques. However investigations discovered that the FAF based JTC is very sensitive to noise in the input scene. Thus, in order to enable the FAF based JTC to accommodate noise in the input scene, this chapter introduces a modified

JTC, in which a modified fringe-adjusted filter (MFAF) is used, thus overcoming the difficulties encountered in the binary JTC technique. This chapter then introduces a SDF based modified fringe adjusted JTC which enables the JTC to accommodate a high degree of image`distortion.

8.2 Joint Transform Correlation

8.2.1 Basic concept

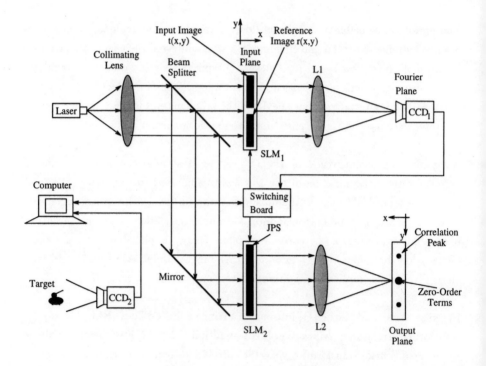

Figure 8.1: *Schematic of the joint transform correlator*

A real time fringe-adjusted JTC is shown in Fig.8.1, where the reference and input images are displayed simultaneously in the input plane using a spatial light modulator (SLM). Assume that $r(x, y + y_0)$ denotes the reference image function and $t(x, y - y_0)$ represents the input image function in the input plane, separated by a distance $2y_0$ along the y axis. The input joint image function $f(x, y)$ can be expressed as

$$f(x, y) = r(x, y + y_0) + t(x, y - y_0) \tag{8.1}$$

Lens L_1 in Fig.8.1 performs the Fourier transform of $f(x, y)$, given by

$$F(u, v) = R(u, v) exp(jvy_0) + T(u, v) exp(-jvy_0) \tag{8.2}$$

where $R(u, v)$ and $T(u, v)$ are the Fourier transforms of $r(x, y)$ and $t(x, y)$, respectively; u and v are mutually independent frequency domain variables scaled by a factor $2\pi/\lambda f$, λ is the wavelength of the collimating light, and f is the focal length of the Fourier transforming lens L_1 and L_2. The joint power spectrum – which is the intensity of the complex light distribution produced in the back focal plane of L_1 – is given by

$$\begin{aligned} |F(u, v)|^2 &= |R(u, v)|^2 + |T(u, v)|^2 \\ &+ R(u, v) T^*(u, v) exp(j2vy_0) \\ &+ R^*(u, v) T(u, v) exp(-j2vy_0) \end{aligned} \tag{8.3}$$

and detected by a square law detector such as a CCD array or liquid crystal light valve. In a classical JTC, the JPS, i.e. Eq.(8.3), is inverse Fourier transformed by lens L_2 to yield the correlation signal. However, in a binary JTC, the JPS is first binarized by applying a nonlinear hard-clipping mask [9] at the Fourier plane before taking the inverse Fourier transform of the JPS

$$|F(u, v)|^2 = \begin{cases} +1, & \text{if } |F(u, v)|^2 \geq T \\ -1, & \text{otherwise} \end{cases} \tag{8.4}$$

where T is the JPS binarization threshold, defined by

$$T = \text{median}[|F(u, v)|^2]. \tag{8.5}$$

In general, the threshold value is selected by making the histogram of the pixel values of the JPS and then picking the median [9]. This process is normally time consuming.

Recently, a JTC based on an amplitude-modulated filter (AMF) [10] was proposed in which the AMF is defined by

$$H_{amf}(u, v) = \frac{1}{|R(u, v)|^2} \tag{8.6}$$

The JPS is multiplied by H_{amf} before the inverse Fourier transform operation is applied to produce the correlation output. This scheme is found to yield better correlation performance than a binary JTC. However, the fact that $|R(u,v)|^{-2}$ may create one or more poles may contribute to other serious problems. To overcome problems occurring with poles in the AMF based JTC, Alam and Karim [11] proposed a fringe-adjusted JTC for which the fringe-adjusted filter (FAF) is defined by

$$H_{faf}(u,v) = \frac{B(u,v)}{A(u,v) + |R(u,v)|^2} \qquad (8.7)$$

where $A(u,v)$ and $B(u,v)$ are either constants or functions. When $B(u,v)$ is properly selected, one can avoid having an optical gain greater than unity. With a very small value of $A(u,v)$, the pole problem is eliminated, whilst at the same time it is possible to achieve very high autocorrelation peaks. The FAF is a real-valued function because it involves only the intensity and has no phase terms; a FAF is therefore suitable for optical implementation. The computations required to produce the FAF may be completed before the input scene is introduced into the input plane of the JTC. Thus, the inclusion of the filter does not have any significant detrimental effect on the processing speed of the system. However, an additional spatial light modulator is necessary to display the FAF function, as shown in Fig.8.2.

A major problem limiting the performance of a FAF based JTC is that it is very sensitive to noise in the input scene. It is well known that the influence of input scene noise is greater for higher spatial frequencies in the Fourier plane of the correlator; unfortunately it is the high frequencies that carry the discriminant information that is vital for unambiguous input scene recognition. When $A(u,v)$ in Eq.(8.7) is set to a small value, the FAF greatly enhances the high frequency components of the JPS; whilst this improves the system performance for a noise free image, it reduces performance for real images where noise is endemic.

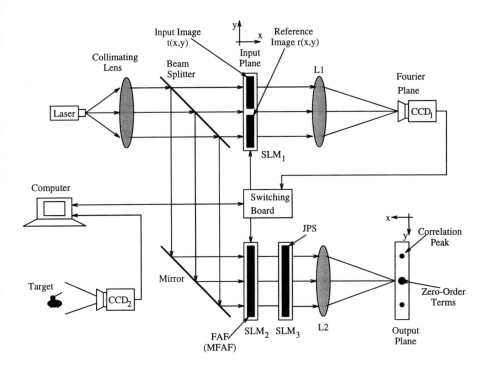

Figure 8.2: *Schematic of the fringe-adjusted joint transform correlator*

8.2.2 Input noise characterisation

Assume that the input scene consists of the reference object with additive noise denoted by $n(x,y)$, thus the input scene can be expressed as

$$t'(x,y) = t(x,y) + n(x,y) \qquad (8.8)$$

The input joint image function $f(x,y)$ now becomes

$$f(x,y) = r(x, y + y_0) + t(x, y - y_0) + n(x, y - y_0) \qquad (8.9)$$

Lens L_1, shown in Fig.8.1, performs the Fourier transform of Eq.(8.9), given by

$$F(u,v) = R(u,v)exp(jvy_0) + T(u,v)exp(-jvy_0) + N(u,v)exp(-jvy_0) \qquad (8.10)$$

where $N(u,v)$ denotes the Fourier transform of the noise function $n(x,y)$. Thus the JPS at the back focal plane of L_1 is then written as

$$
\begin{aligned}
|F(u,v)|^2 &= |R(u,v)|^2 + |T(u,v)|^2 \\
&\quad + 2Real\{R^*(u,v)T(u,v)\}\cos(2vy_0) \\
&\quad + 2Real\{N(u,v)R^*(u,v)\}\cos(2vy_0) \\
&\quad + 2Real\{N(u,v)T^*(u,v)\} + |N(u,v)|^2
\end{aligned}
\tag{8.11}
$$

From Eq.(8.11), it can be seen that noise in the input scene contributes to the last three terms of the output signal, which may adversely affect the correlation peak quality. Comparing Eq.(8.11) with Eq.(8.3), it can be seen that noise in the input scene plays an important role in the JPS which is recorded by a square law detector. The amplitude of the noise is quite small and produces maximum modulation (or interference) of the equally small amplitude higher frequency sector of the JPS.

The FAF accentuates the higher frequency values when $A(u,v)$ is set to a small value, this enhances the relative magnitude of the last three terms in Eq.(8.11) when the input scene is embedded in noise. Thus, for real input images the FAF based JTC will produce a relatively poor correlation peak at the output plane. Usually, the Fourier transform of the reference image concentrates most of the energy at low spatial frequencies with little energy in the high frequencies. This results in the power spectrum of the reference image, i.e. $|R(u,v)|^2$, having an extremely large dynamic range. As $|R(u,v)|^2$ appears in the denominator of the FAF, Eq.(8.7), the dynamic range problem is alleviated somewhat, but system performance does not appear to be robust to noise.

8.3 Modified Fringe-adjusted JTC

To overcome the above problems, a modified fringe-adjusted JTC was proposed by Wang and Chatwin [13]. The modified fringe-adjusted filter (MFAF) is defined by

$$
H_{mfaf}(u,v) = \frac{B(u,v)}{A(u,v) + |R(u,v)|}
\tag{8.12}
$$

Eq.(8.12) still retains the advantages of the FAF. When $B(u,v)$ is properly selected, an optical gain greater than unity can be avoided. The pole problem is also overcome when the value of $A(u,v)$ is selected to be very small whilst still achieving very high autocorrelation peaks at the output plane. Clearly the dynamic range of $|R(u,v)|$ is much smaller than that of $|R(u,v)|^2$, used in the FAF; thus the distribution of energy in the JPS is better optimised to cope with noise. A MFAF based JTC is therefore expected to deliver better noise robustness than one based on the FAF.

The real-valued MFAF is more suitable to display on a spatial light modulator than the FAF as it has a smaller dynamic range. The computations required to generate the MFAF may be completed sufficiently rapidly that its use does not limit the processing speed of the system.

The modified fringe-adjusted JPS is obtained by multiplying the filter function by the JPS. This multiplication is achieved in the same manner as the FAF based JTC [11], illustrated in Fig.8.2. Thus the modified fringe-adjusted JPS may be expressed as

$$
\begin{aligned}
G(u,v) &= H_{mfaf}(u,v)|F(u,v)|^2 \\
&= \frac{B(u,v)}{A(u,v)+|R(u,v)|}[|R(u,v)|^2 + |T(u,v)|^2 \\
&\quad + 2Real\{R^*(u,v)T(u,v)\}\cos(2vy_0)]
\end{aligned}
\tag{8.13}
$$

where the input image $t(x,y)$ is assumed to be the noise free case. If the input object is embedded in background noise $n(x,y)$, using Eq.(8.11), the modified fringe-adjusted JPS is given by,

$$
\begin{aligned}
G(u,v) &= \frac{B(u,v)}{A(u,v)+|R(u,v)|}\Big[|R(u,v)|^2 + |T(u,v)|^2 \\
&\quad +2Real\{R^*(u,v)T(u,v)\}\cos(2vy_0) \\
&\quad +2Real\{N(u,v)R^*(u,v)\}\cos(2vy_0) \\
&\quad +2Real\{N(u,v)T^*(u,v)\} + |N(u,v)|^2\Big]
\end{aligned}
\tag{8.14}
$$

when $B(u,v) = 1$, and $|R(u,v)| \gg A(u,v)$, and the reference is the same as the input target, i.e. $r(x,y) = t(x,y)$, Eq.(8.14) reduces to

$$
\begin{aligned}
G(u,v) &\approx 2|R(u,v)| + 2|R(u,v)|[\cos(2vy_0)] + \frac{|N(u,v)|^2}{|R(u,v)|} \\
&\quad +2Real\{N(u,v)exp(-i\phi_r)\}[1 + \cos(2vy_0)]
\end{aligned}
\tag{8.15}
$$

where ϕ_r denotes the phase of the Fourier transform of the reference image. Taking the inverse Fourier transform of Eq.(8.15) yields the output signal containing the desired correlation patterns. It can be seen from Eq.(8.15) that the second term is just like the phase-only filter [14], as

$$
\begin{aligned}
2|R(u,v)|[\cos(2vy_0)] = \; & exp(-i\phi_r)R(u,v)exp(i2vy_0) \\
& + [exp(-i\phi_r)R(u,v)exp(i2vy_0)]^* \qquad (8.16)
\end{aligned}
$$

This produces the two desired correlation peaks, with the same performance as the phase-only filter, but with a separation distance of $4y_0$ along the y axis. This is a particularly attractive characteristic of the MFAF based JTC.

For the same condition, the FAF based JTC is expressed as

$$
\begin{aligned}
G(u,v) \approx \; & 2 + 2\cos(2vy_0) + \frac{|N(u,v)|^2}{|R(u,v)|^2} \\
& + \frac{2}{|R(u,v)|}Real\{N(u,v)exp(-i\phi_r)\}[1+\cos(2vy_0)] \qquad (8.17)
\end{aligned}
$$

The second term is very attractive because it is actually an inverse filter. However, since noise has its greatest effect at higher frequencies in the frequency domain, it is evident from Eq.(8.17) that the noise effect in the last two terms is greatly enhanced because of the very small value of $|R(u,v)|^2$ at high frequencies (usually $|R(u,v)|^2 \ll 1.0$). The MFAF based JTC, Eq.(8.15), reduces the noise effect by a factor of $1/|R(u,v)|$. Notice that $1/|R(u,v)| \gg 1.0$ for the higher frequency components.

From Eq.(8.15), it can also be seen that a zero order and noise term will be present in the output plane. It therefore would appear to be a simple matter to block the zero-order term by using an optical stop in the output plane. However, when the input image is corrupted by noise, the zero-order term will become more complicated; the use of an optical stop may not be effective; along with simulation results further explanation of this will be given in the next section.

Although the deleterious effect of noise on the JTC has been reduced by using the MFAF rather than the FAF, the noise term, i.e. last two terms of Eq.(8.15), may still result in poor target detection when the input scene is embedded in severe background noise. To further reduce the noise effect in the output plane, and at the same time to eliminate the zero-order term, another architecture is suggested. This is achieved by displaying the input scene at the input plane of the JTC in the absence of the reference image and then recording the input-scene-only power spectrum, expressed as

$$
\begin{aligned}
|I(u,v)|^2 &= |T(u,v)exp(jvy_0) + N(u,v)exp(-jvy_0)|^2 \\
&= |T(u,v)|^2 + |N(u,v)|^2 + 2Real\{N(u,v)T^*(u,v)\} \quad (8.18)
\end{aligned}
$$

and then displaying the reference image only to produce its power spectrum $|R(u,v)|^2$. When the input-scene-only power spectrum, Eq.(8.18), and the reference image power spectrum, $|R(u,v)|^2$, are subtracted from the noise corrupted JPS expressed by Eq.(8.11), the resultant modified JPS can be expressed as

$$
\begin{aligned}
P(u,v) &= |F(u,v)|^2 - |R(u,v)|^2 - |I(u,v)|^2 \\
&= 2Real\{T(u,v)R^*(u,v)\}\cos(2vy_0) \\
&\quad + 2Real\{N(u,v)R^*(u,v)\}\cos(2vy_0) \quad (8.19)
\end{aligned}
$$

where computation involving the reference image power spectrum $|R(u,v)|^2$ may be completed before performing the joint transform correlation operation. The subtraction operation can be performed either optically [15] or electronically, using the computer shown in Fig.8.2. When Eq.(8.19) is compared with Eq.(8.11), it can be seen that the noise effect in the JTC is greatly reduced, although not completely eliminated; furthermore, the large zero order term is completely removed. Using simulation results the next section illustrates how the subtraction method greatly improves the ability of the JTC to accommodate noise in the input scene.

When this modified JPS, Eq.(8.19), is multiplied by the MFAF, i.e. Eq.(8.12), the final modified fringe-adjusted JPS becomes

$$
\begin{aligned}
P(u,v) &= \frac{2B(u,v)}{A(u,v) + |R(u,v)|}[Real\{T(u,v)R^*(u,v)\}\cos(2vy_0) \\
&\quad + Real\{N(u,v)R^*(u,v)\}\cos(2vy_0)] \quad (8.20)
\end{aligned}
$$

Lens L_2 in Fig.8.2 takes the inverse Fourier transform of Eq.(8.20) to produce correlation patterns with reduced noise terms at the output plane.

An alternative hybrid architecture for implementation of the modified fringe-adjusted filter based JTC is shown in Fig.8.3. Three separate CCDs are used to capture: the joint transform power spectrum, the power spectrum of the input scene and power spectrum of the reference image. These power spectra are sent to the computer simultaneously in order to evaluate the MFAF-JPS. Providing the CCDs have a large dynamic range, the power spectra of the input and reference images can be electronically removed from the JPS by pixelwise subtraction. The modified fringe-adjusted joint power spectrum is displayed on SLM$_2$, Fig.8.3, which is then optically addressed by a monochromatic plane wave to produce the desired correlation patterns at the output plane via the Fourier transforming lens L_2 shown in Fig.8.3. The computer, shown in Fig.8.3, can also be replaced by a custom designed high speed microprocessor, so as to improve the processing speed of the system. Notice that the MFAF can be produced directly from the power spectrum of the reference image captured by CCD$_1$ and then electronically multiplied by the JPS; thus the reference image can be updated in real time, thereby making this system more flexible.

8.3.1   Multi-object modified fringe-adjusted JTC

If the input scene contains n objects $t_1(x - x_1, y - y_1)$, $t_2(x - x_2, y - y_2)$, $\ldots t_n(x - x_n, y - y_n)$, and noise $n(x, y - y_0)$, the joint input image may be expressed as

$$f(x, y) = r(x, y + y_0) + \sum_{i=1}^{n} t_i(x - x_i, y - y_i) + n(x, y - y_0) \tag{8.21}$$

the corresponding JPS is given by

$$
\begin{aligned}
|F(u, v)|^2 \;=\;& |R(u, v)|^2 + \sum_{i=1}^{n} |T_i(u, v)|^2 \\
& + 2 \sum_{i=1}^{n} Real\{T_i(u, v)R^*(u, v)\} \cos[ux_i + v(y_0 + y_i)] \\
& + \sum_{i=1}^{n} \sum_{k=1}^{n} Real\{T_i(u, v)T_k^*(u, v)\} \cos[ux_i + v(y_i - y_k)] \\
& + 2 Real\{N(u, v)R^*(u, v)\} \cos(2vy_0) + |N(u, v)|^2 \\
& + 2 \sum_{i=1}^{n} Real\{N(u, v)T_i^*(u, v)\} \cos[ux_0 + v(y_0 - y_i)]
\end{aligned}
\tag{8.22}
$$

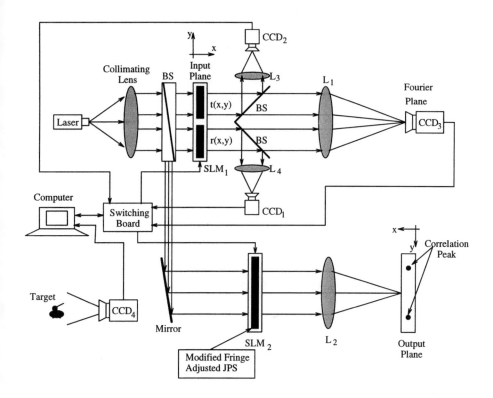

Figure 8.3: *Schematic of an alternative real time fringe-adjusted JTC*

where $i \neq k$ and $T_i(u, v)$ denotes the Fourier transform of $t_i(x, y)$. The correlation output will contain the following terms: autocorrelations of the reference and the input objects, the cross correlations between the reference and the input objects, the cross correlations between the different input objects and various noise terms. The last four terms may produce false alarms in the correlation plane, especially the noise terms. Such false alarms can be avoided, or reduced, by eliminating the cross correlation terms between the different input objects and reducing the noise terms. This can be achieved by subtracting the input-scene-only power spectrum and reference object power spectrum from the JPS expressed by Eq.(8.22); this results in

$$
\begin{aligned}
P(u, v) \;=\; & 2 \sum_{i=1}^{n} Real\{T_i(u,v)R^*(u,v)\} \cos[ux_i + v(y_0 + y_i)] \\
& + 2Real\{N(u,v)R^*(u,v)\} \cos(2vy_0)
\end{aligned}
\tag{8.23}
$$

When this modified JPS, Eq.(8.23), is multiplied by MFAF, i.e. Eq.(8.12), the final modified fringe-adjusted JPS for multiple input objects gives

$$G(u,v) = \frac{2B(u,v)}{A(u,v) + |R(u,v)|}[\sum_{i=1}^{n} Real\{T_i(u,v)R^*(u,v)\}\cos[ux_i + v(y_0 + y_i)]$$

$$+ Real\{N(u,v)R^*(u,v)\}\cos(2vy_0)] \qquad (8.24)$$

From Eq.(8.19) or Eq.(8.20) and Eq.(8.23) or Eq.(8.24), it is evident that noise in the output plane is independent of the multiple objects in the input scene; it comes only from the convolution of the reference object with the noise. This very attractive result illustrates a method of reducing the deleterious effect of noise on the performance of the JTC system.

8.4   Results from Modified FAFJTC

To investigate the performance of the proposed modified fringe-adjusted JTC, the following three cases are considered: 1) an input scene with a single noise free object, 2) an input scene with a single severely noise corrupted object, and 3) an input scene containing multiple objects in a noisy background. The results are compared with the FAF based JTC. For both the MFAF and FAF based JTCs, $A(u,v)$ was taken to be 1×10^{-6} to overcome the pole problem, and $B(u,v)$ was set to unity. In all cases, the correlation peak intensity was normalised with respect to the total energy of the output plane; so that a perfect autocorrelation would use the full dynamic range of the 256 grey levels (i.e. 8-bit) and all correlation outputs are fully resolved to give a meaningful comparison of the performance of the different filters investigated.

8.4.1   Input scene with noise free single object

For the single-object input scene, a 30×48 pixel, noise free, image of a Bradley APC vehicle was used as the reference image, as shown in Fig.8.4(a). The same vehicle, with the same resolution, was taken as the target image. The two images were combined and zero padded to form a 128×128 pixel array joint image. This joint input image was introduced to SLM$_1$ (shown in Fig.8.3) at the input plane, and then the power spectra of the joint image, input image and reference image were captured by CCD$_3$, CCD$_2$ and CCD$_1$, respectively, as shown in Fig.8.3. The computation of the MFAF or FAF, the power spectrum subtraction, and the multiplication operations are completed by the computer. The final modified fringe-adjusted JPS is inverse Fourier transformed to yield the desired correlation output.

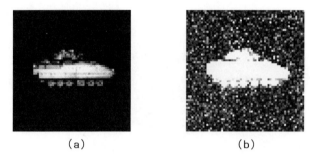

(a)   (b)

Figure 8.4: *Bradley APC images used in the simulation, (a) noise free APC image, (b) noise corrupted APC image with the signal energy to the noise energy ratio of 0.21*

The correlation output for the MFAF based JTC is shown in Fig.8.5(a), which shows that the output correlation peaks are extremely well defined, showing that the target can be detected without ambiguity. For comparison, the correlation output for the FAF based JTC is also shown in Fig.8.5(b). It can be seen from Fig.8.5(a) and (b) that the FAF based JTC delivers better performance than the MFAF based JTC when the input scene has zero noise content. The performance is quantified by the results tabulated in Table 8.1, where API denotes the autocorrelation peak intensity, PSR is the correlation peak to secondary peak ratio, PRMS is defined by Eq.(3.18) which is also the correlation peak to noise ratio, and PNI is the number of pixels inside the correlation peak at the full width at half of its maximum value (FWHM).

From Table 8.1, it can be seen that the correlation peak quality of the FAF based JTC is much better than that of the MFAF based JTC; this is because multiplication of the FAF with the JPS greatly enhances the high frequency components of the

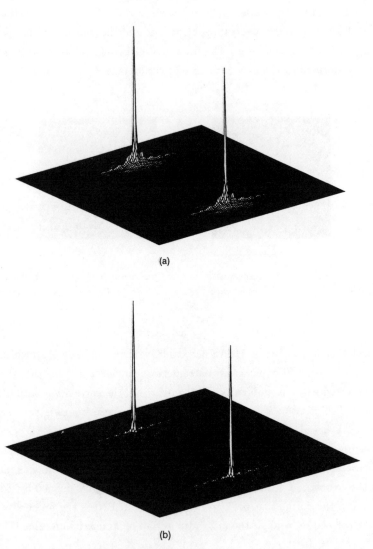

(a)

(b)

Figure 8.5: *3-D plot of correlation output functions when the input scene is free of noise, (a) from the MFAF based JTC, (b) from the FAF based JTC*

Table 8.1: *Quantified results from an input scene with a noise free single object*

JTC type	API	PSR	PRMS	PNI
MFAF based JTC	11.90	24.95	839.43	1
FAF based JTC	54.25	100.54	6024.6	1

modified JPS. However, there is no doubt that, from Table 8.1 and Fig.8.5(a), the MFAF based JTC delivers good correlation performance and very effectively detects the target in the input scene. The PNI metric is found to be 1 which is equal to that of the FAF based JTC.

8.4.2 Input scene with a single noise corrupted object

An effective correlation system should be able to accommodate noise in the input scene; this means that if the target is embedded in a noisy background, the correlator can still recognise the noise corrupted target. In this subsection, the noise robustness of the MFAF based JTC is investigated and compared with that of the FAF based JTC. The noisy input scene is shown in Fig.8.4(b), in which a 30×48 pixel array of the Bradley APC vehicle is severely corrupted by noise, the ratio of target signal energy to noise energy is 0.21. It is evident from scrutinising Fig.8.4(b) that this is a difficult pattern recognition problem.

First of all the MFAF based JTC, with no subtraction of the input image and reference image power spectra from the joint image power spectrum, is investigated. Fig.8.6(a) gives the 3-D plot of the correlation output from the MFAF based JTC. From Fig.8.6(a), it can be seen that a large and broad zero-order term is present in the output plane; the correlation peaks are embedded in a severely noise corrupted background, which makes their detection a difficult task. It is evident from Fig.8.6(a) that the use of an optical stop to block the zero-order term would not be very effective. For comparison, when the noisy image of Fig.8.4(b) is input into the FAF based JTC, the 3-D plot of the output correlation function is shown in Fig.8.6(b). Clearly the FAF based JTC is extremely sensitive to noise in the input scene, as the correlation peaks are completely lost in the output plane noise. From Fig.8.6(a),

Table 8.2: *Quantified results from an input scene with a noise corrupted single object*

JTC type	API	PSR	PRMS	PNI
MFAF based JTC	0.691	3.20	44.51	1
FAF based JTC	0.634	1.82	20.40	1

the MFAF based JTC produces two correlation peaks at the output plane which, although they are embedded in noise, are detectable.

When the power spectra of the input image and the reference image are subtracted from the joint image power spectrum, the 3-D plot of the correlation output function for the MFAF based JTC is given in Fig.8.7(a), it gives an excellent result. Compared with Fig.8.6(a), it is evident that the subtraction technique is extremely useful in reducing the deleterious effect of noise on the JTC. It can also be seen from Fig.8.7(a) that the zero order term is completely removed from the output plane and that the correlation signal can be detected using a simple threshold detector. For the same case, Fig.8.7(b) shows the 3-D plot of the correlation output function using the FAF based JTC. Two correlation peaks are evident in the output plane but they are seriously corrupted by noise; this makes their detection quite difficult. It can be concluded, from Fig.8.7(a) and 8.7(b), that the MFAF based JTC is far more robust to noise than the FAF based JTC. Furthermore, the results prove that the subtraction technique is very effective in reducing noise in the output correlation plane.

The performance of both the MFAF and FAF based JTCs, Fig.8.7(a) and 8.7(b), is quantified by the results tabulated in Table 8.2. From Table 8.2, it can be seen that when the target is severely corrupted by noise in the input scene, the autocorrelation peak intensity produced by the MFAF based JTC (with a value of 0.691) is approximately 10% higher that that produced by the FAF based JTC (with a value of 0.634). The autocorrelation peak to secondary peak ratio and the correlation peak to noise ratio from the MFAF based JTC is found to be almost twice that of the FAF based JTC. Notice that the PSR value from the FAF based JTC is 1.82 which is less than 2.0, which means that the secondary peak intensity is greater than half that of the correlation peak intensity. This may lead to false alarms if

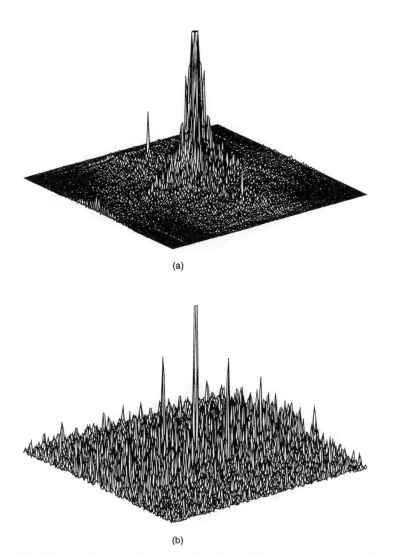

(a)

(b)

Figure 8.6: *3-D plot of correlation output functions with no power spectra subtraction when the input scene is noise corrupted, (a) from the MFAF based JTC, (b) from the FAF based JTC*

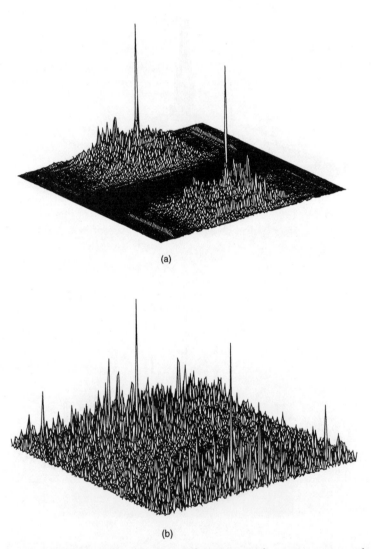

(a)

(b)

Figure 8.7: *3-D plot of correlation output functions with power spectra subtraction from a noise corrupted input scene, (a) from the MFAF based JTC, (b) from the FAF based JTC*

the thresholding value of a detector used to detect the correlation signal is set to PSR=2.0, whereas the MFAF based JTC, with PSR= 3.20, will detect the target without ambiguity.

8.4.3 Multi-object input scene with background noise

When the input scene contains noise free multiple objects, Fig.8.8 (only a 128×192 pixel array is shown, this is zero padded to give a 256×256 pixel array for the simulations), the MFAF based JTC delivers very good performance, the correlation peak intensity from the target object is extremely well defined with only a very small signal from the non-target objects; for brevity, this case is not reported herein. This subsection concentrates on the MFAF based JTC, with a multiple-object input which is severely corrupted by noise. The joint image input consists of a number of tanks with the reference image separated from the input scene which contains several different tanks; however, the input scene is severely corrupted by noise with signal energy to noise energy ratio of 0.4, as shown in Fig.8.9. Note that one of the objects in the input scene, which happens to be the object located at the bottom left position, is identical to the reference vehicle, i.e. the Bradley APC vehicle, if the input scene was not corrupted by noise.

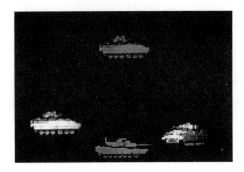

Figure 8.8: *Noise free multiple object input scene used in the simulation*

When Fig.8.9 was used as the input to the MFAF based JTC, the final correlation output is given by Fig.8.10(a). For comparison, Fig.8.10(b) gives the correlation

Figure 8.9: *Noise corrupted multiple object input scene with signal energy to noise energy ratio of 0.4 used in the simulation*

Table 8.3: *Quantified results from an input scene with multiple noise corrupted objects*

JTC type	API	PSR	PRMS	PNI
MFAF based JTC	0.283	3.29	72.66	1
FAF based JTC	0.230	1.80	29.80	1

output from the FAF based JTC. From Fig.8.10, it can be seen that the MFAF based JTC delivers a better ability to accommodate noise in the input scene than the FAF based JTC. Table 8.3 gives the quantified results from Fig.8.10(a) and Fig.8.10(b). It can be seen from this table that the target correlation peak intensity produced by the MFAF based JTC is approximately 20% higher than that produced by the FAF based JTC. The correlation peak intensity from the target object is 3.29 times that of the secondary peak intensity; hence, the MFAF based JTC can detect the target from the noise corrupted multiple-object input scene, without ambiguity, using a thresholding detector set to half the maximum correlation peak height, whereas the PSR value for the FAF based JTC is only 1.80, which means that there are several secondary peaks higher than half the value of the maximum correlation peak; this may cause false alarms when detecting the target from the input scene shown in Fig.8.9.

The PRMS metric quantifies the noise robustness of the correlator at the output plane. From Table 8.3, the MFAF based JTC gives a PRMS of 72.66, which is

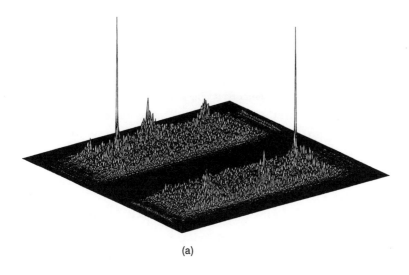

(a)

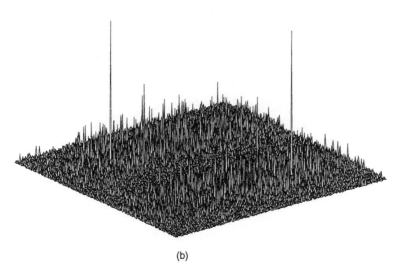

(b)

Figure 8.10: *3-D plot of correlation output functions with power spectra subtraction from a noise corrupted multi-object input scene, (a) from the MFAF based JTC, (b) from the FAF based JTC*

approximately two and half times greater than that for the FAF based JTC (29.80). Thus, the MFAF based JTC delivers a far greater capability to accommodate noise in the input scene, with multiple objects, than the FAF based JTC.

In all cases, the full width of the correlation peak intensity at half of its maximum is found to be 1×1 for both the MFAF and FAF based JTCs, either with the single object input or with the multiple-object input. Hence, the position of the target object within the input scene can be located with high accuracy.

8.5 Synthetic Discriminant Function MFAJTC

Joint transform correlators preserve the shift invariant pattern recognition property, but have high sensitivity to other distortions in the input image, such as in-plane rotations, out-of-plane rotations, and scale variations. Therefore, it is expected that the joint transform correlator is not able to provide a high degree of image distortion invariance. In the VanderLugt-type correlators (matched filtering architectures), synthetic discriminant function (SDF) filters [16],[17],[18],[19],[20],[21] have been used to accommodate these distortions. However, SDF filters normally consist of both the amplitude and phase information from a training image set; this gives rise to some difficulty in fabricating the filter. Furthermore, the SDF filter must be aligned with the optical Fourier transform of the input image. These practical issues limit its application for real time optical implementations. Recently, Javidi [22] successfully applied the SDF to a JTC system in which the SDF was used as a reference object in a bipolar nonlinear joint transform correlator. His SDF based binary JTC uses thresholding at both the input and the Fourier plane. The great advantage of this system is that there is no need to fabricate the matched spatial filter *a priori*. A SDF based binary JTC [22] was found to be superior to a classical SDF based JTC in terms of the correlation peak intensity, peak width, and discrimination ability between the training set images and the nontarget images. Whilst the system successfully manages to classify a single class of object, it does not satisfy the equal correlation peaks (ECP) criterion, and fails with multi-class problems. The fringe binarization of the joint power spectrum (JPS) in the SDF based binary JTC is responsible for this difficulty.

This section introduces the application of the spatial synthetic discriminant function to the MFAJTC, which not only delivers better correlation performance in terms of correlation peak intensity, peak width, and discrimination ability between one class of images and another class of images, but also has the ability to function successfully with multi-class problems and produce equal correlation peak heights for images of the same class.

8.5.1 SDF-based JTC

The classical JTC is sensitive to distortions of the input image such as in-plane rotation, out-of-plane rotation, and scale variations. To enable the JTC to accommodate these input image distortions, the synthetic discriminant function technique, used in the VanderLugt-type correlators, can be applied to the JTC system in the object space as long as the autocorrelation patterns produced by the first two terms of Eq.(8.3) are spatially separated from the desired cross-correlation patterns produced by the last two terms of Eq.(8.3). This requirement can be met if the distance between the reference image and the input image at the input plane of the JTC is sufficiently large; this assumes that the SLM has an adequate space bandwidth product. Assume that a set of centred training images, $r_n(x, y)$, $n = 1, ..., k$, spanning the desired distortion invariant feature range is used to construct the spatial SDF $r(x, y)$ [16],[17],[19]; thus, the JTC reference image is synthesized from this training set. The desired cross-correlation response of $r(x, y + y_0)$ is a constant, c_n, for each training image $r_n(x, y - y_0)$, thus

$$\int \int R_n(u, v) R^*(u, v) exp(-j2vy_0) du dv = c_n \qquad (8.25)$$

or

$$\int \int R_n^*(u, v) R(u, v) exp(+j2vy_0) du dv = c_n \qquad (8.26)$$

where $R(u, v)$ and $R_n(u, v)$ are the Fourier transforms of the spatial SDF $r(x, y)$ and the nth training image $r_n(x, y)$. Typically, $r(x, y)$ is constrained to be a linear combination of the training image set,

$$r(x, y) = \sum_{n=1}^{k} a_n r_n(x, y) \qquad (8.27)$$

By substituting Eq.(8.27) into Eq.(8.25) or Eq.(8.26), the coefficients a_n ($n = 1, 2, ..., k$) can be shown to be

$$\mathbf{a} = \mathbf{R}^{-1}\mathbf{c} \tag{8.28}$$

where $\mathbf{a} = [a_1, a_2, \ldots, a_k]^T$, $\mathbf{c} = [c_1, c_2, \ldots, c_k]^T$, and $\mathbf{R}$ is the correlation matrix having elements

$$R_{mn} = \int \int R_m(u,v) R_n^*(u,v) exp(j2vy_0) du dv \tag{8.29}$$

Therefore, the SDF $r(x,y)$ is determined by substituting the coefficients, obtained by solving Eq.(8.28), back into Eq.(8.27). The resultant spatial SDF $r(x,y)$ is displayed at the input plane of the JTC side by side with the input scene; this provides a reference function with a high degree of distortion invariance.

One of the main problems with the classical JTC is the presence of a strong zero-order peak in the output plane — that corresponds to the sum of the autocorrelations of the reference and the input signals — which almost overlaps the desired correlation signals [23]. This may cause a problem in that the JTC is not able to produce equal correlation peaks for all image input distortions. This difficulty can be alleviated by using a large space bandwidth product SLM to display the joint image. Alternatively, this problem may be overcome using the hybrid architecture shown in Fig.8.3; this arrangement subtracts the power spectra of the reference and the input scenes, i.e. the first two terms of Eq.(8.3), from the power spectrum of the joint image. Thus, if the inputs to the JTC are the reference SDF $r(x,y)$, generated by solving Eq.(8.27) and Eq.(8.28), and the input scene $t(x,y)$, the modified JPS obtained using this system is

$$
\begin{aligned}
|F_m(u,v)|^2 &= R(u,v)T^*(u,v)exp(j2vy_0) + R^*(u,v)T(u,v)exp(-j2vy_0) \\
&= \sum_{n=1}^{k} a_n R_n(u,v) T^*(u,v) exp(j2vy_0) \\
&\quad + \sum_{n=1}^{k} a_n^* R_n^*(u,v) T(u,v) exp(-j2vy_0)
\end{aligned}
\tag{8.30}
$$

From Eq.(8.30), it can be seen that the zero-order term at the output plane is completely removed. Therefore, an SLM with a smaller space bandwidth product SLM will meet the requirement that the two desired correlation signals are separated in the output plane.

8.5.2   SDF-based modified fringe-adjusted JTC

The above SDF based JTC produces very broad output cross-correlation peaks at the output plane and as a result it is difficult to locate the precise position of the target in the input scene and discriminate one class of images from another. To solve this problem, Javidi [22] proposed a SDF based binary JTC which uses thresholding at both the input and the Fourier plane. A SDF based binary JTC was found to be superior to a SDF based classical JTC in terms of the correlation peak intensity, peak width, and discrimination ability between the training image set and the nontarget images. However, one of the main problems with the SDF based binary JTC is that it does not satisfy the ECP rule for the same class of image inputs. Furthermore, it may lose its discrimination ability for multi-class problems (more than 2 classes).

Very recently, in order to overcome the difficulties involved in the SDF based binary JTC, Wang and Chatwin [24] proposed a SDF based fringe-adjusted JTC which uses a modified fringe-adjusted filter (MFAF) in the optical setup illustrated by Fig.8.3. We already know that this MFAF is generated from the power spectrum of the reference image captured by CCD_2, shown in Fig.8.3 and defined by

$$H(u,v) = \frac{B(u,v)}{A(u,v) + |R(u,v)|} \tag{8.31}$$

When the spatial SDF $r(x,y)$ is utilised in this system, Eq.(8.31) becomes

$$H(u,v) = \frac{B(u,v)}{A(u,v) + \left| \sum\limits_{n=1}^{k} a_n R_n(u,v) \right|} \tag{8.32}$$

Thus the SDF based fringe-adjusted JPS is obtained by multiplying the function, Eq.(8.32), by the JPS expressed by Eq.(8.30)

$$G(u,v) = \frac{B(u,v)}{A(u,v) + \left| \sum\limits_{n=1}^{k} a_n R_n(u,v) \right|} \left[\sum\limits_{n=1}^{k} a_n R_n(u,v) T^*(u,v) exp(j2vy_0) \right.$$

$$\left. + \sum\limits_{n=1}^{k} a_n^* R_n^*(u,v) T(u,v) exp(-j2vy_0) \right] \tag{8.33}$$

When $B(u, v) = 1$ and $|R(u, v)| \gg A(u, v)$, Eq.(8.33) reduces to

$$
G(u, v) \approx \sum_{m=1}^{k} a_m \frac{R_m(u, v)T^*(u, v)}{\left|\sum_{n=1}^{k} a_n R_n(u, v)\right|} exp(j2vy_0)
$$

$$
+ \sum_{m=1}^{k} a_m^* \frac{R_m^*(u, v)T(u, v)}{\left|\sum_{n=1}^{k} a_n R_n(u, v)\right|} exp(-j2vy_0)
$$

$$
= T^*(u, v)exp[j\phi(u, v)]exp(j2vy_0)
$$

$$
+T(u, v)exp[-j\phi(u, v)]exp(-j2vy_0) \qquad (8.34)
$$

where $\phi(u, v)$ denotes the phase of the Fourier transform of the reference SDF $r(x, y)$. According to the above section, taking the inverse Fourier transform of Eq.(8.34) should produce ECPs for any $t(x, y)$ belonging to the same class. Unfortunately, the solution set of $\mathbf{a}$, solved using Eq.(8.28), in the SDF based classical JTC is not the solution in the SDF based fringe-adjusted JTC. Our aim is that the SDF-based modified fringe-adjusted JTC will produce the constant correlation peak, c_l, for each training image $r_l(x, y)$, $l = 1, 2, \ldots, k$, i.e.

$$
\sum_{m=1}^{k} \int \int \frac{a_m R_m(u, v)}{\left|\sum_{n=1}^{k} a_n R_n(u, v)\right|} R_l(u, v)exp(j2vy_0) = c_l \qquad (8.35)
$$

where $l = 1, 2, \ldots, k$. Eq.(8.35) is a system of nonlinear equations which may be solved using an iterative procedure [25] based on the Newton-Raphson algorithm. The synthesis coefficients $\mathbf{a}$ for the SDF $r(x, y)$ are constrained to be real, and the accuracy of the coefficients is improved using the iterative formula

$$
a_l^{i+1} = a_l^i + \alpha[c_l - c_0(\frac{m_l^i}{m_0^i})] \qquad (8.36)
$$

where i is the iteration number, α is a damping constant, and m_l^i is the modulus of the peak correlation response of image input $r_l(x, y - y_0)$ with the spatial SDF $r(x, y + y_0)$ constructed with $\mathbf{a}^i$. This relaxation algorithm was used with success in the SDF filter based correlator in Chapter 6 and Chapter 7. In the simulations, 12 iterations were found to be sufficient to achieve equal correlation peak heights (to within 1% error) for all training set images.

Once the coefficients **a** are determined using the relaxation algorithm given by Eq.(8.36), the spatial SDF $r(x, y)$ is synthesised using Eq.(8.27) and then displayed side by side with the input scene on the input SLM_1 of Fig.8.3. The modified joint image power spectrum is thus obtained by multiplying Eq.(8.32), (which is generated from the power spectrum of the spatial SDF $r(x, y)$ captured by CCD_2 shown in Fig.8.3) by the joint image power spectrum. This is then displayed on SLM_2 and optically addressed by a plane, parallel laser beam, which will produce the desired correlation signal at the output plane if the input image belongs to the desired class of images.

8.5.3 SDF-based MFAJTC with multi-object input

If the input scene contains m objects $t_1(x - x_1, y - y_1)$, $t_2(x - x_2, y - y_2)$, ..., $t_m(x - x_m, y - y_m)$, the joint input image of the SDF based JTC may be expressed as

$$f(x, y) = \sum_{n=1}^{k} a_n r_n(x, y + y_0) + \sum_{i=1}^{m} t_i(x - x_i, y - y_i) \qquad (8.37)$$

The corresponding JPS is given by

$$\begin{aligned} |F(u, v)|^2 &= |R(u, v)|^2 + \sum_{i=1}^{m} |T_i(u, v)|^2 \\ &\quad + 2\sum_{i=1}^{m} Real\{T_i(u, v)R^*(u, v)\}\cos[ux_i + v(y_0 + y_i)] \\ &\quad + \sum_{i=1}^{m}\sum_{k=1}^{m} Real\{T_i(u, v)T_k^*(u, v)\}\cos[ux_i + v(y_i - y_k)] \quad (8.38) \end{aligned}$$

where $i \neq k$ and

$$R(u, v) = FT\left\{\sum_{n=1}^{k} a_n r_n(x, y + y_0)\right\}, \qquad (8.39)$$

and FT means Fourier transform operation. The correlation output of Eq.(8.38) will contain the following terms: autocorrelations of the reference spatial SDF $r(x, y)$, and the input objects $t_i(x, y)$, $i = 1, 2, \ldots, m$; the cross correlations between the reference SDF $r(x, y)$ and the input objects $t_i(x, y)$, the cross correlations between the different input objects. The last term may produce false alarms in the correlation plane. Such false alarms can be avoided using the architecture shown in Fig.8.3, which subtracts the power spectrum of the multi-object scene captured by CCD_1 from the JPS. Thus, the modified SDF-based JPS results in

$$P(u,v) = 2\sum_{i=1}^{m} Real\{T_i(u,v)R^*(u,v)\}\cos[ux_i + v(y_0 + y_i)] \qquad (8.40)$$

When this modified SDF-based JPS, Eq.(8.40), is multiplied by the SDF-based FAF, i.e. Eq.(8.32), the final SDF-based modified fringe-adjusted JPS for the multiple input objects gives

$$G(u,v) = \frac{2B(u,v)}{A(u,v) + |R(u,v)|}\sum_{i=1}^{m} Real\{T_i(u,v)R^*(u,v)\}\cos[ux_i + v(y_0 + y_i)] \quad (8.41)$$

Therefore, if the multi-object input scene contains the different classes of the desired images, the SDF-based modified fringe-adjusted JTC will give different correlation peak heights corresponding to the different class of images; for a particular class the peak heights will be equal.

8.5.4 Results from SDF-based MFAJTC

To investigate the performance of the proposed SDF-based MFAJTC, the following two cases are considered: (1) an input scene with a single object from the training image set, (2) an input scene containing multiple classes of object. The results are compared with the SDF-based classical JTC (CJTC) and the SDF-based binary JTC (BJTC). For the SDF-based MFAJTC, $A(u,v)$ was taken to be 1×10^{-6} to overcome the pole problem, and $B(u,v)$ was set to unity. For the SDF-based BJTC, the JPS median was used as the threshold for binarization.

The training image set used in the simulations consists of in-plane rotated images of the Bradley APC vehicle. Each image is centred and normalised to unit energy. The APC vehicle was rotated from $0°$ to $95°$ in increments of $5°$, the images were encoded with a resolution of 64×64 pixels. Views of the vehicle at $0°$, $15°$, $30°$, $50°$, $70°$ and $90°$ are given in Fig.8.11.

The training image set, Bradley APC vehicle ranging from $0°$ to $95°$ in increments of $5°$, is divided into two classes. The first class of image includes ten in-plane rotated

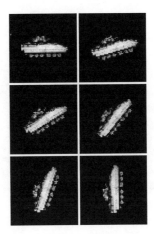

Figure 8.11: *Views of the Bradley APC vehicle (from left to right and top to bottom) at 0°, 15°, 30°, 50°, 70° and 90°*

images of the Bradley APC vehicle ranging from 0° to 45° with increments of 5°; the rest of the in-plane rotated training image set belongs to the second class of images. Thus, SDF reference image $r(x,y)$ is constructed from these two classes of images, with the correlation peak intensity from the first class of images being controlled to be twice that of the second class of images. The spatial SDFs $r(x,y)$ for the MFAJTC, CJTC and BJTC are shown in Fig.8.12(a), (b) and (c), respectively; the SDF $r(x,y)$ is displayed in the input plane of the JTC side by side with the input scene to produce the output correlation results.

Table 8.4 illustrates quantitative results from the correlation tests for the SDF-based MFAJTC, CJTC and BJTC with the input scene from individual training set images, respectively. It can be seen from this table that the SDF-based MFAJTC presents reasonably good results; the equal correlation peak rule for the same class of images is well satisfied; and from the PNI measure, the correlation peaks produced are relatively narrow. Thus the two classes of image can be classified without ambiguity using the SDF-based MFAJTC. For the SDF-based CJTC, as expected, the equal correlation peak criterion for the same image class is well satisfied; however, the correlation peaks are very broad and the peak to secondary peak ratio is lower.

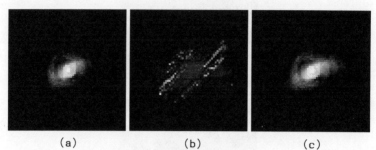

(a)   (b)   (c)

Figure 8.12: *Spatial SDF reference function $r(x, y)$ from (a) the fringe-adjusted JTC, (b) the classical JTC and (c) the binary JTC*

Table 8.4: *Quantified results using individual training set images as the input scene*

	SDF-based MFAJTC				SDF-based CJTC				SDF-based BJTC			
Input	CPI	PSR	PRMS	PNI	CPI	PSR	PRMS	PNI	CPI	PSR	PRMS	PNI
0°	19.72	3.45	157.69	1	1.00	1.18	24.32	205	89.30	12.29	370.97	1
5°	20.09	3.92	160.37	2	1.00	1.23	23.78	217	90.49	9.78	376.15	1
10°	19.93	2.36	159.17	3	1.03	1.26	24.08	215	71.82	4.62	295.71	1
15°	19.87	2.07	158.75	3	1.02	1.25	23.78	222	97.52	11.95	406.82	1
20°	19.89	2.05	158.82	1	1.03	1.20	24.13	221	114.72	12.46	482.78	1
25°	19.87	2.77	158.71	2	1.01	1.01	24.00	216	91.58	8.56	380.89	1
30°	19.84	2.74	158.78	1	1.02	1.18	24.98	201	97.72	9.40	407.65	1
35°	19.97	2.97	160.17	1	1.01	1.17	25.78	179	119.53	12.29	504.27	1
40°	19.71	3.35	157.81	1	1.00	1.52	26.50	149	105.43	9.85	441.57	1
45°	20.07	2.44	160.35	1	1.00	1.51	27.96	113	107.21	13.03	449.43	1
50°	10.60	1.61	83.46	4	0.50	0.48	7.30	802	14.83	1.44	59.37	4
55°	10.64	1.71	84.20	3	0.50	0.52	7.57	808	9.91	1.18	39.57	16
60°	10.67	1.60	85.11	2	0.51	0.56	7.93	804	9.90	0.91	39.52	17
65°	10.70	1.46	86.12	1	0.50	0.60	8.23	803	15.19	1.43	60.83	5
70°	10.62	1.56	85.37	6	0.50	0.64	8.49	808	11.03	1.09	44.06	15
75°	10.66	1.96	86.45	4	0.50	0.67	8.87	802	19.71	2.21	79.07	1
80°	10.69	1.90	87.20	5	0.50	0.69	9.15	796	15.72	1.74	62.97	3
85°	10.62	1.93	87.69	6	0.50	0.77	9.44	789	15.72	1.68	62.95	4
90°	10.66	2.29	88.48	7	0.50	0.79	9.59	778	10.05	0.88	30.67	26
95°	10.69	2.17	88.95	1	0.50	0.82	9.72	750	20.22	2.15	81.13	1

Notice that the SDF-based MFAJTC has a correlation peak intensity average of 19.90 and 10.66 for the first class and the second class of images respectively, whereas the SDF-based CJTC only gives 1.01 and 0.50 respectively. The PRMSs for the SDF-based CJTC are considerably less than those for the SDF-based MFAJTC. The SDF-based CJTC has an average PSR of 1.25 and 0.65 for the first class and the second-class of images respectively; whereas, the SDF-based MFAJTC delivers a better average PSR of 2.85 and 1.82, respectively. Note that although the SDF-based CJTC satisfies the equal correlation peaks criterion for the second class of images, the sidelobe peaks are almost twice that of the desired correlation peak, making them difficult to distinguish from the sidelobe noise.

For the SDF-based BJTC, it is evident from Table 8.4 that the correlation peaks do not satisfy the ECP rule; the maximum variation of the correlation peaks is 40% and 51% for the first class and second class of images respectively. It can be seen from this table that, for the first class of images, the SDF-based BJTC delivers better results than either the CJTC or the MFAJTC; however, it cannot classify the second class of image as some correlation peaks are totally buried in the output background noise. Thus overall, the SDF-based MFAJTC delivers the best results.

The worst cases of the correlation output from the SDF-based MFAJTC, CJTC and BJTC are shown in Fig.8.13. All the correlation results from the second class of images are normalised to their corresponding correlation peak height from the first class. It can be seen from these 3-D plots of the output correlations, that the MFAJTC can classify the two classes of image with a relatively narrow correlation peak even in the worst case (see Fig.8.13(a) and Fig.8.13(b)). However, correlations from the SDF-based CJTC are not well localised and the desired correlation peak is almost half the height of the secondary peak (see Fig.8.13(d)); the SDF-based BJTC loses the correlation peak in the background noise for the second class of images (see Fig.8.13(f)).

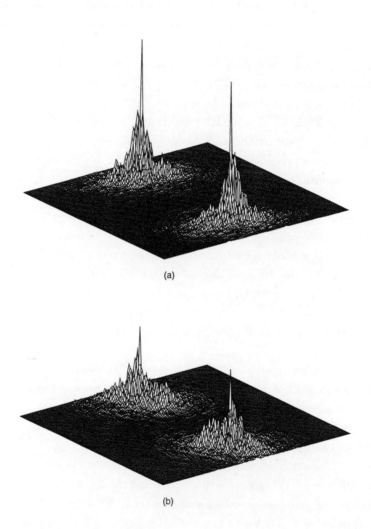

(a)

(b)

Figure 8.13: *The worst-case correlation results for the SDF-based MFAJTC: (a) from first class set, (b) from second class set; the SDF-based CJTC: (c) from first class set, (d) from second class set; and the SDF-based BJTC: (e) from first class set, (f) from second class set; respectively*

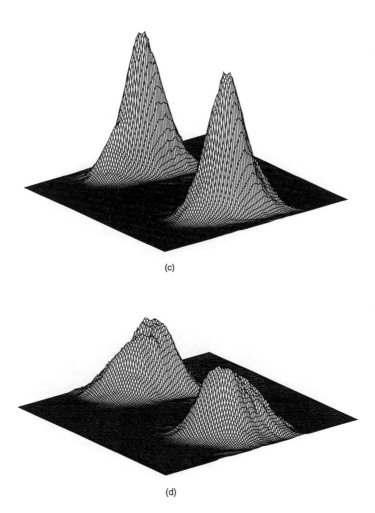

(c)

(d)

Figure 8.13: *Continued*

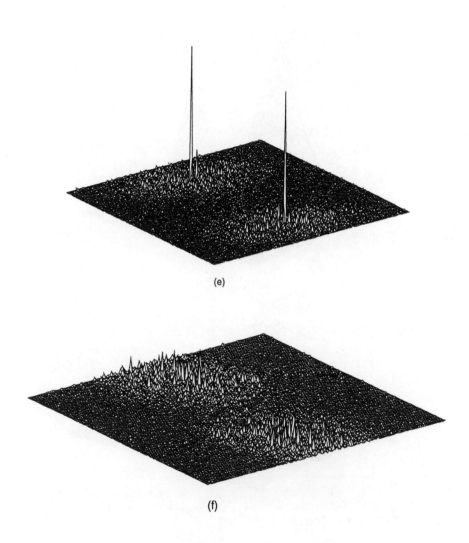

(e)

(f)

Figure 8.13: *Continued*

Table 8.5: *Quantified results from an input scene with multiple objects*

	first object		second object		third object		
SDF type	CPI	PNI	CPI	PNI	CPI	PNI	MLI
MFAJTC	6.49	1	6.60	1	3.28	2	1.70
CJTC	1.00	162	1.03	232	0.66	704	0.85
BJTC	25.04	1	18.13	1	3.51	2	5.49

Input scene with multiple objects

This subsection concentrates on the SDF-based MFAJTC with a multiple-object input containing several different classes of object and a nontarget object. The multiple-object input scene is shown in Fig.8.14 which contains: two objects from the first class of images located at the right side of the figure (rightmost is object 1 and just right of centre is object 2); one object (object 3) from the second class of images located at the left side; bottom centre is a nontarget object (Abrams MI tank, object 4). This multiple-object scene is displayed side by side with the SDF reference scene $r(x, y)$ to produce the correlation output.

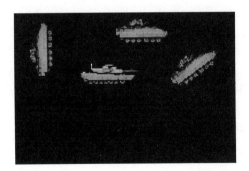

Figure 8.14: *Multiple-object input scene used in simulation*

When Fig.8.14 was used as the input scene to the SDF-based MFAJTC, the final correlation output is given by Fig.8.15(a). For comparison, the results from the SDF-based CJTC and BJTC are shown in Fig.8.15(b) and Fig.8.15(c), respectively.

In terms of classifying the different objects and rejecting the nontarget object in the multiple-object input scene, it can be seen from Fig.8.15 that the SDF-based MFAJTC delivers the best results; whereas, discrimination problems occurred for the SDF-based CJTC and BJTC. Table 8.5 gives the quantified results from Fig.8.15(a), (b) and (c). In the table, MLI refers to the maximum side lobe peak intensity, other than that from the 1st, 2nd and 3rd objects, in the output plane; all the peak values in the table are normalised to the correlation peak value produced by the first object for the SDF-based CJTC. From Table 8.5, the SDF-based MFAJTC produced almost the same correlation peak heights, with PNI=1 pixel, for the 1st and 2nd objects which are from the same class, and produced a half height correlation peak (as designed) from the second class for the 3rd object with PNI= 2 pixels; the maximum side lobe intensity (MLI) in the output plane is 1.70 which is 1.93 times lower than that from the 3rd object. Thus, the SDF based MFAJTC successfully classifies the different desired objects and rejects the nontarget object in the multiple input scene when a thresholding detector is used. The SDF-based CJTC produced correlation peaks that are very broad (minimum PNI= 162 pixels) making it difficult to precisely locate the target in the input scene; furthermore, the maximum side lobe peak intensity, with a value of 0.85, (which is actually from the nontarget object in the input scene) is 1.23 times that produced by the 3rd object with the value of 0.66. Thus the SDF-based CJTC is unable to distinguish the 3rd object from the nontarget object in the multiple object input scene. For the SDF-based BJTC, not only are the correlation peaks produced by the same class of objects of unequal height, but the correlation peak produced by the 3rd object is totally embedded in the background noise. Thus overall, for the multi-object input scene, the SDF-based MFAJTC delivers better performance than either the SDF-based CJTC or BJTC; furthermore, the SDF based MFAJTC can be designed to control the correlation peak height for a different class of objects so as to successfully recognise/classify them and reject the nontarget object in the input scene.

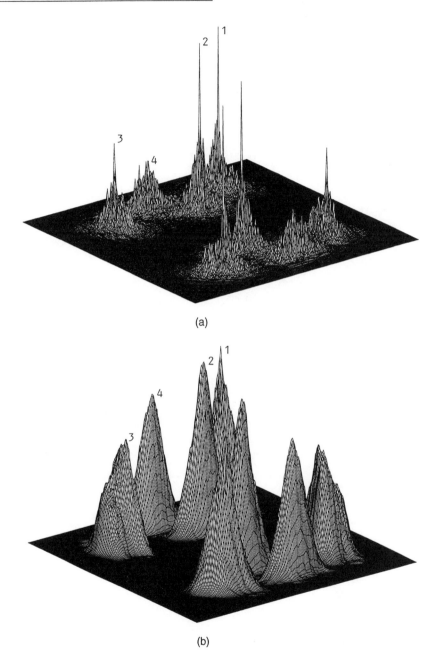

Figure 8.15: *3-D plot of correlation output functions with a multi-object input scene, (a) from the SDF-based MFAJTC, (b) from the SDF-based CJTC, (c) from the SDF-based BJTC, respectively*

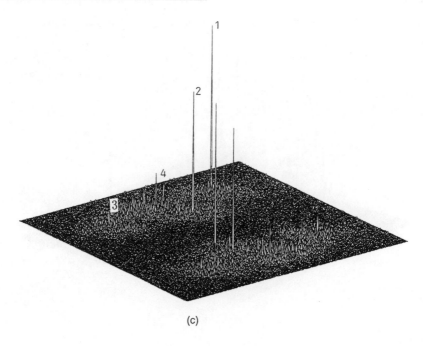

(c)

Figure 8.15: *Continued*

Bibliography

[1] C.S. Weaver and J.W. Goodman, "A technique for optically convolving two functions", *Appl. Opt.* **5**, 1248-1249(1966).

[2] F.T.S. Yu and X.J. Lu, "A real time programmable joint transform correlator", *Opt. Commun.* **52**, 10-16 (1984).

[3] F.T.S. Yu, S. Jutamulia, T.W. Lin, and D.A. Gregory, "Adaptive real-time pattern recognition using a Liquid Crystal TV based joint transform correlator", *Appl. Opt.* **26**, 1370-1372(1987).

[4] B. Javidi and J.L. Horner, "Signal spatial light modulator joint transform correlator", *Appl. Opt.* **28**, 1027-1032(1989).

[5] B. Javidi, "Nonlinear joint power spectrum based optical correlation", *Appl. Opt.* **28**, 2358-2367(1989).

[6] B. Javidi and J. Wang, "Quantization and truncation effects on binary joint transform correlation", *Opt. Commun.* **84**, 374-382(1991).

[7] K.H. Fielding and J.L. Horner, "1-f binary joint transform correlator", *Opt. Eng.* **29**, 1081-1087(1990).

[8] W.B. Bhan and D.L. Flannery, "Basic design elements of binary joint transform correlation and selected optimization techniques", in *Optical Information Processing Systems and Architectures II*, B. Javidi, ed., Proc. Soc. Photo-Opt. Instrum. Eng. **1347**, 344-356(1990).

[9] B. Javidi, and C.J. Kuo, "Joint transform image correlation using a binary spatial light modulator at the Fourier plane", *Appl. Opt.* **27**, 663-665(1988).

[10] D. Feng, H. Zhao, and S. Xia, "Amplitude-modulated JTC for improving correlation discrimination", *Opt. Commun.* **86**, 260-264(1991).

[11] M.S. Alam, and M.A. Karim, "Fringe-adjusted joint transform correlation", *Appl. Opt.* **32**, 4344-4350(1993).

[12] M.S. Alam, and M.A. Karim, " Joint transform correlation under varying illumination", *Appl. Opt.* **32**, 4351-4356(1993).

[13] R.K. Wang, L. Shang, and C.R. Chatwin, "Modified fringe-adjusted joint transform correlation to accommodate noise in the input scene", *Appl. Opt.*, in press.

[14] J.L. Horner, and P.D. Gianino, "Phase-only matched filtering", *Appl. Opt.* **23**, 812-816(1984).

[15] H.K. Liu, and T.H. Chao, "Optical image subtraction techniques, 1975-1985", *Proc. SPIE* **638**, 55-65(1986).

[16] C.F. Hester and D. Casasent, "Multivariant technique for multiclass pattern recognition", *Appl. Opt.* **19**, 1758-1761(1980).

[17] D. Casasent, "Unified synthetic discriminant function computational formulation", *Appl. Opt.* **23**, 1620-1627(1984).

[18] D. Casasent and W.-T. Chang, "Correlation synthetic discriminant functions", *Appl. Opt.* **25**, 2343-2350(1986).

[19] Z. Bahri and B.V.K.Vijaya Kumar, "Generalized synthetic discriminant functions", *J.Opt.Soc.Am.* **A5**, 562-571(1988).

[20] D. Jared and D. Ennis, "Inclusion of filter modulation in the synthetic discriminant function construction", *Appl. Opt.* **28**, 232-239(1989).

[21] R.K. Wang, C.R. Chatwin and M.Y. Huang, "Modified filter synthetic discriminant functions for improved optical correlator performance", *Appl. Opt.* **33**, 7646-7654(1994).

[22] B. Javidi, "Synthetic discriminant function–based binary nonlinear optical correlator", *Appl. Opt.* **28**, 2490-2493(1989).

[23] F.T.J. Johnson, T.H. Barnes, T. Eiju, T.G. Haskell, and K. Matsuda, "Analysis of a joint transform correlator using a phase-only spatial light modulator", *Opt. Eng.* **30**, 1947-1957(1991).

[24] R.K. Wang, C.R. Chatwin, and L. Shang, "Synthetic Discriminant Function Fringe-adjusted Joint Transform Correlation", *Opt. Eng.* **34(10)** (1995), in press.

[25] G.F. Schils, and D.W. Sweeney, "Iterative technique for the synthesis of optical correlator filters", *J. Opt. Soc. Am.* **A3**, 1433-1442(1986).

Index

A

accuracy 125, 246

adaptive filtering 85-102

additive noise 21, 112, 182, 225

ambiguity 78, 98, 142, 162, 233, 239, 240, 249

amplitude
  distribution 38, 42
  encoding 151
  information 18, 50, 87, 101, 150, 151, 153, 155, 178, 182
  mode 18, 151
  modulation 16, 18, 51, 61, 153
  transmittance 37, 38, 40, 41

amplitude compensated matched filter 50, 74, 182

amplitude modulated filter 223

B

back focal plane 33, 35, 36, 38, 40, 219, 223

bandlimit 87

bandpass 57, 61, 136
  filtering 51
  spatial frequency 19, 66

binarization 47, 221, 248
  fringe 242

binary
  coding 155
  phase only filter 18, 45-46, 105, 123, 142, 150
  quantization 131, 150

spatial light modulator 135

Bragg matching constraint 54

C

central zone 21, 124

classical matched filter 45-45, 50, 85, 87, 123

classical matched filter modulation 127

coherent
  illumination 220
  light 15
  optical beam 16
  optical correlation 42-43

coherent optical data processing 37

complex conjugate 44, 86

complex function 16, 41, 123

complex matched filter (see: classical matched filter)

computer generated hologram 44

continuous Fourier transform 25-27

convolution 17, 31, 43, 51, 232
  operation 64, 184
  theorem 32, 184

correlation 43
  theorem 15, 32, 126

correlation peak detectability 50

cutting quality 206

D

detection accuracy 19, 72, 79, 98

difference of Gaussian function 64

difference of Gaussian filter 61-68

diffraction 42
  efficiency 17, 48, 54, 56
  integral 33
discrete Fourier transform 27-30
discrimination ability 72-73, 79, 81, 98, 101, 112, 117, 143-145, 159-165, 188, 246
distortion range 111, 136-143, 154-159, 194-200
distortion invariance (see: distortion range)
dynamic range 41, 152, 220, 226, 232

E
edge enhancement 17, 50, 51, 57, 91, 130, 136, 189
encoding constraints 21, 124
error 182
Euclidean distance 152

F
false alarm 138, 198, 221, 231, 236, 240, 247
filter function 20, 40, 118, 227
filter SDF 125-126
focal length 38, 223
Fourier transform 25-33
Fourier transform lens 33-37
Fourier transform pair 28, 29
Fresnel approximation 34
fringe-adjusted filter 224
fringe-adjusted JTC 222-224, 245
full width half maximum 72, 78, 97, 189, 233

G
Gaussian white noise 77, 90
Gaussian function 64

Gram-Schmidt procedure 110

H
Hartley transform 47
highpass filter 46, 126
high-speed hybrid optical correlation 142
hologram filter 52, 54, 56, 61
holographic recording 40-42
Horner efficiency 45, 72, 97, 104, 189
hybrid architecture 15, 230

I
illumination: uniform 37
image distortion 104, 183, 196, 222, 243
impulse response 39, 57, 91, 108, 136, 191
in-class image 162, 165, 169, 191, 193, 196, 197
in-plane rotation 19, 104, 123, 146, 242
intra-class 183
intra-in-class 196
intra-out-of-class 196
inverse filter 74, 119, 228
iterative 87, 90, 92, 99, 248
  relaxation algorithm 125

J
joint input image 230, 233, 247
joint power spectrum 220, 223
joint transform correlation 219-258

L
laser cutting 200, 211, 212
laser cutting process 200, 206
linear combination 108
liquid crystal light valve 219

liquid crystal television 18, 46, 124, 150
location accuracy 117, 242
low-pass filter 36

M
magneto-optic SLM 46, 48, 105
matched spatial filter 182, 186, 189, 213, (also see: classical matched filter)
minimum average correlation energy 116
minimum average correlation energy filter 116, 117
minimum-variance SDF 20, 115
modified filter SDF 123-173
modified fringe-adjusted filter 222, 226-242, 245
modified fringe-adjusted JTC 226-232, 245, 247
monochromatic plane wave 37, 40, 52, 230
multi-object input scene 239, 248

N
noise corrupted image 77, 81, 92, 169, 170, 173, 222, 235, 240
noise resistance of filter 167-173
noise robustness 18, 74, 79, 85, 86, 87, 97, 227, 235, 240
nonlinear filter 130
nonlinear hard-clipping 223

O
out-of-class image 56, 110, 159, 160, 167, 169, 186, 193, 194, 196, 198, 200, 210
out-of-plane rotation 112, 123, 242

P

peak to secondary peak ratio 77, 89
phase 26
    mode 18, 46, 151
    information 18, 50, 85, 87, 130, 153, 159, 173, 178, 182, 242
phase only filter 45-46, 50, 85, 104, 123, 182
photographic film 16
photo-refractive filter 51-61
projection SDF 106
propagation number 34
pupil function 35
pupil mask 39

Q
quantization 18, 221
    effects 220

R
Rayleigh criterion 166

S
scale mismatch 104
shift invariant system 31
signal to noise ratio 17, 44, 50, 68, 74, 77, 90, 97
space bandwith product 54, 111, 243, 244
spatial bandwith product (see: space bandwith product)
spatial light modulator 16, 17, 20, 44, 47, 183
spatial frequency 31
successive algorithm 129
synthetic discriminant function 105, 106, 165, 191, 196, 243

T

target discrimination (see: discrimination ability)
ternary matched filter 45
threshold 223
thresholding detector 236, 240, 256
transfer function 39, 42, 44, 185
training image set 19, 110, 129, 133, 192, 193, 242, 245, 248
training image spacing 153, 165-167, 178, 196, 198

U
uniqueness 79, 98

V
VanderLugt correlator 16, 52, 219 (also see: classical matched filter)

W
Wiener filter 184, 185
Wiener filter correlation 182-200

Z
zero order 228, 229, 236

Index

Apostolidis, A 84
Arsenault, H.H 119
Awwal, A.A.S 24, 216
AuYeung, J 83

Bahri, Z 24, 117, 120, 127, 129, 179,
        180, 216, 260
Barnes, T.H 181, 261
Bartelt, H.O 49, 84, 180
Bhan, W.B 259
Blackledge, J.M 217
Bollapraggada, S 121
Bracewell, R.N 49
Braunecker, B 106, 120
Breipohl, A.M 122
Brown, G.R 23

Caelli, T.M 112, 120
Campos, J 120
Caufield, H.J 17 23
Casasent, D 23, 24, 106, 108, 115, 119,
        120, 121, 122, 179, 217, 260
Cathey, W.T 49
Chang, W.T 23, 115, 120, 179, 217,
        260
Chao, T.H 181, 217, 260
Chatwin, C.R 18, 21, 23, 24, 51, 52,
        83, 84, 103, 115, 122, 124, 131,
        142, 150, 153, 180, 181, 217,
        218, 226, 245, 260, 261
Chavel, P 181
Chlanska-Macukow, K 216

Choa, E.O 180
Connelly, J.M 24 216
Cooper, I 52, 84
Cottrell, D.M 47, 49

Davis, J.A 49
Day, T 49
Dickey, F.M 24, 216
Downie, J.D 180, 218

Eiju, T 181, 261
Ennis, D 20, 21, 24, 179, 218, 260
Ersoy, O.K 180

Farn, W.W 216
Fekete, D 83
Feng, D 260
Fielding, K.H 221, 259
Flannery, D.L 135, 180, 181, 221, 259
Flavin, M.A 180

Gianino, P. D. 17, 23, 24, 49, 83, 103,
        121, 179, 216, 217, 260
Goodman, J.W 49, 108, 120, 121, 122,
        216, 219, 259
Gregory, D.A 166, 181, 259

Haskell, T.G 261
Hassebrook, L 113, 121
Hauck, R.W 120

Hester, C.F 23, 106, 108, 121, 179, 217, 260
Hildreth, E 84
Horner, J.L 17, 20, 23, 24, 45, 47, 49, 83, 84, 103, 121, 179, 180, 183, 216, 217, 220, 221, 259, 260
Hostetler, L 121
Huang, M.Y 24, 83 ,103, 180, 218, 260
Huignard, J.P 52, 84
Hunt, B.R 217

Iwaki, T 83
Iyer, A 120

Jahan, S.R 24, 216
James, M.L 121
Jared, D 20, 21, 24, 124, 166, 168, 173, 179, 218, 260
Javidi, B 84, 103, 220, 242, 245, 259, 260
Johnson, F.T.J 261
Juday, R.D 152, 181
Jutamulia, S 259

Karim, M.A 24, 216, 221, 224, 260
Keller, P.E 181
Keshava, N 180
Kirsch, J.C 181
Korn, G.A 121
Korn, T.M 121
Kumar,B.V.K 24, 111, 112, 113, 115, 117, 120, 121, 127, 129, 179, 180, 216, 217, 260
Kuo, C.J 259

Laude, V 152, 181
Leger, J.R 49, 103, 216
Lilly, R.A 49

Liu, H.K 112, 181, 260
Liu, Z.Q 120
Lohmann, A.W 23, 120
Loomis, J.S 180, 181
Loudin, J.A 181
Lu, X.J 219, 259

Ma, P.W 180, 218
Mahalanobis, A 24, 116, 121, 217
Mallick, S 84
Maloney, W.T 105, 120
Marr, D 84
Matsuda, K 181, 261
Maze, S 181
McCall, M 84
Mills, S 181
Milkovich, M.E 180, 181
Mitsuoka, Y 83
Mostafavi, H 111, 122
Mu, G.G 24, 83, 85, 103, 216

Nicholson, M 52, 84
North, D.O 122

Ooyawa, N 181

Paek, E.G 49, 83, 122, 180
Papoulis, A 49, 84, 103
Paris, D.P 23
Pepper, D 52 83
Petts, C 84
Pochapsky, E 111, 112, 121
Psaltis, D 47, 49, 83, 122, 180

Rajbenbach, H 84
Ravichandran, G 120, 121, 122
Refregier, Ph 84, 122, 181
Reid, M.B 180, 218

Romero, L.A 24, 216
Rosen, J 217
Ross, W 181
Roude, D 84
Rozzi, W 179

Schils, G.F 180, 217, 261
Scott, B.F 180
Shamir, J 217
Shang, L 260, 261
Shanmugan, K.S 122
Sharma, V 24
Smith, F 111, 122
Smith, G.M 121
Solymer, L 84
Stewart, G.W 122
Sweeney, D.W 180, 217, 261

Tam, E.C 181

VanderLugt, A. 15, 23, 49, 50, 83, 103,
        122, 179, 216
Venkatesh, S.S 49, 83, 122, 180,

Wang, J 220, 259
Wang, R.K 21, 24, 83, 103, 115, 122,
        124, 150, 180, 181, 218, 226,
        245, 260, 261
Wang, X.M 24, 83, 103, 216
Wang, Z.Q 24, 83, 103, 216
Weaver, C.S 122, 219, 259
Witka, T 216
Wolford, J.C 121

Xia, S 260

Yariv, A 83

Yaroslavsky, L.P 21, 24, 182, 217
Yoon, Y 180
Young, R.C.D 18, 23, 51, 52, 83, 84,
        131, 142, 153, 180, 217, 218
Yu, F.T.S 108, 122, 181, 219, 220, 259

Zhao, H 260
Zimmerman, D 180